JEWS
and the
FRENCH FOREIGN LEGION

By
ZOSA SZAJKOWSKI

KTAV PUBLISHING HOUSE, INC.
NEW YORK, NEW YORK
1975

© COPYRIGHT 1975
ZOSA SZAJKOWSKI

Library of Congress Cataloging in Publication Data

Szajkowski, Zosa, 1911-
  Jews and the French Foreign Legion.

  Bibliography: p.
  1. Jews as soldiers. 2. World War, 1939-1945—Jews.
3. France. Armée. Légion étrangère. 4. Jews in France—
Persecutions. 5. Szajkowski, Zosa, 1911-   I. Title.
D810.J4S935   940.54′05   74-32011
ISBN 0-87068-270-9

PRINTED IN THE UNITED STATES OF AMERICA

TABLE OF CONTENTS

I.	The World Forgetting, by the World Forgotten	1
II.	Their Heroism Lies in Their Suffering	7
III.	We are French *Soldiers* but Not French *Citizens*	11
IV.	The Legion Works, the Legion Gets No Pay!	14
V.	The Right to Plunder	17
VI.	Jews Among the Old-Time Legionnaires	22
VII.	Volunteers for the Defense of France	24
VIII.	Engagé pour la Gamelle	28
IX.	The Revolt of Carency	30
X.	Union Sacré in an Atmosphere of War-Time Antisemitism	38
XI.	Americans in the French Foreign Legion	45
XII.	In the Atmosphere of Munich	56
XIII.	Again in the Foreign Legion	60
XIV.	Forced Volunteers	64
XV.	With Republican Spaniards	69
XVI.	Demobilized for the Antechambers of Death Camps	76
XVII.	In North Africa—"This Hostile Place with a Perfumed Name"	83
XVIII.	Building the Trans-Saharan Railroad	87
XIX.	A Most Atrocious Camp	101
XX.	North Africa Liberated—Internees Punished for Hoisting the American Flag	115
XXI.	Suffering and Death After the Liberation	151
XXII.	Join the Foreign Legion or Go to Prison	172
XXIII.	The World Will Never Understand	178
XXIV.	The Joint Commission on Political Prisoners and Refugees	183
XXV.	Anything Which Might Offend French Susceptibilities Has Been Omitted	191
XXVI.	Volunteers Forced Not to Fight	208

XXVII.	"Incredible" Politics of Compromise	214
	Postscript	227
	Illustrations	119
	Appendix	230
	Notes	250
	Sources	261
	Index	269

The research for this book was made possible by a grant from the Lucius N. Littauer Foundation, Mr. Harry Starr, President, and sponsored by the National Foundation for Jewish Culture, Dr. Harry I. Barron, Secretary.

I. "The World Forgetting, By the World Forgotten"

The French Foreign Legion was officially created on March 10, 1831. France needed troops for the pacification of Algeria and accepted the suggestion of a Belgian adventurer who called himself Baron de Boëgard to use foreign troops. The Baron, assuming the rank of lieutenant-general, collected around him a band of mercenaries and other adventurers, and so the Foreign Legion was born.

One could mention many "glorious" pages in the history of the Legion. April 30, for example, is a big day in the legionnaire's life. France had decided to conquer Mexico and offer, with the help of bayonets, the Mexican throne to Maximilian, brother of Emperor Joseph of Austria. On April 30, 1863, sixty-two legionnaires stood off two thousand Mexicans for nine hours.[1] In honor of this glorious battle, which took place at Camerone, the legionnaires are given a good meal, plenty of red *pinard* (the cheap red wine), and time to sleep it off.

Life in the Legion was portrayed in the press, in songs, novels, stories, movies, and other propaganda media as one of constant excitement; a dangerous life but nevertheless full of the unexpected.

Col. Fernand V. M. Maire wrote that a former officer of the Legion, having been transferred to Paris, dreamt about "his Legion . . . his beautiful Legion of bygone times, but still alive deep in his heart." He was a brave officer and the Legion was proud of his becoming a legionnaire, but he was also a debtor to the Legion for enabling him to become a pure legionnaire.[2]

Were not a king of Serbia, a prince of Monaco, a president of Peru, and the adopted son of Maxim Gorky former legionnaires? Even a Spanish bishop served in the Legion. He used to play the organ in the chapel of Sidi-bel-Abbès (in order to play well he had to be drunk).[3] The most colorful officer of the Legion was Prince Aage, an authentic prince of Denmark, commander of the 1st Battalion of the 3rd Regiment of the Legion. He was an international celebrity. Visitors would travel hundreds of miles out of their way to meet the famous, tall, romantic prince of the

Foreign Legion. Aage, a good dancer, was the only legionnaire whose name was always in the gossip columns, linked to some international beauty. He gained the reputation of being able to drink any of his fellow legionnaires under the table. In town, he and his non-commissioned officers "mixed in with the legionnaires on thundering binges, and they staggered off to bed together." The next morning the legionnaires would parade, pale and groaning, with hangovers like pneumatic drills. "In an army where drink was God, Aage's battalion was a byword as the drunkenest and meanest of all."[4]

Perhaps the story of Lord Edward Montagu is more realistic. In 1934, the 29-year old son of the Duke of Manchester tried to enlist in the French Foreign Legion. He was fond of adventure of any kind, and was in financial difficulties. His sister, Lady Louise, tried to dissuade him. Finally in 1935 he signed up for five years, but was rejected and the bad ship went back to his family.[5]

The ill-informed British novelist of the 1860's Ouida (Louise de La Ramée) romanticized the Legion of Dukes, love and adventure in her novel *Under Two Flags* and so began the international legion vogue.[6] In Roland Pertwee's 1927 novel *Gentlemen March,* Nicco signed up for the Legion. In real life he was a British Lord in grief at the loss of his love. But all ended well. Before he died he was assured of his love and honored by the Queen.[7]

The film *Beau Geste* adopted by Herbert Brenon from Percival Christopher Wren's 1925 novel of the same title gave, according to Mordaunt Hall of the New York *Times,* "a true conception of life" in the French Foreign Legion, the brutality of a non-commissioned officer, the courage of the legionnaires "who remained faithful to the tricolor." Even the brutal sergeant had his good sides, courage and strategy. Watching on the screen the African desert, almost feeling the baked sands and the perspiration running down the faces of the legionnaires, one could feel only sympathy "for the men of the many nations who bury themselves in the Foreign Legion to escape prison, to forget love affairs, or for the mere sake of hoped-for adventure." One almost agrees that "the chance of an attack by the Arabs is almost a welcome piece of news, because of the bitter ennui of life in the fort." Howard Thompson wrote in the New York *Times* (September 8, 1966) about a 1966 production by Douglas Heyer that the story "retains a curiously appealing, old-fashioned dignity."[8] During the showing of *Beau Geste* in England, a former legionnaire, dressed in the uniform of a real legionnaire, stood in the foyer and answered questions. He was even presented to the Duke of York, the later King. Many spectators liked even the *Ten Tall Men,* an unorthodox 1951 film based on a story by James Warner Bellah and Willis Goldbeck, in which Burt Lancaster, Gilbert Roland and Kieron Moore were primarily trying to present to the spectators a bushel of fun with a flavor of the Foreign Legion.[9]

A British ex-legionnaire wrote: "No other regiment in France can approach the Legion for smartness at drill on parade."[10] Indeed, during parades in Casablanca, Paris, Marseilles, or other large cities, the legionnaires marched in a desert step to tunes of the marching song *Le Boudin,* which some consider to be sinister while others think of as melancholic, exalting, romantic:

> Tiens, voilà du boudin,
> Voilà du boudin,
> Voilà du boudin.

On such rare occasions women threw flowers at the white *kepis* (military caps worn by legionnaires). After the parade, a prostitute, or even an honest woman, often spent the night with a legionnaire—*Mon Légionnaire,* and made him forget the frequent fighting, thirst, hunger, heat of the day and cold of the night in the African *bled* and the terrible loneliness which only a legionnaire feels—the *cafard*.

When Marie Dubois was singing *Mon Légionnaire* ("He was tall . . . he was handsome . . . he smelled good of the warm sand . . . on his neck: Not seen, not taken in . . . in his heart: own self . . .," etc., etc.) the audience became sentimental and more than one person silently shed a tear.

Such parades, however, had little resemblance to the real legionnaires in North Africa, which Isabelle Eberhardt thus described: "Then the legionnaires came, emaciated and tiresome, with a hollow look, feverish, their capotes faded and worn out, with their old equipment, tired, covered with dust. . . ."[11]

One former legionnaire called the act of signing up for the five years in the Legion *piquer une tête à la Légion* (to take a header), to hang up one's past on the coat-stand and look at it as a dangling corpse. It meant to forsake at dawn a sleeping playmate, silently close the door on a brief intimacy of one week or one night; it meant to go and sell his skin to the recruiting sergeant of a professional army. "Sign here!," said the sergeant without even looking at the face of a tormented or resolved man who was about to throw away five years of his life. And he signed in order to be initiated into the mysteries of the Legion which was supposed to be the refuge of men without a fatherland, of outlaws, of tramps, of princes, of those who had gone astray, and of desperate lovers.[12]

Did the prospective legionnaire know the contents of the contract? According to another former legionnaire, each man had to sign six times, but over the top copy a blank sheet of paper had been laid in each case, leaving only the signature spaces available in echelon. "Judging by the size of the paper there must have been a lot which we did not see."[13]

Some men did join the Legion looking for adventure. Fighting was part of their life, they belonged to those who could be described as "born fighters." Perhaps there were even many such legionnaires, although one former legionnaire wrote that "they were obviously fish out of water, and did not fit into the frame of the Legion at all."[14] The thrill at finding that he was actually taking part in a real, good, old-fashioned fight, wrote P. C. Wren, "just the sort of thing one reads about, 'this was what I came for,' I said to myself, 'the genuine thing! What splendid luck! A real fight with real Arabs in a real desert! It doesn't seem real.' But it was, and he got, what is known vulgarly as a bellyfull."[15]

The legionnaire was actually a mercenary, whose real driving force was a love of fighting. "They fought, when the rest of the world thought of peace, in arduous colonial wars, of whose causes they knew little or nothing. . . . After the war . . . but there isn't any real after the war. War and peace are so alike . . ."[16]

Men escaped into the Legion from a wife or parents, to forget a woman they loved or hated, or to escape punishment for a crime. A captain of the Legion wrote: "The world forgetting, by the world forgotten. Such is the stuff from which legionnaires are made."[17] The ex-legionnaire Francis A. Waterhouse recalled how he was arrested in France and a gendarme told him he need not go to prison if he would tell the authorities that he wished to join the Legion. He consented and they suspended his sentence to let him join "this *beautiful* Legion of theirs."[18] Another ex-legionnaire told the story of a legionnaire who got drunk and was made to sign an I.O.U., which was really an enlistment in the Legion.[19] In 1928, Mrs. J. J. Fitzgerald tried to obtain the discharge of her son Willy Sadek from the Legion. Willy became a friend of another legionnaire, Bernard Ellis from England. Bernard signed up for the Legion while he was under 18 and the British Foreign Office obtained his release. On June 18, 1928, Sonia Ellis, Bernard's mother, wrote to Mrs. Fitzgerald:

In regards to Willy he told Bernard that he had leave from his ship and went to *Paris,* had a merry evening found himself robbed and unable to pay the fine. Penalty *Prison* or join the French Legion! Should this thing be true, I admire the boy more than I can say, as he did not wish to disgrace his mother by having the stigma of *Prison* over him, which would have otherwise been the case, under the circumstances they got this boy in under a trick for had he applied to the American Consul and explained the circumstances, the child would never have got himself where he is, to me your Willy is still a kiddie, only I who have been in the same plight as yourself, know what you are going through. It took me six months to get him out had to agree to pay for all the time he was in the Legion also the moneys he received on joining also for his fare for his return home. All that was nothing as long as I got him home [20]

"Only a psychologist could tell what process went on in my mind while I was asleep," wrote Brian Stuart. When he went to bed, no thought of enlisting in the Legion had crossed his mind. Yet, he awoke in the morning with the fixed idea to do so.[21]

Most men who joined the Legion tried to obliterate their past and sign up under an assumed name and nationality. The French authorities were aware of the situation and were willing to ignore it. Among the "famous" legionnaires was the assassin of the German Foreign Minister Walter von Rathenau who became an adjutant-chief, the highest rank among the non-commissioned officers. Thus, the Legion collected all kinds of criminals from many countries. The prospective legionnaire is not even forced to remember the names of his parents, or to state his profession. In the Legion no questions about a legionnaire's past were asked and thus he was able to escape punishment for a crime. Officially Frenchmen could serve in the Foreign Legion, but for the same reason many Frenchmen, even deserters from the regular French army, had joined the Legion. After a certain time in the Legion these Frenchmen were even permitted to regain their real identities and return to their units in the regular army.

According to the instructions governing the enlistment in the Legion, published in the *Journal Officiel* of August 2, 1937, foreigners had to possess a birth certificate or an equivalent document and asserting that their parents or legal guardians consented to their enlistment if they were 18 to 20 years of age. However, a declaration in which the party concerned certified that he was at least 20 years old was also accepted by the Legion.

Any French reservist, whatever his grade, could enlist in the Legion as private for five years, as a *foreigner.* Reserve officers had to resign their reserve commissions. Non-commissioned officers who were about to be dismissed from the regular French army for disciplinary reasons, could resign as NCO's and enlist as privates in the Legion. However, Frenchmen who had not yet completed their term of compulsory service and wanted to enlist in the Legion as Frenchmen had to obtain special permission from the Ministry of War.

To the historian, the survival of the Legion, with the system it represented, must appear an extraordinary anomaly. Why did men sign up? For the money? The pay was very low. For glory? The legionnaire lived and died unknown. For ambition? "No legionary has ever risen from the ranks to command the armies of France. For the gallant life of the 'free companion?' He endures toil, privation under the strictest discipline in the waste places of the earth, among hostile peoples, from whose hatred only fear protects him."[22]

In 1974, a criminal named Guy Neumeyer was found guilty on 15 counts, including armed burglary, holdups, muggings and gunfights with the police. According to the police and his lawyer, Neumeyer is "afraid of nothing" and has "an unbelievable contempt for danger." His lawyer said that in the French colonial era, such a young man "might have become a hero fighting alongside the Foreign Legion" in Africa or the Middle East.[23]

II. "Their Heroism Lies In Their Suffering"

One American officer wrote that the life of the legionnaire had many hardships. Discipline was severe, because many of these "fine adventurers," who had often broken the laws of their country, had to be handled firmly. In spite of the "misstatement of some newspapers who are frankly hostile to the Legion," the severity was not inhuman. It was only necessary to visit any garrison of the Legion to see that the life of the legionnaires was the same life as of the French soldiers.

> There, as everywhere, the officer looks out for the well-being of his men. The composition of the troops and the more frequent serious offenses against discipline evidently necessitate more severe punishments which however are according to the same scale as that for French regiments. This is true, especially in garrison, detested by the legionnaire who greatly prefers the life of physical hardship but full of unforeseen happenings of the wild. There only he feels himself truly a soldier, conscious of his strength and his usefulness and ready to risk his life gaily. It is in battle that the legionnaires show all their best military qualities: skill, courage, confidence, devotion, and a feeling of union. In action the legionnaire demonstrates the respect which he has for his officers, and never in any troops has the famous maxim: "all for one, one for all" been more scrupulously observed, nor caused more brilliant deeds. The Foreign Legion is truly an organization of the elite.[24]

However, Reginald R. Forbes entitled a chapter of his memoirs of the Legion "Soldiers or Convicts."[25] The former legionary Mervyn Pellew was of the opinion that the system at the Legion aimed

> at breaking a man's spirit, breaking his self-respect, breaking his hopes, breaking every quality in him that savours of humanity, and leaving him nothing but a kind of perverted pride in the harshness and brute-force of the body which has taken away his dearest possession, his individuality and turned him into an unthinking, pitiless fighting-machine, efficient and sullen.[26]

The Legion was famous for its cruel forms of punishment. J. M. Sothern told of the following punishment known as *la crapaudine:* Five or six legionnaires suspected of selling arms to the Arabs were placed in a kneeling position in a small trench, tight against each other, with their wrists lashed to their ankles behind their backs. Bare-headed and stripped to the waist, with jam smeared over their faces in order to attract ants and flies, they were left in the sun for several days. After three days one died, a second had his hand amputated on account of gangrene poisoning having set in, and a third went mad. Erwin Rosen, also an ex-legionnaire, thus described the *crapaudine:* the man to be punished was tied up in a bundle, his hands and feet tied together on his back till they formed a sort of semicircle. Another form of punishment was the *silo*. It consisted of a funnel-shaped hole in the ground, broad at the top and pointed towards the bottom. Into this hole the legionnaire was thrown, without a blanket or any other protection against the rain, cold and sun. He was left there for several days, unable to lie down. Often a *silo* prisoner died in the hole. According to Michael Alexander, a Britisher, the punishment known as *la tombe* (the legionnaire was forced to dig a grave in the sand and lie in it for three nights with hands and ankles tied) was officially abolished after protest from the United Nations, but was still practiced in the 1950's in out-of-the-way camps.[27]

One former legionnaire described how his comrade Cordoba was punished for allegedly having stolen something belonging to an officer: A group of legionnaires, after enduring the strain of a drill as punishment, were given a tin mug of water each. As Cordoba's turn came an officer took the mug and dropped a handful of salt in the water and ordered him to drink it. Because Cordoba dared to protest he was tied up and flogged until his back was a mess of ploughed flesh, salt was rubbed into the flesh and then he was put on the rack. The former legionnaire thus described the rack:

> This rack is a wooden frame in which a man can be fixed as though in a vice. It is so constructed that his arms are fastened stretched out, and, at the same time pulled slightly backward—an exceedingly awkward position, after a short time. When he is fixed in the rack, a bag of wet sand, weighing about 36 pounds, is strapped on to the nape of the neck and fastened by a harness which is contrived so that it pulls the victim's head forward and downward, until his chin rests on his breastbone.

All this happened six weeks before the court-martial at which Cordoba appeared in chains, held up by two guards. The court-martial found him to be innocent. The same ex-legionnaire described another form of punishment: the man, stripped to the waist, was kneeling beside a T-shaped frame driven in the ground. His neck was fastened down to the centre and his two wrists to the extreme ends of it. On either side of his kneeling form a stake had been driven into the ground, and his waist was fastened to stakes driven to the ground on either side, the result being that he was unable to move any part of his body. A long pole twenty feet in height had been stuck into the ground, and on the top of it an old petrol tin had been fastened. It was pierced in the bottom in such a manner that every few minutes a drop of water fell on the man's spine, below the nape of the neck. After a while the drops of water provoked a terrible pain, like a very hot dagger, and waiting for the next drop was the most terrible part of this torture.[28]

An ex-legionnaire thus described how a legionnaire, a Dane named Anderson, a good soldier, on the verge of *cafard,* was punished for flinging his shovel at a sadistic officer, a "devil who gloried in seeing pain and suffering." He was locked up in the hottest cell, with his hands and feet manacled. All that day the captain came to the cell every fifteen minutes and jeered at the poor devil. The Dane did not utter a word, even though he had not been given the half pint of tepid water which other prisoners were given.

> By noon the next day, the sun blazed down so that rifle barrels or galvanized iron blistered the hands if touched. At one o'clock, the Dane was taken out of his cell by the four sergeants, stripped to the skin and *buried naked in the sand* with only his face free. For the first hour that brave chap mocked the captain and his sergeants. Then his face suddenly became bloodshot and he let out the most dreadful shriek from his blue lips. The legionnaires stood around awestricken, glaring at him while he let out peal after peal, crying for mercy from a devil who knew no mercy. "If," he cried in awful sobs, "you will release me from this blazing pit, from this oven which is burning me and driving me mad, I will kiss your feet every time you ask me. I will do anything, say anything . . ." and all the time the captain stood beside his grave and grinned. Anderson was not released until night. Then he was a gibbering idiot.[29]

"Their heroism lies in their suffering," wrote the former legionnaire Francis Arthur Waterhouse.[30] A young legionnaire, who disobeyed an order, received twenty lashes each day for three days. Then he was tied up to the wheel of a gun and left in the blazing sun for eight hours.[31]

Those who tried to escape and failed, wasted away in prison. Deserters who were caught were dragged back at the tail of a horse with a halter around their necks. Two legionnaires who had tried to escape from a ship were entirely dressed, with full equipment and packs, bound hand and foot, and imprisoned in a chamber above the boiler room. This happened in a region only two degrees from the equator; it was like putting them in an oven or roasting them over a fire.[32]

For a time, self-mutilation was one common way of getting out of the Legion. Those who chose this way cared little if they became handicapped and disabled for life as long as they got out of the Legion. But later things changed and a legionnaire who wounded himself was court-martialed and sentenced up to five years in prison.[33]

Legionnaires were often punished by being sent to the *bats d'Af* (battalions of Africa), disciplinary units to which France sent many of her criminals and about which Albert Londres wrote that it surpasses the worst that Dante saw in his inferno. Colomb-Béchar was the site of the *Compagnie de Discipline* of the Legion. It is one of the hottest corners of North Africa. "There is no more monstrous evil under the sun than the Penal Battalion," wrote Roy Baker.[34] Sholem Schwartzbard, who served in the Legion during World War I, nicknamed the disciplinary battalion "African Siberia." He recalled a legionnaire of Belgian origin who had signed up for five years, but was sentenced to five years in "African Siberia" for talking back to a brutal corporal; there he was sentenced to another five years. Once, during a forced march, he was unable to continue. For this he received another three years, and another time five more years. When World War I broke out he was permitted to join a regiment fighting in France. He was dreaming of being transferred to the Belgian army, not dying for France which made a wreck of him. (On March 20, 1940, Charles H. Heisler, American consul at Tunis, reported that soldiers of the French disciplinary *Bataillon d'Afrique*, stationed in the southern military district of Tunisia, rioted and hanged their colonel.)[35]

III. "We Are French *Soldiers* But Not French *Citizens*"

The legionnaire's credo was thus summed up in a Legion song:

> Soldats de la Légion
> De la Légion Etrangère,
> N'ayant pas de nation
> La France est notre Mère.
>
> [Soldiers of the Legion,
> Of the Foreign Legion
> Having no country,
> France is our Mother.][36]

But was France the legionnaire's Mother? Edmond Genet, the first American pilot killed during World War I wrote: "We are French *soldiers* but not French *citizens*."[37] "Whom shall I defend—/Where will be my fatherland?" asked the Jewish legionnaire Sholem Schwartzbard while on guard duty somewhere in the Vosges mountains during World War I.[38] The motto on the flags of the regular French army is "Honor and Fatherland." Not so in the Legion. The motto on the regimental flags is "Honor and Discipline."

There is something gruesome in the expression *il se fait tuer* used by some "historians" in writing about Jewish legionnaires killed in action, as if they were seeking death as their goal.[39] Sholem Schwartzbard wrote: "Only death threatens on every corner—who is asking for more?"[40]

An American officer wrote that all other soldiers "step aside for the legionnaires; and the Legion shows them a way, or shows them how to die. . . . other regiments sometimes conquer, the Legion always knows how to die."[41] A British author wrote that the legionnaire

> may be said to have chosen Death as his bride. For Death is, indeed, the bride of the Legion, as was well expressed by General de Négrier in his famous words before a battle: "Mais vous autres, légionnaires, vous êtes soldats pour mourir, et je vous envoie ou l'on meurt." Any man who comes to the Legion

11

should know that he comes to die, or at least that there is small hope of escape. The actual motto of the Legion is "Honneur et Fidélité: Valeur et Discipline"; perhaps an alternative motto would be: "Morituri vos salutant."[42]

Death is the theme of a Legion song:

> Nos anciens ont su mourir
> Pour la gloire de la Légion,
> Vous saurez tous perir
> Suivant la tradition.
>
> [Our ancients know how to die
> for the glory of the Legion,
> You will all know how to perish
> According to tradition.]

The most important training in the Legion consisted of long hours of marching. The Legion was proud of its marches; sometimes legionnaires marched over forty kilometers a day, often in full kit. One legionnaire thus summed up the marching of "the two-legged cavalry," a nickname earned by the Legion:

> "March anyhow you damn well like. Humped back, toes turned in or out, but—damn you march!" If you are hungry, and hunger pangs are gnawing your stomach; if your tongue is parched and hanging out, well bad luck, but it is no excuse for not marching. If you *think* that you are dead tired, utterly exhausted: if your feet are blistered or even bleeding, well!—that is really too bad, but it is no reason for not marching.

However, the legionnaire was permitted to carry his rifle as he pleased, on the shoulder or by the sling. He was allowed to carry his knapsack as he wished, to wear his coat opened or buttoned. The legionnaires could smoke, talk or sing.[43] In fact, during World War II we were encouraged to march in groups according to nationalities and sing our songs in Yiddish, Italian, Spanish or other languages.

Many writers compared the Foreign Legion and its marches to hell. Walter Kanitz summed up the life of the legionnaire with the following words: the *cafard,* forced marches, the danger of dying of thrist in the desert of North Africa or having his throat cut by a hostile Arab—

> all this is far from the glory and adventure so frequently associated with the idea of service in the Legion. There is nothing glorious or adventurous about the

marches of the Legion. It is hard, tough work, requiring superhuman endurance. Between an implacable enemy and the iron claws of the Corps' discipline the legionnaire fights a losing battle against a murderous climate. His living conditions are much more primitive than those of a criminal in a penitentiary and his chances of survival are less than slim. If he survives, he survives as a physical or mental wreck. This is the glory and adventure of the Legion![44]

One ex-legionnaire characterized the Legion's marches as a "ruthless practice . . . If you fall and can't take care of yourself—if you can't get up under your own power or are not discovered in time—you die where you fall. Colonials are sent back to First Aid and dressing stations; imperials are sent back. But legionnaires get back by themselves." To this the legionnaire added the immortal words: "'Marche ou crève!' which translated means simply, 'March or die!'"[45]

"To fall out of a march" was to commit one of the most serious offenses known to the Legion, "punished in characteristic fashion by dragging the laggard along at the tail of a cart or a mule."[46]

IV. "The Legion Works, the Legion Gets No Pay!"

Wine is the legionnaire's only escape from reality, the only way of forgetting his misery. In order to have his bottle of *pinard* he is willing to steal or engage in homosexuality, and, in rare cases, even to commit murder. One ex-legionnaire recalled an old legionnaire begging for a franc, "a lousy franc! so that I can buy some *pinard* in the canteen . . . give me five sous, friend . . . only five sous."[47] The more a legionnaire drinks the more thirstier he becomes. The *cafard* brings out the *soif* (thirst) and the wine brings out an even greater *cafard*. There is no end to this vicious circle. *Cafard* is the dread, black homesickness which drives the legionnaire to do desperate things. Everything could be explained by an attack of *cafard*. It was the official excuse for tolerance of drunkenness. "Legionnaires were drunk on duty, and they were drunk off duty. Whole companies would march drunk, fight drunk, die drunk. No one was considered drunk in the Legion provided he could get to bed, on all fours if necessary. Drink to the Legion meant something different than it did to any other army. It was the only way of achieving the oblivion that made life bearable." They got drunk on cheap, raw, red wine called *pinard*. The old legionnaires even scorched French cigarettes with rum. The Philadelphia *Record* recalled the "sinister frankness" of a sergeant of the Legion who admonished a new recruit this way:

> It is when you are insane that you must be careful . . . yes, all good legionnaires go insane at times—then they kill themselves, kill their comrades, or defy a sergeant . . . we call it "le cafard"—the cockroach. It crawls round and round in the brain, and the greater the heat, the monotony, the hardship, the overwork, the overmarching, and the drink—the faster goes the beetle and the more it tickles. Then the man says, "J'ai le cafard," and runs amuck, or commits suicide, or deserts, or defies a sergeant . . .[48]

Women were another escape, although more expensive. There was no lack of bordellos in North Africa, near the camps and even in tents. For a long time the medical corps took care of the sexual needs of the men but it did not distribute individual first-aid kits to legionnaires. Arab girls were plentiful and they were cheap. The lucky ones among the legionnaires had their own Arab mistresses or wives who often followed their men on the move. One ex-legionnaire recalled:

> Like most of the other legionnaires I'd never had a chance to meet a real girl. French shopkeepers and civil servants and minor employees in the local business houses kept their women well away from the Legion. They thought we were dirt. And some of us were.[49]

In 1929, an American officer stated:

> Many legionnaires love the life full of unforeseen events which awaits them in Morocco; we are therefore not surprised that there are many reenlistments among the men who have accomplished their first five years of service. In fact, outside of the NCOs, about one quarter of the strength of the regiment is made up of reenlisted men. It would not be saying the truth to attribute only to the desire for an adventurous life the love which many legionnaires show for their career. In reality there are many who are lured by and remain in the Legion because of the certainty of good pay . . . These various pecuniary advantages are particularly appreciated by the legionnaires. It is therefore not surprising that many renew their first contract of enlistment, assured as they are to live a life which they like on account of its roughness and its dangers but which frees them entirely for the present and partially for the future of worry in the struggle for life.[50]

In reality the "good pay" was part of the legend about the Legion. What actually happened to a legionnaire after having served five years? According to an Englishman who had served in the Legion, the discharged legionnaire landed in Paris or in another city, or on the borders of Germany, poorly clad, often in bad health, most probably shivering with cold:

> Then he begins to long for his old pal *pinard,* for a few litres of that in his belly alongside of a bowl of the Legion's soup. He craves for the warmth and sunshine of Africa and for the company of old comrades—tough as they may have been. He probably has no relations to go to after five years in the Legion, and his term of service has not made him more capable of getting a job in civil life. Worn out, hungry, lonely, craving for the company of friends, at last he re-enlists and goes back to Africa and the Legion. There at least he will be clothed, fed, meet old pals, make new ones and eke out an existence, until old man Death comes for him.[51]

The pay was very small, so small that the legionnaire could not afford the barest necessities. Most chroniclers of the Legion wrote that the food was, if not good, then, at least, plentiful. One chronicler, however, wrote that "Food was scarce."[52]

According to Erwin Rosen, a German-American who had served in the Legion, the luckiest man was the one who kept up some sort of communications with his family or friends and was able to get a small money order. "The Legion works—the Legion gets no pay!," an Arabian spahi told him once. Shortly before World War I, a legionnaire was paid five centimes (1/20 of a franc) a day which was about one cent, a fiftieth part of the daily pay of an American soldier. When one takes into consideration that the legionnaire was a "paid" mercenary his "pay" seemed grotesque.[53]

In 1935, legionnaires were paid 0.25 francs per day during the first year; 1.20 after one year's service; 2.20 after three years; 2.95 after five years; 3.45 after ten years. The following bonuses were given: 1,000 francs, of which 600 were paid after three months' service. The remaining 400 francs were paid out during the rest of the first year of service. After five years of service, a yearly bonus of 300 francs was given. After fifteen years' service the legionnaire was entitled to a pension, the amount of which depended upon the duration of his service and the number of his campaigns.[54]

V. "The Right to Plunder"

In every army there are individuals of a criminal nature who are ready to loot, rape and kill. With the exception of the armies of Czarist Russia, Poland and other East European countries where tens of thousands of Jews were killed during pogroms, the Turkish army which massacred the Armenians, and the German Army during World War II, such acts were not army policy but were acts committed by individuals. Usually such acts were severely punished. In the Foreign Legion looting, raping and killing were a part of life. Such acts were explained as a reaction against atrocities committed by Arabs. However, such forms of revenge could hardly be excused if they were committed by an army of a civilized country. Killing of innocents was common after a battle. One legionnaire recalled that about eighty Druses had been taken prisoner and were made to assist in work after a battle in Syria. Then, when they had completed their job, they were finished off by the Algerians, squads of whom were acting as execution parties. Not a single prisoner was allowed to live. The legionnaire explained the reason for the massacre:

> Five women were caught with two legionnaires. These women had long, razor-sharp knives in their hands. The two legionnaires were spread-eagled out on the floor: hands and feet were kept in position by large nails which these harpies had driven through them into the floor. They were nearly dead after having suffered the most terrible tortures at the hands of the women. As the Algerian Tirailleurs [of the French Army] entered, these women stood back from their awful amusement, blood dropping from the knives they held in their hands. Every one of the women was covered with blood from head to foot. They expected no quarter but sprang at the soldiers as they entered. They were bayoneted where they stood fighting like fiends until the last one was killed.

The looting, rape and torture followed:

> Hot bayonets applied to the feet of men who are too silent will make the most stubborn talk and remember things which he thinks that he has forgotten. Dead bodies properly rifled will give up gemmounted daggers and scimitars . . . We burnt, pillaged, shot, and often tortured every man whom we caught with a weapon—even a small knife. La belle France was pretty desperate and she can

be as merciless as any when roused to the extent that she was at that time. Actually France was fighting with her back to the wall, for she knew better than any country, that if things went against her in Syria, others would take advantage of her disasters. Day after day we went out on these merciless punishing expeditions. It was always the same. We would be fired at from every wall and piece of cover; it did no good. Murder, rape, death, torture, kill, kill, kill; was all it amounted to with either side.[55]

Another ex-legionnaire recalled that after a battle, the officer ordered his men to collect the babies of the villages and throw them into the river. There the officer shot them.[56]

Bennet J. Doty, an American ex-legionnaire, told the story of the looting of a Druse village which had refused to pay taxes:

Some of the old legionnaires were elated. They had heard rare things of such expeditions. They knew that if the tax was still refused, in spite of such formal asking, then everything in the village was taken and the houses burned. This meant loot. You returned with goats, sheep, horses and chicken; sometimes if you were lucky, with trinkets, linen and silk. There were stories of men having found jewelry, of another having found a pot of gold coins. The old devils of my sections wet their lips with anticipation. Not that they were misers, apt to hoard gold. But gold meant lots of wine and plenty of dancing girls . . . they hoped the village notables would refuse to pay the taxes, so that we could do a little looting.

The village did pay the taxes and the legionnaires felt cheated. They marched back, disconsolate. Politically the expedition was a success; from the point of view of the legionnaires it was a dead loss. Sometime later the legionnaires had their chance; there was a bloody battle. But "if it has been a decent battle, there is also loot." One legionnaire actually came across someone's hidden treasure in a cellar of the village—coins mixed with trinkets and jewelry worth nearly five thousand francs. "For months afterwards, whenever he was where it could be done, he was to get gloriously drunk till the result of his frugal morning's labor at last was dissipated."

Doty tried to desert, was caught, and sentenced to eight years of forced labor. But an American correspondent and the American consul intervened for him and he was permitted to leave the Legion.[57]

Ex-legionnaire Francis Arthur Waterhouse described a primitive expedition in Damascus after which "the looting, murdering, capturing, raiding, and raping lasted altogether about four hours."[58]

Reginald R. Forbes described a scene of looting. The officer told them: "Take what you want—and who you want, and if anyone questions your right—shoot!" The head man of the Moroccan village who protested was shot, "and the awful business of pillage and rape began."[59]

A captain of the Legion and its admirer wrote in 1930:

> But life in the Legion has its compensations, of their rights and privileges granted them by unwritten law the legionnaires are jealous and their officers are scrupulous. In passing, it may be said that the one privilege which the Legion prized above all is that which the French term the *droit de pillage* [the right to plunder]. The Legion alone of the troops of any civilized army today has this privilege, and, so far as I know, has always had it. When the Legion takes a town, it takes it. And how! What soldier has not thrilled at the thought of loot?[60]

Some ex-legionnaires and both French and foreign observers have had kind words for the French Foreign Legion. Walter Kanitz wrote:

> On the whole it can be said that regardless of the nationality of the volunteer the Legion has been a new fatherland for everyone who knocked at its door. It was a mother, stern and hard maybe, but a mother nevertheless to the thousands of hungry, the thousands of desperate, the thousands of persecuted which the troubled economy and turbulent politics of Europe have shed and discarded over the 120 years of the Legion's existence. Legio Patria Nostra! La Légion Etrangère, immense melting pot, became the home, the last refuge and ultimate protection for the men without a country.[61]

In the opinion of one observer this was a *"troupe d'élite,* which has been the admiration of all . . . Never can such a glory fade, for it is among the proudest of all the glories of the French army."[62] The Legion was even suggested as a model for an international force.[63]

The number of defenders of the Legion was especially great among the Frenchmen. However, even many Frenchmen objected, and still object, to the use of foreigners in a special Legion. They are shocked by the very idea of an army consisting of deserters from other armies, criminals, and other desperate individuals. Germany and other countries, especially Germany, have attacked the French government on the grounds that the Foreign Legion was against international law and the treatment of foreign nationals in the Legion was inhuman. Germany was especially bitter because the majority of legionnaires was always German.[64]

At the end of 1921, Swiss newspapers carried warnings from the police that French agents were recruiting men for the Foreign Legion, particularly in the canton of Solothurn. This recruitment was believed in Switzerland to be a pernicious evil, as the Swiss claimed that many excellent young men from decent homes were caught up by the fine promises of these recruiting agents, and very few of them were heard of again once they enlisted with the Legion. The Swiss claimed that the standards of living, food, housing conditions, etc., were abominable and below those which any Swiss was accustomed to, and that the standard of morality was such that most young men were ruined forever. The Swiss did not feel the same toward the Dutch foreign legion for service in the Dutch East Indies, this due to the fact that after a certain number of years' service a man received a decent pension.[65]

In 1926, Alfred Lensch, a nephew of a professor of law at Yale, was a student at the University of Freiburg, Germany, when he made a trip to Switzerland. While there, he met a recruiting emissary of the Legion and the suspicion was that he enlisted in the Legion. His uncle asked the State Department to locate Lensch.[66]

The majority of ex-legionnaires who wrote about the Legion felt only animosity for the Legion. Fritz Klose wrote: "Over in Africa are 40,000 Germans—slaves to the French masters and outcasts from Society."[67] Reginard R. Forbes wrote:

> I do not like France or the French; I never yet met a legionnaire who did. I consider that the maintenance of such a force as the Foreign Legion is in itself a blot upon the nation; and the atrocities which I saw during my service have bred in me a hatred of the country and people who can permit such things.[68]

In the opinion of Heintz Pol, an American writer, "to enter in the Foreign Legion has always been regarded as something dishonorable."[69]

Mention should be made of the Spanish Foreign Legion, which followed the example of the French Foreign Legion.

On September 4, 1920, at a time when Spain had difficulties in Spanish Morocco, Colonel (later General) Don José Millán Astray organized the Spanish Foreign Legion, or Tercio de Extranjeros, as it was known throughout Spain. The headquarters of the Legion was at Centa, in Spanish Morocco, and it was patterned after the French Foreign Legion. In the words of Millán Astray, the legionnaires consisted of

> the strugglers with life, adventurers, dreamers, the hopeful and the hopeless . . . they come because things are too complex for them, because of passions,

necessity, vice, social disarrangement, the thirst for glory, the craving to live fully or the desire to die; because of desperations and hunger; because of the pay and a secure lodging.

One ex-legionnaire called the Spanish Foreign Legion "the hell of the earth." The hymn of the Spanish Legion starts off with: "Legionarios a luchar! Legionarios a morir!" (Legionnaires, on to conflict! Legionnaires, on to death!). It was Colonel Francisco Franco who led the Legion through the war with the Riffs and later perfected and enlarged it. It was at the Officers' Club in Centa that Franco made plans to attack the republic. The infamous role of the Legion in the Spanish civil war is only too well known.[70] The *Voelkischer Beobachter* of April 19, 1937, published a photograph of the following inscription on the tombstone of a legionnaire killed in the Spanish Civil War: "Viva La Muerte."

VI. Jews Among the Old-Time Legionnaires

With the exception of World Wars I and II, when aliens desiring to fight for France were forced to enlist in the Foreign Legion, few Jews lost their way in the Legion.

On February 14, 1889, a Russian Jewish student named Wolf Abedovitch signed up for five years in the Legion, served in Algeria, and was honorably discharged on February 12, 1894. He then worked as a cap maker and later as a watch repairman. He used to write Yiddish and Hebrew poetry that was recited at literary events in Paris.[71] Erwin Rosen, a German-American legionnaire, told the story of a Rumanian Jewish legionnaire named Abramovici who before 1914 "had a spark of humor left in him" that was rare in the Legion. He was the first, the last, and the only legionnaire who ever succeeded in never doing any work and who was saved from punishment by his inherent gift of humor.[72] Victor Emmanuel Chapman, an American legionnaire, wrote on September 26, 1914: "A typical Parisian *apache* (ruffian) has taken a fancy to me. He is a naturalized Russian Jew, but got in as a foreigner because he served a turn in prison and did not want to be sent to Algiers."[73]

In 1937, the Polish Jew Mendl Erlich, in danger of expulsion from France as an illegal immigrant, signed up for the Legion and served in North Africa until after the War. One should imagine that many other people joined the Legion in order to avoid expulsion which at that time threatened many illegal immigrants.[73a]

A. Liddel Hart wrote that after World War II there was a Jewish legionnaire in Indochina who used to sing Nazi songs.[74] Geoffrey Bocca, himself a legionnaire, told the following story of an Israeli *sabra* and professional soldier who served after World War II in the Legion. Because Jews were rare in the Legion he was nicknamed *Jew*. Although he kept to himself he was well liked by his comrades who gave him the greatest accolade legionnaires can bestow. They called him *un bon baroudeur*, a good scrapper. At that time the Legion and the French paratroopers had much admiration for the Israeli Army, dating from a brief alliance sealed in blood at Suez. The Jews even maintained a comradeship with a former Nazi. "He wasn't a bad fellow," the Jews told Bocca. "But he could not understand complexity. He was capable of either hate or doglike devotion. There were no gradations in between. You were a bastard or a comrade. He hated the French, and despised the Legion, and because he could not pigeonhole me in any of the dockets associated with France or the Legion, he followed me around." He even cleaned the Jew's rifle. Then he deserted. The Jew went out into the bled to try and get him back but the Arabs got him first and slit his throat. Nobody liked him except the Jew and when he died he mourned him. He risked his own life for a good-for-nothing. Had the Jew been taken prisoner by the Arabs, his fate, as a Jew and a legionnaire, was something that did not bear contemplating. To Bocca, the Jew was a mysterious man who fulfilled completely Vigny's view that "the warrior's hardness is an iron mask, concealing a noble countenance, a stone dungeon enclosing a royal prisoner." Sometime later, in Paris, Bocca spoke about the Jewish legionnaire to a woman diplomat from the Israeli embassy. Although he pointed out that he had gone into deadly danger in order to bring his friend back to the Legion, she was not impressed. "He must have been a pretty disreputable specimen of Jew," she said. "Only criminals join that dreadful army." Bocca noted: "I don't know why I was taken by surprise, but I was. I knew that the Legion's admiration for Israel was not reciprocated."[75]

Charles E. Mercier told the following strange story of the enlistment in the Legion of a Rumanian Jew named Eliahu Itzkovitz. During World War II Eliahu was thrown together with his parents and three brothers into a concentration camp operated by the Rumanian Iron Guard. His parents and brothers perished there at the hands of a Rumanian named Stanescu. Eliahu survived, emigrated to Israel and became a paratrooper in the Israeli Army. His dream was to find Stanescu and kill him. One day he learned that Stanescu enlisted in the French Foreign Legion and served in Vietnam. He obtained a transfer to the Israeli Navy and when his ship was in an Italian port he deserted, crossed into France and joined the Legion. Finally he located Stanescu and killed him. He served out his term in the Legion and presented himself to the Israeli military attaché in Paris and told him the story. In view of the circumstances an Israeli court-martial sentenced Eliahu only to one year imprisonment.[76]

As noted earlier, during World War I aliens were forced to join the French Foreign Legion. Among them were many immigrant Jews.

VII. Volunteers for the Defense of France

As early as June 2, 1914, the Yiddish publication *Letste Nayes (Latest News)* published an appeal by Sacha Malinets to create a "regiment of Slav volunteers." The issue of August 2, 1914 stated: "If we are not yet Frenchmen by law, we are with our heart and soul," and appealed to Jews to enlist. The poet L. de Bercy wrote in Gustave Hervé's *La Guerre Sociale* of August 26, 1914, "And where there are citizens, one will hear Nicolai's Jews." On July 31, 1914, a meeting was organized by nineteen Italian immigrants in the Café Globe for the purpose of enlisting foreign volunteers. Four of the organizers were Russian Jews. On the first day of enlistment there were 1,564 volunteers, 917 of them Jews. The majority of the Russian Jewish volunteers enlisted for the defense of France although they were anti-militarists. The first group of 150 Russian volunteers, half of them Jews, called itself "détachement socialiste" (Socialist detachment). Later the name was changed to "détachement républicain." The first meeting of these volunteers was held on August 1914 in a cooperative restaurant of Russian emigrés on rue des Cordelières. Later, a recruiting center was opened in a club of left-wing groups on rue de la Reine Blanche. This center published the following declaration:

> We Russian socialists are joining the French Army, fully conscious of the political importance of our decision . . . The autocratic and feudal governments of Germany and Austria who prepared and provoked this war represent the main forces of imperialism in the world . . . Their defeat will be a decisive triumph for democracy.

The first military instruction was given to these volunteers in a movie house on rue Tolbiac. The Socialist *L'Humanité* of September 20, 1914, published a letter by three "Polish" Socialists (Z. Leder, J. Tenenbaum, M. Kohn) who explained that they enlisted in order to fight not for the Czar of Russia but for French democracy. Many non-political immigrants went to the Russian Embassy to enlist. There a sign told them that only non-Jews were permitted to enter; Jews were directed elsewhere.

Rumanian Jews opened a recruiting office at Jacques Flax's restaurant on 10 rue Mésangerie. Another group of Rumanian Jews calling itself *Groupe de volontaires Juifs Russo-Roumains du 18e* opened a recruiting office at the Café Weissmann, on 82 rue Marcadet. This group posted broadsides on the streets containing the following appeal:

> Fellow Jews! France, the land of Liberty, Equality and Fraternity, the first country in the world to grant Jews the Rights of Man—this dear country where we and our families have found sanctuary and happiness—France is now in a state of war! What are we going to do to prove our love and loyalty to this second Fatherland of ours? Shall we sit with folded arms while the French people has risen as one man to the defense of the Fatherland? No! For even though we are not yet legally French, we are French in spirit . . . Together then, hand in hand and single of purpose, to the service of France.

There were even a few private recruiting offices. A certain Leibovitchi of 25 rue Custin recruited 800 Jews. On Montmartre, where many foreign-born Jews resided, a Jewish butcher rode on a horse decorated with the French and the blue and white flags, carrying placards calling upon Jews to join the French armed forces. On August 1, 1914, a group of Jews paraded through the Place de la Bastille carrying a placard with an appeal to fight for France. Sholem Schwartzbard, who was himself a volunteer, wrote a song in which the Jewish volunteers were compared to the Maccabees.

Jewish volunteers even came from neutral countries. On August 2, 1919, a group of Russian Jews arrived at Morteaux (Doubs) from Switzerland. From there they left for Bourg-en-Bresse to enlist. In Brussels a group of eighty-two Russian refugees enlisted at the French consulate.

There were not only Russian-Jewish volunteers. Many Jews from Rumania, Syria, and other nations desired to defend France. (After Russian Jews were allowed to be transferred from the Foreign Legion to regular French units they remained in the Legion. The Franco-Jewish weekly, *L'Univers Israélite,* suggested that these Jews, too, should be transferred into French regiments.)

A committee at 68 rue Sedaine registered a contingent of six hundred Turkish Jews. Many other Jews of the Ottoman Empire volunteered for service. (Those who had been discharged were not, like non-Jewish Ottomans, sent home, but were sent to Mascara for internment.)[77]

A *régiment de marche* (marching regiment) was formed with three battalions who signed up *pour la durée de la guerre* (for the duration of the war). A fourth battalion was later sent from Algeria, formed mainly with "duration" volunteers who signed up there. These four battalions formed the First *Régiment de Marche* of the French Foreign Legion stationed in the Palace of the Popes in Avignon. The First Regiment of the Legion had been transported to France in 1914, recruited till it numbered 4,000 men, and then "thrown into the furnace."

> In its first action, charging in the face of machine gun fire, across trenches and barbed wire, it had been virtually annihilated. Recruited up to strength again, it had gone on thus through the entire war, depleted almost to nothing over and over again—a sort of sacrificial corps, ever at the worst place.

Officers and non-commissioned officers of the 2nd *Régiment Etranger* were sent to Rouen to train volunteers. Later they moved to Toulouse where the 2nd *Régiment de Marche* was formed with three battalions of volunteers from France and a fourth from Algeria. These two regiments were attached to a Moroccan Division. After the first two regiments were sent to the front, a third *Régiment de Marche* of the Foreign Legion was formed with Paris firemen as the cadre. This regiment was regarded as the black sheep of the Legion. It was composed entirely of aliens who volunteered at the outbreak of the war and commanded, because of lack of trained officers to fill the cadres of the vastly expanded army, by officers of the Paris fire brigade. It never took part in a major action and was disbanded in July 1915.

In November 1914, Giuseppe Garibaldi, a grandson of the famed Italian liberator, brought a large number of Italian volunteers into France. They, too, were placed in the Foreign Legion, in the popularly called "Garibaldi Brigade." By May 1915, when Italy entered the war, the Italian brigade had lost 429 men. Many others were wounded. Italians who had enlisted earlier wanted to join the armed forces of their own country when she entered the conflict, but it took a long time to obtain permission for such transfers.

In November 1915, as a result of the departure of Italian, Belgian, some Russian, and other nationals for service with their respective armies, the four regiments were consolidated into one called, "Marching Regiment of the Foreign Legion." When the war started, the New York *Times* of May 24, 1917, recalled, six battalions of legionnaires forming two regiments had been sent to the front. "Now only three battalions remain forming one regiment."

Just how many men the Legion lost in World War I is not known.

According to one source, of 44,150 aliens who served in the Legion during the war nearly 31,000 were killed, wounded, or were reported missing in action.[78]

Mention should also be made of the Tunisian Jews. They could not be mobilized without the Bey's permission because Tunisia was only a French protectorate. However, many Tunisian Jews expressed a desire to sign up as volunteers on the condition that they be granted French citizenship and serve in regular French regiments. Even so, many Jews volunteered for the French Foreign Legion. (Later, Tunisian Jews suffered much from antisemitic propaganda that claimed they took away commerce from Frenchmen in Tunisia who were drafted.) After the war they organized an association of former Jewish volunteers (Association Tunisienne des Anciens Combattants Volontaires).[79]

VIII. "Engagé Pour la Gamelle"

Sholem Schwartzbard, the man who shot Petlura in 1926 to avenge the victims of the pogroms in the Ukraine, wrote in his memoirs that the Foreign Legion attracted many kinds of people:

> escaped criminals, liberated prisoners, thieves, drunkards, men who had lost their human feelings and sought to lose themselves in the Legion, where they no longer had to be accountable to public opinion. Their only duty was to obey a terrible inhuman soldierly discipline. Through their task of "civilizing" the quiet people of Africa—killing men, raping women—and also through all kinds of military denunciations, they obtained a low grade, became corporals and obtained medals. This became their sole morale, the only meaning of their lives.[80]

The great majority of legionnaires who fought in France were volunteers for the duration of the war who were forced to join the Legion. Some of the officers and non-commissioned officers of the staff were Frenchmen who had the misfortune to have served in the Legion. Some of them, but not all, had committed some infraction against the law after leaving the Legion. They felt unhappy and bitter because of having been thrown again into the Legion which they had tried to forget. But the majority of the staff consisted of *anciens,* old legionnaires who were brought over from African bases. The mixing of the old legionnaires with the volunteers, or "duration" legionnaires, provoked many conflicts. Thus the regiments of the Legion serving in France were composed of three different groups who had nothing in common in civilian life and distrusted each other while in uniform.

The Jewish volunteers were told over and over again that it was not the desire to fight for France that had brought them to the Legion, but the search for food. "You came only for the *gamelle*" (mess kit, a tin-plated bowl with a cover, strapped at the top of the pack). This phrase was constantly thrown at the volunteers by the Legion's old timers. In one unit a group of Jewish volunteers organized a protest meeting. On Yom Kippur (the Day of Atonement), the most solemn Jewish holiday and fast day, they fasted and in the evening did not eat at the Legion's mess but broke the fast with their own food, paid for with their own money: white bread, salami and beer. They took a photograph of one legionnaire named Friedman who had come from Switzerland, holding a mess kit with the following legend: *Engagé pour la gamelle* (enlisted for the mess kit).[81]

The dream of every Jewish legionnaire was to be transferred to a regular French regiment. Pierre Goldfarb, born in Warsaw, who came to France in the beginning of 1914, also signed up for the Legion. From the front he wrote: "France was for me a friend. That is why I defend her with the greatest courage and if I remain here, I will tell my parents: victim of his duty!" In another letter the same volunteer expressed his desire to be part of a "regular" regiment, "As I am a soldier and am fighting for France it will make me happy to be called soldier and non legionnaire; and when I will go through the campaign one could not tell me that I served in a regiment which has no flag." *L'Univers Israélite* noted that the letter contained a sentiment of honor and dignity beneath the frustration.[82]

Many of the Jewish volunteers had spent many years in France. They had emigrated to France as children, had gone to schools there, but had not become French citizens because of the strict French naturalization laws. Such was the case of Marcel Pessin who had graduated in 1910 with honors from the Jewish Vocational School of Rue Rosiers. When the war broke out he signed up with the Legion for the duration of the war. He served there one year. As a result of a wound *(à la suite d'une blessure)*, he was happy to be transferred to a French regiment, where he was wounded three more times and later killed in combat.[83]

Some tried to excuse the French authorities: they were too busy to think about the sensitive alien volunteers and their desire not to serve in the Legion. It was hard, however, to find an excuse for such a shortsighted policy.[84]

IX. The Revolt of Carency

Carency was the site of a bloody battle that took place on May 9, 1915. Thousands of volunteers in the Foreign Legion were attached to a Moroccan Division which was engaged on this front. This was a heroic battle, according to some; a terrible, bloody debacle, according to others. Of about 4,000 Jewish volunteers, only 900 came out alive. Capt. Brevit of the 1st Régminet Etranger told a British officer after the combat of Carency that the Jewish soldiers were "the best and bravest soldiers under his command."

In an hour and a half the Moroccan Division advanced four-and-a-half kilometers and reached the objective: cote 140 was taken! It was considered a great victory, the first victory of the war. One historian wrote of the battle of Carency—and a bulletin of the Association of former Jewish legionnaires repeated it—"Never before was an attack undertaken with such cheerful ardour."[85]

Officially Carency became a synonym for bravery, and afterwards the associations of former Jewish volunteers celebrated the memory of the battle of Carency with patriotic ceremonies. On May 9, 1925, a monument was erected on "Hill 140," where the famous battle took place, in memory of all who had died there. There was another side to the history of this front as well. Soon after the battle of Carency large groups of both Jewish and non-Jewish volunteers of the 2nd Regiment refused to move up to the front; they asked for transfers from the Legion to regular French army units, even to Russia. Many Jewish legionnaires were court-martialed, nine were executed, and over twenty of them were sentenced to long years of hard labor. Among the nine who were executed was Maurice Sloutchewsky, a member of the cap makers union. (One hundred and seventy of the union's 1,000 members had signed up for the Legion.) In a short letter addressed to his comrades of the union he expressed hope that the death sentence would be commuted to imprisonment. Then he added a postscript: "I am leaving for the scaffold."[86]

Sholem Schwartzbard related in his memoirs that the legionnaires were told of a circular giving all Russian citizens who had volunteered for the

Legion the right to ask for a transfer to regular French units or to Russia. The rumor reached them while they were in the trenches, after the first attack of May 9, 1915, and before the second attack of June 16. By then only a little over 930 of the original legionnaires in the regiment remained alive. Right after the first attack the Italians started to rebel and were sent away. Then the Greeks, too, refused to fight, but they did not openly revolt. The Jewish legionnaires saw a ray of hope in the circular and they decided to demand transfers. Legionnaires of other nationalities encouraged them to do so hoping that the circular would also apply to them. Instead of being transferred they were ordered to get ready for a new attack. The Jewish legionnaires refused to move. They assembled in a grove and demanded an explanation as to why they were not transferred. The officers, including the colonel himself, came to plead with the legionnaires. He told them that Frenchmen and Russians were fighting the same enemy. "But not in the Foreign Legion," they replied. A short time later the legionnaires were locked up in a large stable guarded by Senegalese troops. The officers blamed Jewish revolutionaries for the revolt. In reality those responsible were a Russian officer and two Russian non-commissioned officers who were the first to tell their comrades of the existence of the circular. In the stable they discussed whether or not they should give up. Finally, the general of the division himself came to plead with them. Paris had found out about the revolt in the 2nd regiment on May 9 and the execution of the nine legionnaires, and the authorities had, in all probability, been ordered to avoid new executions by being lenient with the legionnaires. The latter decided to rejoin their units.[87]

News about the nine executions reached Paris quickly. Those foreign-born Jews who had not yet volunteered now refused to do so. Under the influence of anti-Jewish groups, the French government decided, in July 1915, to take strong measures against those foreigners who did not volunteer for the Foreign Legion. They were to be investigated by the police and—in case they still refused to volunteer—to be expelled to Russia. Some Russian Jews left at that time for the United States and for Spain. The situation was much discussed in the press. While the reactionary press attacked the Russian Jews who refused to join the Foreign Legion, the liberal press came to their defense.

Russian Jews started to receive summonses to come to the police stations and were threatened with being sent to concentration camps *(camps de concentration)* if they would not go back to serve in the Russian army or sign up for the Foreign Legion. "Which minister authorized the prefect of police to give such orders to his commissioners?" asked Gustave Hervé in *La Guerre Sociale*. He characterized the police action as an "enormous stupidity." These Jews were political refugees who had escaped from Russian pogroms. "In our Foreign Legion?" asked Hervé, "thousands of them did just that in the beginning of the war when Paris was menaced by the German advance. Ah, they were well rewarded. A heartless and brainless administration" lost its head in August and provided for these sensitive volunteers to defend republican France with a cadre of officers and N.C.O.'s taken from the Legion, men accustomed to a disciplinary life of Algeria and Morocco, devils and human wrecks who had signed up in peacetime as mercenaries in the Legion. These sensitive volunteers were called *sales youpins* (dirty sheenies), *mangeurs de gamelle* (mess kit eaters). Now one dares to ask the Russian Jews who are familiar with the tragic events of the Legion—the Jewish Legion—near Carency, to sign up for the Foreign Legion! Hervé thus made an allusion to the revolt and execution of nine legionnaires. He warned of the shock that these facts would produce among the Jews of the United States and demanded that sanctions be imposed on police functionaries and others responsible for this blemish on France and the republic. "We are begging everywhere for sympathy," Hervé wrote. "The infamous menace addressed to our Russian-Jewish refugees will bring us no sympathy from two-and-a-half million American Jews, so influential in New York!" He thus addressed himself to the Jewish legionnaires:

> Forgive those miserable non-coms who have been calling you *sales youpins* and *mangeurs de gamelle,* you who came forward of your own free will full of enthusiasm, ready to give your blood for France, the symbol in your eyes of all liberty, all moral grandeur. Forgive them, for they knew not what they did.

La Guerre Sociale of July 3, 1915, printed a cartoon by Grandjean entitled, "The Eternal Wandering Jews," showing a group of Russian Jews listening to a police commissioner telling them: "You say that you had escaped from Russia because of pogroms? I don't care! Right of asylum? I don't care!"[88]

The trade unionist *La Bataille Syndicaliste* of June 27, 1915, wrote about the Russian Jewish legionnaires:

> One knows everything those who enlisted in the beginning of the war had to

undergo. We are aware of the degradation they were put to by the non-commissioned officers from Algeria and Morocco. We are also aware how many of these *mangeurs de gamelle,* as they were called by the imbeciles commissioned to train them, were killed in action. They offered their lives to defend France, in exchange they were given only venom, and even worse. And one would like that the Russian Jews who knew how the first volunteers of their race were treated, and who know of the horrible drama which stained with blood the Jewish Legion, not far from Carency—a drama about which I do not want to speak because of patriotic shame, but which is already known to the entire Jewish colony—one would like that they enlist in the Foreign Legion!

A large paragraph of the article was censored. Marius Moutet wrote in the Socialist daily *L'Humanité* of July 1, 1915:

The Russians were the most numerous among the enlistments in the army of the Republic; the revolutionaries could have formed entire battalions. However, their enthusiasm was oddly chilled because they were unappreciated and misjudged. Those who unwisely went back to Russia were not given forgiveness, Bourtzev is still in Siberia. In France, enlistments were accepted in the Legion. These men who offered themselves to fight for the republican ideal in the republican army, subjected to the command of non-commissioned officers who are used to lead men of a very different nature; the legionnaires of Morocco and the desert were their companions. Instead of a discipline applied to free citizens, with deference to their legitimate sensitiveness, they found a conception of arbitrary, brutal, authoritative discipline and mechanical submission.

In *L'Humanité* of April 10, 1916, Docteur Enemesse characterized the campaign against foreigners of Paris as reactionary, contemptible and inhuman. He was especially shocked by the irresponsible accusation that the Russian refugees who did not enlist were spies. If this is true, he wrote, and it can be proven, then they should not be permitted to enlist in the army but be executed. On June 10, 1916, Enemesse wrote that the measure suggested in November 1915 by the City Council of Paris to deport those who refused to enlist in the Legion would be *méprisable et inhumaine.*

The well-known Paris daily, *Petit Parisien,* published on June 27, 1915, the following statement by J. Rakover, president of the Society of Jewish Merchants at the *Carreau du Temple:*

Their enlistment in the Foreign Legion had been accepted. Their intention was to join a military unit serving France . . . But the junior officers treated them quite crudely . . . so much so that their friends and coreligionists in Paris were deterred from joining the Legion.

Rakover complained that volunteers were even sent to the Legion in Algeria, at Saida and Sidi-Bel-Abbès. A representative of the newspaper *Le Petit Parisien* was informed at the prefecture of police and the Ministry of the Interior that this was true. Russian Jews, he was told, could go back to serve in Russia but if they want to serve in France they must enlist in the Foreign Legion.

The Paris periodical *L'Echo du 9e* wrote in its issue of July 1, 1915 that Jews protested against the Foreign Legion, saying, "Let us join the ranks of the French Army, not the Foreign Legion . . . Sending us to the Legion is contrary to everything that the French spirit of democracy stands for." The conservative and influential *Le Temps* of November 29, 1915 called upon the authorities not to repeat with foreigners of allied countries the blunder with the Alsatians who were interned in "evacuation" camps. It concluded, "Let us be severe with our friends as much as with ourselves, but let us not deceive the firm confidence of those for whom we symbolize in the world the spirit of liberty, justice and sound democracy."

In November 1915 was created the Committee of Political and Professional Organization of Russian Citizens in Paris (Immigrants' Committee) which took up the defense of both Jewish and non-Jewish Russian nationals. An executive committee of nine members met with Jean Longuet, Marius Moutet and other Socialist deputies. The Committee published an appeal warning against any panic.[89]

On October 27, 1916, the Deputies Gratien Candace, Henri Galli and Poirier de Narcay tried to make the parliament vote in favor of a law forcing the enlistment of foreigners. As the question of service of British and Italian nationals had been already regulated the proposed measure was directed mainly against Russian and Rumanian Jews. Marius Moutet, a Socialist deputy, recalled that the question was very sensitive because of an antisemitic campaign in the press and "unfortunate acts." Moutet had in mind the affair of forcing the volunteers to serve in the Legion and the subsequent executions at Carency.[90] The number of prospective alien volunteers was greatly exaggerated by the xenophobic propagandists. Leon Bailby wrote in *L'Intransigeant* of August 24 and September 4, 1916, that a mobilization of foreigners in Paris would give France 100,000 more soldiers.

The French government was forced to do something in order to avoid anti-French propaganda in neutral countries. A special commission was created for the purpose of investigating the conflict. Brelet of the Conseil d'Etat was appointed president. Some of the other members were J. H. Busson Billaut, Professor Emile Durkheim and representatives of governmental bodies. As a result of the commission's recommendations the French Government decided not to expel the foreigners who had refused to sign up for the Foreign Legion. It was also made easier for legionnaires to ask for transfers to regular French army units.[91]

On the anniversary of the battle of Carency, in which Jewish legionnaires took a considerable part and suffered the heaviest losses, the "Amicale des Volontaires Juifs" organized a public meeting at which Ferdinand Buisson, President of the "Ligue Pour la Défense des Droits de L'homme et du Citoyen" presided. The deputy Jean Longuet made the following speech:

> If we remember that 10,000 Jewish volunteers came to sacrifice their lives for our country, we fail to understand how can people, who should have understood and known the situation, how these people can throw accusations against Jews and especially against Russian Jews.
>
> Not having been compelled by any law whatever, 10,000 healthy men arose to our defence without vacillating a moment before the horrors of modern warfare. How many, many of them have already fallen in the plains of the North and in the valleys of Lorraine, where the horrible battle of this monstrous War seems never to finish.
>
> 10,000 men abandoned their wives and children for the defense of a pure idea. They wanted to be thankful to republican France which had given them an asylum.
>
> Have we appreciated the heroism of these brave men who sacrificed themselves? . . . To all the Allied Armies, the Jews have given more than a million men, i.e., an army which exceeds the armies of Roumania and Bulgaria combined. For giving their help to the Allies these two countries have increased every day their claims. What have we given to the Jewish nation for the million soldiers they have given to the cause of the Allies?
>
> When the War is over and mankind returns to civilized life, will we be forced to state that this catastrophe has changed nothing; shall we forget all those who lost their lives on the fields of Carency and elsewhere for liberty, defended by old democratic England and republican France?
>
> We celebrate to-day citizens who fell for the idea of justice, which was born in the heart of the Jewish nation . . .

The Conjoint Foreign Committee of the Board of Deputies of British Jews and the Anglo-Jewish Association, which had released a report on the above-mentioned commemoration, also distributed a list of military distinctions conferred upon Jewish legionnaires. Following are but a few examples:

Mikhail Kulman of Odessa. Military Cross. He was mentioned in the order of the day as follows: "He is an example of daring and dash. He bravely attacked the enemy; after having been wounded, he continued throwing hand grenades and saved his deadly injured comrade. After recovery, returned to the fighting line."

M. Naidman, Ilia Lax, and Solomon Poliakov were mentioned in the order of the day as follows: "On July 21st, they undertook a reconnaissance notwithstanding the destructive fire of the enemy, and then ably participated in the attack of their company, holding out the artillery fire to the very end of the battle." All three awarded the Military Crosses.

A. Svirsky was wounded three times, but returned each time to the fighting line. Awarded the Military Cross, was mentioned in the order of the day as follows: "He is a splendid example of energy and endurance under the enemy shells."

Isaak Ventura, participated in the attack of September, 25th, 1915 and was mentioned in the order of the day. "He is a brave and good soldier, displayed excellent military qualities and contempt of danger during the attack."

Leopold Kahan, mentioned in the order of the day as follows: "A model soldier of perfect audacity and faithfulness. Behaved excellently during the trying days of October 6th and 11th."

Engineer M. Rotstein. Was the organizer of the volunteer movement in France. In the Foreign Legion he very soon distinguished himself and was made corporal. When his regiment of the Foreign Legion was dissolved, he was transferred to a regiment in Champagne where he participated in many attacks and was promoted to the degree of an officer. He was given the Military Cross and made a Chevalier de la Légion d'Honneur.

Elia Cruker, was mentioned in the order of the day as follows: "During the night of October 15th, he secured the lines of communication under a heavy shelling of the enemy."

Adolph Mikhovsky, was awarded the Military Cross and mentioned as follows: "Repeatedly displayed much bravery and indifference to danger and presence of mind. On September 5th, 1915, he brought out of the firing line his Commander who was mortally wounded."

Simon Elishkovsky. Participated in the battle at Artois, was wounded and promoted corporal. After having recovered, he returned to Russia, was wounded again and awarded the St. George's Cross.

Mark Leibovitch. Awarded the Military Cross for bravery and endurance.

Mark Shönberg, he was mentioned in the order of the day as follows: "Russian subject, volunteered at the beginning of the War. Very brave and performed much very dangerous reconnoitering. Gravely wounded on November 10th, 1915."

Doctor J. Shat. When a student at the University of Paris, he entered as an ordinary soldier the Foreign Legion at the outbreak of the War, but towards the end of 1914 he was made a doctor and transferred to Verdun, where he remained all the time. He was wounded. Awarded the Military Cross and was thrice mentioned in the order of the day.

M. Hirsch (a Roumanian Jew). Father of eight children. Entered with his eldest son.

Corporal Poliakov (a book-keeper from Riga). Wounded. Awarded the Military Medal, Military Cross and St. George's Cross. Twice mentioned in the order of the day.

Paul Berkovitch. Displayed excellent military qualities and during military parade was quite unexpectedly for himself promoted as corporal.

The Conjoint Committee also quoted from the Paris newspaper *La Victoire:*

We must admit that not a single Jewish volunteer, however distinguished by his superiors was admitted to the cadet schools, though other Russian subjects, Russians by birth were admitted. The Russian Military Attaché could certainly explain this.

And from a Russian-Jewish weekly:

Isaak Friedmann. Participated in many battles in France. As it was impossible for him to be transferred from the Foreign Legion to an ordinary regiment, he returned to Russia. He was wounded at the Russian front and is in a hospital in Vologda. At the beginning of the War, very many soldiers of the Foreign Legion preferred to be transferred to Russia rather than remain in the Legion.[91a]

At that time France suffered from a general atmosphere of suspicion and lack of individual freedom. Every alien was regarded as a possible German spy. Gustave Hervé protested against the internment of thousands of people who had a right to expect better treatment. Many of them were Italians and Poles persecuted by Germany and Austria and "Jews from Galicia, from Bukovina, who escaped from antisemitism to France." Many of those evacuated by force from Paris were trying to enlist in the army. Even Alsatians were forcibly evacuated while France claimed to be fighting for Alsace-Lorraine. (Among the Alsatians who enlisted were many Jews.) A Franco-Jewish publication complained that many Alsatians and aliens were interned as a result of uncontrolled denunciations. After release from internment their dossiers were not destroyed.[92]

X. Union Sacré in an Atmosphere of War-Time Antisemitism

Prof. Victor Basch stated during his mission to the United States that no trace of antisemitism was left in France. Whatever conditions may have been in the past there was nothing but admiration for the Jews who had been fighting and dying for their country.[93] However, the Franco-Jewish weekly, *L'Univers Israélite,* noted that the campaign to force aliens to volunteer for the Legion was not directed at all aliens (not at Chinese and Spaniards, for example), but only against alien Jews. It was the result of a well-organized antisemitic campaign in the press which completely ignored the *union sacré.*[94] Jewish tailors were refused work at factories making uniforms. At a meeting of the tailors' union the slogan *La France aux Francais* (France for Frenchmen) was heard.[95] Gustave Thiéry suggested in the organ of Catholic jurists that foreigners be forbidden from purchasing land in order to "preserve France for Frenchmen."[96] Léon Daudet, leader of the monarchist and antisemitic *Action Française,* attacked the "insubordinate Russian Jews" many of whom, he claimed, were really German Jews. Daudet even claimed that non-Russian Jews praised his campaign. (Indeed, there existed a Jewish group of *Action Française*.)[97]

The French Jews were completely paralyzed by the desire of their government to avoid any criticism on matters concerning the war. Yet, in spite of the traditional reluctance to criticize the government, the strong censorship and its enthusiasm for the *union sacré,* the Franco-Jewish publications reported about the scandals of the Legion. Emile Cahen asked in the *Archives Israélites* if the right cadres were chosen to lead the volunteers in combat. After many Russian nationals were transferred to the regular army units the Rumanian, Dutch, Syrian and other nationals forcibly remained in the Legion. After Carency, Mathieu Wolf, a Jewish army chaplain, organized a religious service for 500 of them. He wrote that his only hope was that they would be granted French citizenship or, at least, be allowed to serve in the regular French army.[98]

One would imagine that the Franco-Jewish leaders would quietly intercede with the authorities. But they were not willing to break the *union sacré*.

The first to protest against the scandal of the Legion were Gustave Hervé, a former Anarco-Syndicalist who, after the outbreak of the war gave up his antimilitarist convictions. In his organ, *La Guerre Sociale (The Social War)*, which became violently anti-German, Hervé took up the cause of the volunteers and accused the authorities of conducting a shortsighted and dangerous policy. *L'Humanité*, official organ of the Socialist Party, joined the campaign. It was impossible for the two Franco-Jewish publications to keep quiet. All they had to do was to reprint some of the articles published by Hervé. The editor of *L'Univers Israélite* added his own remarks to two articles published by Hervé, but the remarks were censored and the articles appeared with blank spaces.[99]

La Guerre Sociale published letters written by Jewish legionnaires which were reprinted in the Franco-Jewish publications. One legionnaire wrote on May 16, 1915, after a victorious attack by the Legion: "All our friends, the Russian Jews were killed or are wounded. From 4,000 Jews in our brigade only 190 remain. May God keep us!" One letter was written by the legionnaire Lévy-Aaron Litwak, a Russian Jew, after the battle of Arras. He expressed his admiration and love for France, but his bitterness as well for being forced to serve in the Legion. He and his comrades were constantly reminded that they had enlisted for *la gamelle*. The Jewish volunteers paid a high price, not for *la gamelle*, but as Jews and soldiers, "so the entire world could see Jews dying for the liberty, for the ideal." Shortly afterwards, Litwak was killed in another battle.[100]

Many French officials were afraid that the policy toward Jewish volunteers would create sharp anti-French feelings among the Jews in neutral countries, especially in the United States. There most of the Russian Jews were so strongly anti-Russian that many became pro-German. In fact, the pro-German Jewish press published articles on the persecution of Russian Jews in France. The New York *American* of November 28, 1915, published a letter written by the Anglo-Jewish author Israel Cohen against the treatment of Jewish legionnaires and the executions. Cohen was the Berlin correspondent for the Glasgow *Herald and Globe*, and special correspondent for the *Times*, Manchester *Guardian* and Westminster *Gazette*. At the outbreak of the war he was interned in Ruhleben camp where he wrote to the New York *American*:

Of all the tragedies that have occurred outside the Czar's dominions the most revolting was that in the French Army, in which the Russian Jews, who made up nearly the whole of the so-called "Slavonic" Legion and wished to show their gratitude to their adopted country, were hung to desperation by the taunts of their comrades.

Of all the pacifist and neutral American Yiddish newspapers only one, *Der Tog (The Day)*, which had previously written about the execution, reported on Cohen's letter to the *American*. *The Day* wrote that the last words of the nine were *Vive la France* (Long Live France), and commented that this was French gratitude. The Foreign Legion, *Der Tog* continued, "is the stigma of the French Army, a sanctuary for adventurers, degenerates, criminals, 'former' human beings and some who were never human beings." Into this Legion were assigned political refugees who volunteered for France. The *Varhayt* published a few articles on the persecutions against Russian Jews in France without reporting on the tragedy of Carency. It appealed to American Jews to defend their brethen in France, but nothing was done.[101]

In order to combat the pro-German propaganda among Jews in neutral countries, a special committee was organized in November 1915 in Paris, the *Comité de Propagande Française auprès des Juifs Neutres* (French Propaganda Committee Among Neutral Jews). On December 16, 1915, this Committee decided to change its name to *Comité Français d'Information de d'Action auprès des Juifs des Pays Neutres* (French Information and Action Committee Among Jews in Neutral Countries). Among its leaders were both Jews and non-Jews: George Leugues (former minister and president of the Commission for Foreign Affairs at the French Parliament), Professor Sylvain Lévi, Victor Basch, Ferdinand Buisson (president of the League of Rights of Man and Citizen), Chief Rabbi Israël Lévi, the Socialist Deputy Marius Moutet, Salomon Reinach, and many other well-known personalities.

In 1916, the French propaganda committee sent one of its members, the Socialist Deputy Marius Moutet, to discuss the problem of Russian Jews with Herbert Samuel, Minister of Interior of Great Britain. There a large number of Russian-born Jews refused to volunteer for the defense of Russia where Jews were brutally persecuted. Russian-Jewish immigrants were told that they had to choose between compulsory service in Great Britain or deportation to Russia. Moutet pleaded with the British Government to avoid both steps because it would reinforce pro-German propaganda in the United States. All sixteen Jewish trade unions in London held a conference on August 20, 1916, which adopted the following declaration:

> As Russian Jews, who in their country of origin were deprived of elementary citizen-rights, and subjected to all kinds of restrictions in movement, trade, education, etc., to constant insults, to persecutions, massacres, unspeakable horrors—we consider that deportation to Russia would be for us the most terrible of fates, and for Britain a most inconceivable act of inhumanity. It was owing to these political conditions that we came here, fleeing from brutal laws and criminal violence. We have been victims of the political regime in Russia, and therefore are all political refugees. We cannot believe that the Government of Great Britain, where the Right of Asylum has been sacred for centuries, will overthrow that noble tradition. We must especially emphasize that the Right of Asylum has always been known in history to extend to all those who left their native countries owing to persecutions, and to whom can it apply with more cogency than to ourselves? What political refugees have had grievances greater than ours?

The Yiddish weekly *Pariser Yidishe Vokh* of July 21, 1916, wrote that England was for the Russian Jews "an asylum but not a home . . . it is a terrible irony to demand men to sacrifice themselves for the English government that helps the same government which had driven them out and even now persecutes their brethren."

A committee of Russian-Jews from France who had found a temporary haven in England organized the *Russian-Jewish (French Refugees) Protection Committee*. On August 15, 1916, G. Bernard, honorary secretary, addressed a letter to the *Foreign Jews Protection Committee Against Deportation to Russia and Compulsion* asking to protect also the refugees from France. He accused the French government of making it difficult for them to obtain passports in order to return to France or to emigrate elsewhere.[102]

On July 8, 1915, Alan Seeger, an American legionnaire, noted in his diary: "Rumors of great changes in the regiment which have been going about for a long time, seem now to be coming to a head. The Russians, it seems, are to be sent to the Russian army or allowed to join a French regiment. The same with the Belgians."[103] How many Russian Jewish legionnaires were actually transferred? According to Sholem Schwartzbard only twelve out of thousands of Jewish legionnaires in his regiment were transferred to a regular unit of the French army, the 363rd Regiment.[104]

There was no lack of derogatory remarks about Jewish legionnaires. One British ex-legionnaire wrote that Jews joined the Legion in order to save their possessions because "their nationality was uncertain."[105] The American legionnaire Edmond Genet wrote that there were even "German Jews" in the Legion; many of them can only speak German. "How they get taken in I can't imagine but they are here just the same and most are lazy and good-for-nothing. German is a harsh enough language to hear but when a Jew speaks it it sure sounds ridiculous."[106] He simply mistook Yiddish for German. Genet himself was glad to be transferred from the Legion to the Lafayette Squadron. Another American ex-legionnaire, Paul Ayres Rockwell, wrote that the second regiment of the Legion

> was afflicted with a battalion composed almost entirely of Russian Jews and political exiles, which was permeated from the start with a spirit of revolt and anarchy. Many of its members had enlisted with no idea of ever going to the front. This battalion revolted in the early summer of 1915, and refused to leave for the trenches when ordered to do so. The colonel commanding the regiment gave the battalion forty-eight hours for reflection. As the Russians still refused to march, he then court-martialled and had shot eleven of the ringleaders, all Jews. Two of the rebels executed were the sons of a powerful St. Petersburg Jewish banker. This man appealed to the Imperial Government, to which he had loaned money, and within a week after the ringleaders of the Battalion F mutiny were shot, a Russian general appeared at the regimental headquarters and demanded that all the Russian volunteers in the Legion either be liberated or allowed to transfer to other regiments of the French Army. The Russian Embassy in Paris backed the request, which was granted by the French War Ministry.

Rockwell, who was looking for adventure and signed up for the Foreign Legion (instead of a regular British or Canadian unit) was one of the first to take advantage of the permission given by the French to Americans to be transferred to a French regiment.[107]

The affair of the Legion was discussed during the trial of Louis Jean Malvy, former French Prime Minister who was accused of treason. Gustave Hervé and Marius Moutet recalled then how the bad treatment of the volunteers was used by Germany for its anti-French propaganda in neutral countries.[108]

In the beginning of 1917 was created in Paris a committee of the Russian colony *(Kolonial Komitet)*. In a circular dated February 26, 1917, the committee complained that police visits of homes of Russians became so frequent that their neighbors started to distrust them. Many Russian workers were discharged by their employers. After the Russian Revolution of March 1917 a committee called *Obrona* took charge of the re-emigration to liberated Russia of political refugees, including volunteers in the Foreign Legion who were permitted to be transferred to Russia.

On July 28 and August 10, 1917, an agreement was signed between France and the Provisional government of Russia on the military service of Russian citizens in France and Frenchmen living in Russia. Russians living in France could be drafted into the French army. Although no mention of the Foreign Legion was made in the agreement the fear that France would send Russian draftees to the Legion existed. The Russian ambassador in Paris advised his government that the Russians living in France felt uneasy, that they preferred to serve in Russia or, if that was impossible, in the Russian Army units in France.[109]

By September 1917 Paris had only a few hundred Russian Jews who could be mobilized. Most of the Russian Jews had volunteered for service in the beginning of the war, the political activists had left for Russia, many were employed in war industries or were too old to serve. In spite of this a few antisemitic deputies again demanded the government take measures against the Russians. The agreement between the French and Russian governments gave the Russian citizens living in France the choice of going back to Russia or serving in the French army. However, according to the Russian Embassy in Paris, Russian citizens desiring to remain in France could serve only in the Foreign Legion.[110]

After the Bolshevik Revolution, Russian nationals who were allowed to return to Russia were told to enlist in Denikin's army. A group of 120 Russians who refused to do so were warned that they would be sent to Algeria.[111] In December 1918 a special battalion of the Legion was sent to Northern Russia. The majority of the men were anti-Bolsheviks; when the battalion was disbanded in July 1919 most of them remained to fight with White Russian units against the Red Army.[112]

Some French circles accused the Russian Jewish immigrants who had not enlisted in the French Legion of being responsible for the rebellions that shook the French army at the front in 1917.[113] They ignored the fact that the soldiers had suffered from hunger and extreme fatigue, bad leadership which resulted in very heavy casualties, and had been influenced by the events in Russia.

At the outbreak of World War I a number of Russian Jews who lived in

France sought refuge in Spain. Some of them had refused to return to Russia and take up service in the Czarist army; others had refused to join the French Foreign Legion. For four years they lived quietly in Spain. Then, in January 1919, the Bolshevik scare seized the Spanish government with panic and the expulsion of Russian Jews as well as non-Jews was averted only after many interventions. It seems that the Spanish government had ordered their expulsion at the request of the Allies.[114]

The first association of Jewish volunteers *(La Solidarité des Volontaires Juifs)* was organized during the winter of 1915 by a group of volunteers who held their first meeting at the Café Weissman on rue Marcadet. In the beginning it was a small society, consisting of about thirty members. Each member on leave from the front received 10 francs. Every week 20 or 25 parcels were sent to those in the front lines. After the armistice the Association counted 170 members who held their first commemorative meeting in 1919.

XI. Americans in the French Foreign Legion

In the period before and during World War I, some expatriate Americans, a few of them intellectuals but more of them pseudo-intellectuals, served in the Legion. The officers and non-commissioned officers did not like them. One corporal of the Legion reported that the Americans were the "dirtiest, lousiest, meanest soldiers" of the Legion. "They crawl into their dugout, roll into their blanket and when I call them for duty the language they use would burn a man up if it came true." He hastily transferred to a different battalion where there were fewer Americans. But on the rifle range the Americans invariably held the record. They never fell out on route marches, although one American, Dave King, was once seen marching with feet so sore he could only put "one toe of each foot on the ground." According to one legionnaire, Geoffrey Bocca, the adventurers, the Harvard boys, the pugilists, the scions of old East Coast families put up with the hardships merrily. "To move among cutpurses and men without hope, after the privileged life of America, was a startling change, but, save in a few cases, the very enormity of the shock anesthetized them from the discomforts and the indignities they were called on to suffer." They were shocked and fascinated by the sub-world of aliens among them. Edmond Genet, a small, neatly-made blond youth from New York, wrote to a friend: "There sure is some collection of people in this outfit (1st Regiment, 2nd Company). I think I have met every nationality except Chinese, Indians and Hindus." Russell Kelly wrote of "an Italian who catches rats, skins them, and has them roasted by the cook. I have seen many strange things, but the coldbloodedness of this fairly turns one's stomach."[115]

The French army authorities gladly accepted American enlisted men in the Foreign Legion, at least, as we shall see, until the 1930's. Negroes, for example, were not accepted in the Legion, but an exception was made for American Negroes.[116]

There were about seventy Americans in the Foreign Legion during World War I.

Why did Americans sign up for the Foreign Legion instead of joining the Canadian or British forces? For adventure perhaps. Alan Seeger, a Harvard graduate, explained the reason in a verse written before he was killed by a German sniper:

> I have a rendezvous with Death
> On some scarred slope of battered hill,
> When Spring comes round again this year
> And the first meadow-flowers appear
> . . . But I have a rendezvous with Death
> At midnight in some flaming town,
> When spring trips north again this year,
> And I to my pledged word am true,
> I shall not fail that rendezvous.[117]

Among the Americans in the Legion was a Brooklyn Jew, Herman Chatkoff, who had left for Paris after a disagreement with his parents over his future. He worked for a while on cattle ships. Back in Paris he had no regular job and was washing cars in a garage. He used to joke that he was a professional soldier, having served five years in the Salvation Army. After the war he was back with his family in Brooklyn, and spent some time in an asylum. The American Legion took an interest in him and obtained a special government pension for him.[118]

There were a few other American Jewish legionnaires: George Peixotto, a painter; Sylvain Rosenberg, killed in 1916 at Verdun; George Meyer of Brooklyn, killed in April 1917 near Rheims.[119]

A group of four American legionnaires, among them Herman Chatkoff, David King, Alan Seeger and Rene Phelizot, all were resting behind the lines at Cuiry-lès-Chaudardes when two *anciens* (old-time legionnaires) walked past them and made insulting remarks about volunteers in general and Americans in particular. Phelizot hit one of them and a melee ensued. Phelizot was taken to a military hospital at Fismes where doctors discovered that his skull had been broken. Two days later he died without regaining consciousness. When the Americans at the front found out about his death they went to the machine gun section where the two *anciens* served. Chatkoff caught the man who had struck Phelizot and started stomping him. The military police separated them.[120]

After Carency and similar scandals in the Legion, Americans were transferred from the Legion to regular units in the French army. On September 1, 1917, Alan Seeger noted in his diary:

> Great and unexpected news this morning to report. All American volunteers in the Legion are to be given the privilege of entering a French regiment. I have always been loyal to the Legion, notwithstanding the many obvious drawbacks. . . . It must be admitted that here [in the Legion] discontent has more than the usual to feed upon, where a majority of men who engaged voluntarily were thrown into a regiment made up almost entirely of the dregs of society, refugees from justice and roughs, commanded by *sous-officiers* who treated us all without distinction in the same manner that they were habituated to treat their unruly brood in Africa. I put up with this for a year without complaint, swallowing my pride many a time and thinking only of the day of trial, shutting my eyes to the disadvantages I was under because I thought that on that day the regiment, which I have always believed to be of good fighting stock, would do well and cover us with glory . . .
>
> This has almost induced, in fact, to turn down the offer and stay where I am, since perhaps the greatest glory will be here, and it is for glory alone that I engaged. But on the other hand, after a year of what I have been through, I feel more and more the need of being among Frenchmen, where the patriotic and military tradition is strong, where my good will may have some recognition, and where the demands of a sentimental and romantic nature like my own may be gratified.

On October 25, 1915, Seeger wrote to his mother that most of the other Americans had taken advantage of the permission to transfer into a regular French regiment. "There is much to be said for their decision, but I have remained true to the Legion, where I am content and have good comrades."[121]

According to the New York *Times* of October 28, 1915, a New York legionnaire described the transfer of the American to a regular French line regiment as follows:

> The shattered Legion was reformed to be sent to the Balkans, but could not take the Americans along, as they had enlisted to fight only in France. The American company in making the transfer marched nearly all night and immediately went into the first line trenches.

In November 1914, Norman Prince, an American, conceived the idea of a Lafayette Squadron of American volunteer pilots to serve with the French army. A total of 213 Americans were recruited for the squadron, among them legionnaires who had been transferred. To get into the French air force, a foreigner had to first enlist in the Foreign Legion. Although several Americans were allowed to transfer directly to the flying corps without first serving with the Legion in the trenches, many members of the squadron were former legionnaires. Four of the seven original members of the squadron came from the ranks of the Legion. (Chatkoff left the Legion to become a pilot. Later he was back in the Legion.)[122]

An American who served six months with the Legion during World War I wrote:

> To me the days in the French Foreign Legion stand out among the happiest of my life: the sense of irresponsibility, adventure and risk provided an extraordinary exhilaration.[123]

Two days after the war broke out Edward Morlae, the son of a California-born son of a French immigrant who served as sergeant in the French army in 1870, left Los Angeles for Paris and enlisted in the Foreign Legion. On returning to America, wounded in the neck, he went to Boston where Ellery Sedgwick, editor of the *Atlantic Monthly*, made his acquaintance, heard his story, and asked him to write it up. It was published in the issue of March 1916 and, in the same year, in book form. It was, according to the editor, a very nice story. Morlae wrote:

> Of the Legion I can tell you at first-hand. It is a story of adventurers, of criminals, of fugitives from justice. Some of them are drunkards, some thieves, and some with the mark of Cain upon them find others to keep them company. They are men I know the worst of. And yet I am proud of them—proud of having been one of them; very proud of having commanded some of them . . . In my own section there were men of all races and all nationalities . . . the international stew . . . every man had left a past behind him. But the Americans in the Legion were of a different type. Some of us who volunteered for the war loved fighting, and some of us loved France. I was fond of both.

American legionnaires criticized Morlae but he was praised by Ellery Sedgwick. The New York *Times* noted that the charges of Morlae's former buddies were rather trivial and irrelevant to the literary value of his story.[124]

After World War I, isolated Americans continued to sign up for the Legion. Adrian Liddel Hart, one of them, was of the opinion that it was natural that many Americans should see in the Legion not only a romantic legend but an "expression of the European unity which they persistently advocate—and even an embodiment of some of the impulses which want to create America herself."[125]

In 1931, Major Edward F. Knight of the 77th Regiment, New York Guards, visited the Foreign Legion at Marrakesh and came back with praise for the appearance and perfect drilling of the legionnaires. So did Capt. E. Ernest Dupuy who ridiculed the notion that the Legion was made up of fugitives from justice and men with unsavory pasts. He said: "I have never seen a finer, cleaner-limbed or clear-eyed group of soldiers anywhere."[126]

However, most Americans in the Legion were simply looking for adventure.

Winthrop Lyon Saville, son of Marshall Howard Saville, professor of archeology at Columbia University, joined the Legion in the 1930's after reading the "crazy" stories about it. He signed up as a Canadian under the name of Winthrop Lyon. After serving for five years he declared: "I had a grand time . . . the Legion is not particular about the name or the past of a volunteer, but is very particular about his physical ability."[127]

In 1933, Philipe Ortiz, an American in Paris, whose 19-year-old son Pierre served in the Legion, tried to organize a society to disseminate the "truth" about the famous military body. Ortiz was the founder of the Paris edition of *Vogue*. Pierre was born in New York and his father brought him to France to complete his education. However, the excitement of the Legion appealed to the boy's spirit of adventure more than did the college in Grenoble where he was enrolled.[128]

In July 1925, Colonel Charles Sweeny told how he and six other American aviators were going to Morocco "to see how many Riffians they can kill." The *World* published a letter written by Alfred R. Kuttner protesting against such soldiers of fortune.[129]

Henry Newman of Chicago thus summarized his five years' service in the Legion: "Soldiering in the Legion is only pick and shovel work nowadays, all dirt and no romance of the 'Beau Geste' kind."[130]

During World War I there were about 200 Americans in the French Foreign Legion.

The United States State Department was then and in later years constantly asked by parents and other relatives of American legionnaires to intervene with the French authorities for their discharge from the Legion or their transfer to regular units of the French Army. At first the American Embassy in Paris deemed it improper to intervene in such cases, but later the Embassy received unofficial assurance that the Americans in the Legion would be transferred.[131]

Fred W. Zinn of Galesburg, Mich., went to Europe shortly after finishing college. He was in Paris when the war broke out and, catching the

Legion fever, enlisted. His parents tried for some time to get him released from duty, but without success. In an uncensored letter to his parents dated August 13, 1915, the legionnaire Zinn wrote:

> It is not pleasant to think of the cost of such an operation. That offensive that was made around Arras when the first Etranger was cleaned out cost about 20,000 men and all it made was a little dent in the line which doesn't even show on a map.[132]

Zinn was killed in action.

William E. Dugan was waiting for a transfer from the Legion. On October 30, 1915, he wrote to his parents:

> After a month of action the legion went to the rear for repose, but we, having been put into a Regiment that had just arrived are still in the thick of it and have just come out of 12 hard days in the front line. Where we are now, just back of the French batteries, the constant crash of the shells of the heavy German guns keeps us wondering how long we shall continue to be lucky. Some one reported me to the Embassy in Paris as being badly wounded and a friend of mine received an inquiry about me. I have just replied that I am still alive and uninjured.
>
> The past six weeks have been the hardest and most strenuous I have yet experienced and I look forward with a great deal of anticipation to my long promised permission to Paris. If I ever get there, I shall write a long letter, telling you many things I have not the time or opportunity to write at present.
>
> I have heard several times from Charlie. He says efforts are being made to transfer me to his Regiment, but any steps in that direction are either futile or very slow in results. Having now been at the front 11 months, I am pretty well worn in mind and body and would welcome most anything that would give me a temporary relief. There are few who have been in action as long as our little crowd and scarcely any but what have had furloughs. We are also in the hardest and most disturbed sector on the front, so you can imagine how welcome a little relief would be.
>
> It is getting very cold and as my only bed in this God-forsaken part of the Country is the cold ground, am badly in need of winter clothes. So far the Army have given us nothing. My only shirt is one Ruth Crippen sent me months ago and I am lousy from head to foot, so please, if you would care to send something send small registered packages and I will get them quickly.[133]

William Flournoy Killgore of Arcadia, Louisiana, entered the United States Merchant Marine Service in August 1924, and in the following February deserted at Le Havre, France, and joined the Foreign Legion. His parents wrote Senator Joseph M. Ransdell:

He is now, however, thoroughly disillusioned, and finds himself in a galling position of virtual slavery—to quote from a letter received from him today—'We don't have any breakfast, only a cup of coffee, and for dinner and supper, watery soup, two spoonfuls of meat gravy and a cup of boiled potatoes or beans' while he is required to drill from nine to ten hours a day, not provided with hosiery, has to wear hobnailed shoes, and in consequence his feet are in bad condition, and in addition is under abusive and profane command at the hands of a corporal—for all of which he receives the munificent (?) equivalent in American money of one and one-fourth cents a day.

On October 28, 1925, his mother wrote to Frank B. Kellog, Secretary of State:

My father, Mr. W. U. Richardson of Arcadia, La. has lately purchased some authentic works on international law and finds therein that my son is entitled to discharge, and I have been informed of an instance where a nineteen-year-old boy enlisted in the English army and his discharge was secured and it seems to me an entirely untenable proposition that France has a right to keep a minor American because he was unthinking enough to grant France a temporary advantage. Certainly we know that in actual fact one could not keep possession of a neighbor's child because of a contract made with the child alone. My son is an American ward as well as citizen and ineligible for making binding contracts and by all that is fair and civilized we have a right to claim his release. Having done so much for France, are we, the most outstanding Christian nation in the world, going to tamely submit to her flaunting in our faces such a Medo-Persian law as her claim of superiority in this matter? Where is her gratitude to us? Or respect for this country? In a recent magazine article the statement was made that at one time the U.S. paid a ransom of $50,000.00 for a Greek-American held in detention by a foreign power. I do not know whether he was a naturalized citizen or the American born son of naturalized parents but my son is of unmixed-loyal American ancestry antedating the American Revolution and if the Greek-American and the national honor involved in this case were worth $50,000.00 I certainly think that my son worth rescuing from that foreign power; especially if any value is set upon his potential worth as a future citizen—but if his country fails him in this time of desperate dependence will she have any right to ask or expect his loyal patriotism when he does get out—if he lives and is not maimed for life in the French service? The youth of the present is our citizenship of tomorrow and if democracy has any meaning it should by all fair dealings, be instilled into the *boy* and inspire him with ideals of patriotic loyalty. I want no ransom paid, nor that we have any international complications, but I want my boy, and besides, I need him—we are poor people and my husband's health is failing. As long as I have consciousness to pray to God I shall not give up.

On December 22, 1925, she wrote again to the Secretary of State asking him to intervene in the discharge of her son from "that 'dehumanizing' (to coin a word) foreign legion," where "he was in practical slavery—unworthy of twentieth-century civilization." Killgore had been wounded in the shoulder on July 9th and recommended for a Croix de Guerre for gallantry in action. Finally, after intervention by the Secretary of State, he was discharged after having served ten months in the Legion. Back home, he wrote to the Secretary of State: "I sincerely regret my unhappy adventure and feel that I am greatly indebted to my country as a whole to be the best citizen I can." To a local newspaper Killgore declared:

> The legionnaire is treated like a dog. Sixty-five per cent of the legion's members are German with many English and a sprinkling of Russians, Italians and negroes from America and other countries. Practically every nationality is represented. No oath of allegiance is required. The recruiting officer merely inquires the age and nationality with the name which may be an assumed one. Most of the non-commissioned officers are extremely brutal and take delight in kicking and cuffing the recruit although they seldom try any rough tactics with Americans. To be a non-commissioned officer a legionnaire must be able to speak four or five languages in order to be able to communicate with his men as they are made up of so many nationalities. All commands, however, are given in French. Death is the contemplated lot of the legionnaire and this fact is held before him constantly. The words "Legionnaire, you are going to die for France," are written on almost every wall of the barracks in the training camp in Algeria. I did not know what I was doing when I hooked up with that outfit. If anyone thinks there is any mor or glory about it, he can take my word for it there is nothing of the sort.[134]

(In connection with Killgore's statement that American Negroes were serving in the Legion it should be noted that on April 15, 1921, the Frederic Douglas Council, a New York City Negro organization, adopted a resolution against the use of colonial African colored men "in the various French armies of occupation. The colored youth thus conscripted is forced to sacrifice its life in causes alien to the interests of the colored race. Experience has taught that such conscription is carried on with inevitable hardships and cruelty to the colored populations."[135])

On November 3, 1927, Henry P. Creek, serving in the Legion under the name of Joe P. Miller, wrote to Governor Alvan T. Fuller of Massachusetts:

> I am a lonely American, from Boston, now soldier of the French Foreign

Legion in Morocco . . . I am not as a criminal in the Legion only by hard luck and misfortune I am here now. After the war I went back to Europe and first I joint in 1924 in Barcelona Spain the Spanish Legion and I deserted in 1925 from Tarquist to the French line but the French and Spanish treaty was every deserter from one or another to send him back so I joint the Legion in France. So I ask your Honor in helping me out from this place if possible to you.[136]

In December 1928, Arthur M. Clark, publisher of the Carpinteria (California) *Herald*, wrote to the Secretary of State:

Considerable annoyance was caused by a young American, during the past summer, who joined the French Foreign Legion and deserted. His life was saved by the U.S. Diplomatic Corps but the incident no doubt left a scar which may prove embarrassing to us some time. It is painful to contemplate what might have happened had the French carried out their order of execution and to have had word of it reach the young man's influential relatives. The disaster following the assassination at Sarajevo might have been avoided had a system for handling such cases been established before that time.[137]

In 1932, Robert Young of Long Beach, Cal., left home during a family quarrel and joined the Legion. During his year and a half of service he had been wounded several times and decorated five times for bravery. He escaped, together with an Italian legionnaire named Giuseppe Carusso because he could not stand the stern military discipline and great privations any longer. His companion was slain.[138]

In 1932, enlisting in the French Foreign Legion was barred to Americans who were regarded as potential trouble makers. The Legion's closed-door policy where Americans were concerned was a result of Bennet Doty's much publicized desertion noted above and the subsequent publication of his experiences in book form.[139]

In 1942, the American consular authorities were asked by the parents of an American in the Legion to obtain his discharge.[139a]

On July 19, 1918, Frank S. Butterworth requested that the Secretary of War approve a plan of recruiting in the United States volunteers for the French Foreign Legion to complete one regiment. He believed that "volunteers from America should contribute to carry on the traditions of this unit of the French Army." The War Department did not approve of the project. The laws of the United States permitted a citizen or subject of one of the Allied countries to enlist in the army of their own country, but a citizen of the United States could not enlist in such a regiment as proposed by Butterworth.[140]

The idea of a foreign legion in the United States Army was not in keeping with American tradition. During the Civil War there were several regiments in the service of the United States with designations indicating the foreign origin of the soldiers. While each of these regiments contained men of the same nationality, the soldiers were both naturalized citizens as well as aliens. The army was not looking for soldiers of the same origin to form a regiment; the composition was rather the result of the recruits having come from the same town or state in the United States. In fact, such aliens were recruited and assigned to regular army units.

There were made, however, many plans to form foreign legions in the United States Army during World War I. These legions, however, would not have been organized along the same lines as the French Legion. The army rejected a plan to form United States regiments "composed of those of Germanic descent or affiliations." It was pointed out that the idea was impractical because "it would tend to accentuate bitterness" against those who refused to enlist and there probably were more who would reject the plan than adopt it, "for it is quite unreasonable to expect those of Germanic affiliations to desire to take any active part against their mother country, though content to take no part."[141] Plans to form a brigade of Mexicans and other Latin Americans and a unit of British Colonials (West Indians) were also regarded as impracticable. The formation of a Slavic Legion to cooperate with the American and Canadian armies in Russia and Siberia was rejected. Camp Wadsworth near Spartansburg, South Carolina, was designated as the base to which recruits for the Legion would be assigned, but there were no volunteers.[142] This would have been organized differently than the French Foreign Legion. The American plan permitted the Poles to recruit American volunteers for their legion under the command of Gen. Józef Haller, but not under the jurisdiction of the American flag.[143] The legality of this act can be disputed. Anyway, by their pogromist activities against the Jewish population of Poland these Polish-Americans dishonored the United States which had permitted them to join the Polish Legion.

Above all, one cannot avoid making a comparison between the treatment of Jews and other aliens in the French army and those in the armed forces of the United States. In the United States both Jewish aliens, non-Jewish aliens and American citizens were given equal treatment as soon as they joined as volunteers or were drafted. Aliens owed their adopted country the same duties as did the Americans but were also given the same privileges. They were not inducted in special penalized units.

XII. In the Atmosphere of Munich

In 1921, only 9,670 aliens were naturalized as French citizens. In 1922, 16,456 were naturalized. Naturalized citizens were discriminated against in the armed forces. They were kept out of "secret" branches. Only after living in France for many years as a naturalized citizen could one become an interpreter for the army. Thus, these restrictions served to maintain and further reinforce the practice of the Foreign Legion.[144]

In the 1920's and 1930's France needed troops for its various campaigns in North Africa and other colonial possessions. Again, the existence of the Foreign Legion was most convenient. Because of the depression in Germany and in other countries, there were many volunteers. In addition, a large number of Russian emigrés also joined the Legion, and there was no lack of all kinds of adventurers. The Third German Reich also supplied its quota of trained spies who entered the Legion.

In January 1935, France planned to form a full regiment of Saarlanders. However, in spite of the activities of French recruiting agents among refugees from the Saar in Forbach, Sarreguemines and other cities near the Saar border, there were not enough volunteers. Then, in March 1938, suspicion had been aroused concerning the large numbers of young Germans enlisting in the Foreign Legion and was finding expression in the Paris press. The *République* of March 27, 1938 asked: "Is it not possible that these young men have been charged with the task of seeding the Legion? There may be a method in this sending of Hitlerian agents into an African regiment." However, as the New York *Times* of March 28 noted, the circles of the Legion were of the opinion that such a plan could not work, for very quickly loyalty to the Legion dominated every other loyalty.[145]

After the defeat of the Republican Army in Spain many Spanish refugees interned in France and North Africa enlisted in the Legion in order to escape the hardships of French camps as did many Austrian and German political refugees who were also interned.

In April 1939, France began to recruit Spanish soldier refugees into the French army, or rather, the Foreign Legion. This authorized but limited enlistment was interpreted in some quarters as a French warning to Italy that she would arm masses of refugees if Rome did not take her troops out of Spain.[146]

Before World War I, the Foreign Legion had included only infantry troops. This arrangement fully satisfied the needs of the Legion during the occupation of colonies and mandates. With the law of August 5, 1920, the French parliament authorized the creation of cavalry units within the Legion and two years later, a decree regulated the creation of the First Cavalry Regiment of the Foreign Legion. With a few exceptions, almost all the officers were regular French officers. About a quarter of the NCO's were regulars of the French Cavalry. In the beginning the Cavalry Regiment included a large number of White Russians. For this reason it was called the Cossack regiment, but after a while these Russians were discharged. Basically the Foreign Legion was not better prepared for modern warfare than in August 1914.

In 1938 there were some suggestions put forth that in case of war aliens should be incorporated into the regular French army. Such was the desire expressed at the conference held in March 1939 by the *Union Nationale des Officers Anciens Combattants* (National Union of Veteran Officers) and of the *Combattants Républicains* (Republican Veterans). On March 9, 1939, a law was introduced in Parliament which would permit all aliens to become French citizens and serve in the French Army if they so desired. Senator Charles Reibel went even further: all aliens who were permitted to work in France should serve in the French Army. The press commented in favor of these projects. Later that month, the government published a law in the *Journal Officiel* of March 23, which stated: "All foreigners will be recruited in the French Army." However, no details were given as to how this would be accomplished and when World War II broke out, all alien volunteers had to enlist in the Foreign Legion for the duration of the war.[147]

Nobody was thinking seriously about this terrible injustice to volunteers. At the yearly celebrations of the associations of Jewish volunteers at Carency, nobody thought of saying *kadish* in memory of the nine Jewish legionnaires who were executed for demanding that France behave humanely towards aliens who had volunteered to defend her. Not one voice demanded a revision of the court martial which had sentenced the legionnaires to death. Not one Jewish association tried to trace the whereabouts of the Jewish legionnaires who were imprisoned as a result of the revolt at

Carency and were, most probably, living a miserable life in a punitive Legion battalion in North Africa. Only Sholem Schwartzbard spoke out against these injustices, in his memoirs, which were published abroad in Yiddish.

One "historian" of the Jews in the Foreign Legion wrote:

> The Foreign Legion? Why the selection of this colonial army of harsh discipline, of professional soldiers trained in superhuman heroism? Driving back of hesitating loyalty? Or was it a supreme honor reserved for men of passionate inclination? All these things together, perhaps. But who cares about the scenery, the important thing is to participate in the drama! And as enlisting in the Foreign Legion was permitted to them, they will be legionnaires.[148]

Raymond Raoul Lambert wrote in *La Revue Juive de Genève* that France had a sad history of xenophobia. In time of crisis a government increased taxes and adopted new legislation against foreigners.[149] Indeed, the action against aliens in general and refugees in particular was influenced by the existing antisemitic propaganda. The Jews were accused of preparing a war—a "Jewish war" of vengeance against Germany. In Paris and other cities Jews were attacked in the streets by mobs. "The Jews want the war to revenge themselves on Hitler," was the agitators' cry, taken up even in the crowded working-class sections. Extreme left labor circles as well as Fascist groups encouraged the agitators in order to discredit the government's foreign policy. In a sermon on the occasion of the Munich Agreement of September 29, 1938, Chief Rabbi J. Weill stressed that Jews did not desire a war. An association aiding refugees distributed a leaflet in which refugees were asked not to assemble in public, to avoid speaking German, to sign up for the French Foreign Legion, etc. (Many French Jews were among the most ardent partisans of the Munich Agreement.) The anti-Jewish propaganda was so strong, so obviously influenced by German agents, and so clearly a danger to the country, that in April 1939 the French Government enacted a law prohibiting racial defamation. However, stronger measures—which the Government did not take—were needed in order to cope successfully with the propaganda.

The antisemite Charles Mauras wrote in *Action Française* of November 29, 1939: "Where are the 'residents' in war-time? Surely not in the regiments!"

A law of November 2, 1938, permitted the internment of "undesirable foreigners" in camps *(étrangers indésirables dans les centres spéciaux)*.

The number of internees was already quite large by the end of 1938. Nonetheless, a law of December 31, 1939, expanded the scope of such internment.

Yet the camps were not administered by an anti-Jewish and pro-German government. Ironically, for a time, a Franco-Jewish Minister of the Interior, Georges Mandel, who himself fell victim to the anti-Jewish policy, was in charge of the camps. Needless to say, before the German defeat of France the refugees who were interned were not interned because they were Jews. But most refugees were Jews, and they were often criticized for having left Germany instead of remaining there to fight Hitler. Such an opinion was expressed even by *L'Oeuvre,* a liberal daily "read by almost all the Jews of Paris."

Officially the *concentration camps* of 1939-1940 were rarely referred to by this horrible name. They were imaginatively called "Centers," "Supervised lodging centers," "Reception Centers." Thanks to this hypocrisy—to use the expression of one historian—the system of camps became recognized as a legal institution in a civilized society. The play of words was continued after the Franco-German armistice of June 1941, and so until the very end of the war.

As early as the summer of 1939, more German and Austrian refugees, and even Polish Jews, were interned. The camp of Rieucros was a "tower of Babel." Many refugees taken off the ships, both enemies and neutrals, were put in camps. According to Hicem reports of the end of 1939, about 6,000 Jews were interned at the time in about 70 camps. However, the number of camps is understated. Many refugees were also imprisoned and they were rarely liberated.

When the law of October 4, 1940 gave the Prefects of the free zone the right to intern Jews, there was no shortage of camps. Camps of all sizes were located in hundreds of places. There is enough evidence to state that half of these camps had existed before June 1940.[150]

XIII. Again in the Foreign Legion

After the outbreak of war in 1939, foreign Jews together with non-Jewish immigrants once again were in long lines in front of government offices and voluntary institutions waiting to be recruited. Although there was no recurrence of the attacks of 1938 at this time, a strong anti-Jewish sentiment was felt nonetheless, and foreign Jews avoided the cafes and made themselves scarce on the streets.

All the Jewish parties and organizations, with the exception of the Jewish Communists, called upon the alien Jews to do their duty and volunteer for the French Army. In a single office alone, at 10 rue Lancry, opened by the Union of Jewish Volunteers of 1914-18 and the Federation of Jewish Societies, over ten thousand Jewish volunteers, all of them non-citizens, were registered in ten days. Yiddish placards were posted in the government registration offices and Yiddish translators seated there. Native French Jews and those of foreign birth who had been naturalized did not, of course, have to volunteer.

According to Joseph Ratz there was much confusion in accepting alien volunteers. In fact, in the very beginning, the military authorities did not accept enlisting aliens. Their names were inscribed on special registers and they were told that they would be called when the question of service of aliens would be decided. France had not decided in advance what to do with her tremendous number of aliens in case of war. Private organizations became impatient and opened their own enlistment offices, but they were told to send the volunteers to the army offices.[151]

Men registered as volunteers on the assumption that they would serve in the regular French Army. Even though no decree was published at the outbreak of the war stating that foreigners must volunteer, moral pressure to do so was exerted at every turn. The police stopped people in the streets and not only asked for their regular papers but also for evidence that they had enlisted in the French Army. This is not to say, however, that alien Jews did not volunteer to fight for France. In fact, thousands of them did enlist of their own free will.

These volunteers, however, were not taken into the regular French Army but were attached to the tragically famous Foreign Legion. The mistake of World War I was repeated, and nobody spoke out against it.

The Foreign Legion accepted almost everyone who volunteered for the duration of the war: older men, heads of large families, sickly men who would have been rejected by the regular army and who volunteered in order to escape the pressure on immigrants to enlist.

The novelist, Benjamin Shlevin, described in *The Jews of Belleville* how a group of Jews were stopped at the Place de la République by policemen who checked their identity papers and then demanded to see their enlisting papers. However, not everybody could show such a document for the simple reason that the many recruitment bureaus were unable or unwilling to register all volunteers, and many foreigners had to come back at another time. Meanwhile, they were afraid to show themselves in public. Some people even bribed the guards to let them enter the bureaus of recruitment. One wanted to be in order with the laws regulating the right of foreigners, to be able to demand French citizenship some day. There were many who lived illegally without papers giving the right of residence; some had even been expelled and had come back. These were people who hated borders, consulates, the Hitler regime, which had made of them men without a country, living in the underground and in unemployment. Now, they believed, the time to show their faces had arrived. Surely, France would not refuse volunteers ready to defend the country. Once one got inside the door, the bureaus would accept anybody without asking too many questions. "Sign here," and they all signed their names without reading the document.[152]

I, too, volunteered on September 2, 1939, for the duration of the war. I signed a paper which I had not read, and, after waiting many weeks, was sent to a training center of the Foreign Legion, first to Vancia and then transferred to La Valbonne (near Lyons) where recruits had been trained in the 1914-18 war. The attitude toward Jews was not exactly friendly. Several times antisemitic remarks by a corporal or sergeant would lead to unpleasant incidents. The officers did nothing to remedy the situation.

The officers and non-commissioned officers were almost all brought over from the Foreign Legion in North Africa. They constantly insulted us, the volunteers. One sergeant of my unit called all legionnaires "Salomon" and always yelled, "This is the Legion, not a synagogue!" Some of the non-commissioned officers gladly accepted bribes. Among other insults, it was sneeringly remarked to the Jews that they had joined for the food. The story of 1914-1918 repeated itself. Curiously, even the uniforms given us during the training period had been used during World War I. I was told the story of a Jewish volunteer who was given a jacket bearing the name of his father-in-law, a volunteer in 1914. All this was comic. However, even the rifles were old and rusted. It was almost impossible to keep them clean, and many of these rifles proved useless at the front line.

While waiting to be called up for service, I had a very busy and exciting life. I became influenced by a group of Jewish intellectuals, Russian émigrés, who were connected with the YIVO Institute for Jewish Research in Vilna, Poland. They had left Berlin at the advent of the Third Reich to settle in Paris. Under their influence I had left the Communist movement. They were people to whom the individual was more important than state, party or organization, perhaps because they themselves had been victims of collectivist ideological or political forces. Among them was the historian Elias and Mrs. Rebecca Tcherikower, who befriended me. I think I was a very lucky young man. After having for many years been active in the Communist movement, in disrupting Socialist and Zionist meetings and even collecting funds for the Arabs during the Palestine pogroms in 1929 ("for the victims of Zionist imperialism"), I had now found a group of people and an intellectual climate which gave me a new faith profoundly influencing my life from that time on.

In April 1938, the American Yiddish poet Jacob Glatstein published a poem in which he said "good night" to the world and proclaimed the idea of going "back to the ghetto." A discussion on the value of emancipation started, which found its best expression in two large issues of *Oyfn Sheidweg* (On the Crossroad), edited by Elias Tcherikower and Israel Efroykin. After the advent of the Third Reich, a large number of European intellectuals who had resided in Germany found refuge in France. They were secular Jews, but of a special kind. Most of them had grown up in Russia, been active in Jewish and Russian movements, witnessed the Revolutions of 1905 and 1917, and lost their faith in God. However, they never made a show of their secularism. Many of them still believed that religion was the basis for the endurance of the Jewish people, and some of them even thought of themselves as religious Jews. They suffered because they were unable to break away from the secular ideologies and habits. Among them was Tcherikower. His apartment (at 34 rue Dombasle) became a salon where long debates were conducted on religion versus secularism; on the emancipation, for which Jews had given up their physical and intellectual ghettos, thus opening the way to assimilation, which had weakened the capacity of resistance to enemies; on what should be done in face of the new danger—Nazi Germany; etc., etc. The Communist philosopher Charles Rapoport, who had left the Communist Party, was among the participants in the discussions. I remember how one day he was perusing a volume of Graetz; all of a sudden he said: "What an idiot I was, my entire life I have toiled for strangers." In *Oyfn Scheidweg* Tcherikower developed the idea that the Third Reich was not the first catastrophe in the history of the Jewish people. However, the previous generations had been able to survive because their "religious faith had created a philosophy of suffering and prevented the fall of the Jewish spirit," but ours is "the tragedy of a weak generation." His arguments were refuted by Simon Dubnow in an article published in the second issue, which also contained a reply by Tcherikower. It was then that Tcherikower wrote his study on the Jews during the French Revolution of 1789 in which he described in detail the hesitation of the Ashkenazim to give up their autonomy in exchange for emancipation.

Tcherikower kept on his desk a Bible given to him by his grandfather; he kept it during his wanderings in Palestine, the United States, back to Russia after the Revolution of March 1917, Germany, then France. When the war broke out and I went into the army, he gave me the Bible, saying: "It will keep you safe." Later, when I was wounded, I lost the Bible and also an amulet with the inscription "YIVO" given to me by Mrs. Tcherikower.

XIV. Forced Volunteers

Those who volunteered because they had no other choice were influenced not only by fear of serving in the Foreign Legion, but also by propaganda of the Jewish Communists against the "imperialistic war." There were, indeed, many Communists among us and they called themselves VF's (*voluntaires forcés*—forced volunteers). They were always reading newspapers, eager to find some indication of a quick end to the "imperialistic war." They held meetings and even published a mimeographed bulletin. The anti-Communists tried not to provoke them. They were afraid that the discovery of a Communist organization among the Jewish volunteers would result in arrests, perhaps even executions, most certainly in anti-Jewish propaganda. However, the Communists would constantly provoke their adversaries and even warn them that on the front line a bullet cannot always be traced to the rifle that fired it.

One Jew, who had served during World War I as a volunteer in the Foreign Legion, was now a naturalized citizen having been drafted into the Legion as an adjutant. He tried to force us to give him the names of the Communist ringleaders. We told him that as much as we disliked them the very suggestion that we play the role of informers was distasteful to us. Finally, we had to enlist the help of the Jewish chaplain, René Hirschler, in order to force the adjutant to abandon his plan.

In my dairy I had noted:

> After our arrival at the camp of Vancia, near Lyons, we had to pass a final medical examination. Those really unfit for service in the Legion were to be sent back to Paris. The chief physician at the camp was a naturalized Polish Jew, L. Hufnagel, who had been active in the Association of Polish Jews in France. With a few rare exceptions he accepted everyone for service in the Legion.
>
> Those who thought of themselves as "forced volunteers" disliked the very name of this Jewish captain and told all kinds of stories about him. On the way to Vancia the train stopped at the Dijon railroad station and there we met a few volunteers on their way back to Paris. They told us a fantastic story: the Jewish physician is on leave, and the non-Jewish physician who replaced him is rejecting a very large number of Jewish volunteers. He is an antisemite who dislikes the idea of having too many Jews in the Legion. If one wishes to be

JEWS AND THE FRENCH FOREIGN LEGION 65

rejected, one has only to complain about something. Such was really the situation at Vancia and nobody knew the real reasons. According to some gossips it was in order to get rid of as many Jews as possible and force them to join the Polish Army in France. Anyway, the Jewish captain came back and the massive rejections of Jewish volunteers were immediately stopped.

From another entry in my diary:

The wives of the wealthy *volontaires forcés* (forced volunteers) left their children with *nourrices* (foster mothers) and came to stay in the villages near the barracks and other cantonments where their husbands were training. They paid extravagant prices for the privilege of having a private room where they could spend the nights with their husbands. The latter had to pay bribes to the non-commissioned officers for overnight passes, be back in time for reveille and listen to the endless jokes at their expense. It was as if through love-making these couples were trying to make themselves believe that the war would never become a reality for them. Such legionnaires refused to eat the army food which contained bromide, a substance which lessened sexual desire. In general the food in the Legion before we went to the front was, if not always good, then at least plentiful and if one could find out from the mess sergeant which food contained the daily ration of bromide, the bread, wine or soup, then even this fear could be avoided. But the *volontaires forcés* did not trust such a system and waited for the evening to eat at a local cafe. Those *volontaires forcés* who could not afford to bring over their wives also avoided the army food. What if this imperialistic war were to end suddenly and they would be sent home? God knows what effect the bromide may have on them!

The legionnaire Albert Rothsztein of the 51st company stationed at St.-Maurice-de-Gourdans, in civilian life a tailor, wrote a song that ended with the following stanza:

> Fun trinken dem vain un esen di zup,
> Faln bay unds mener di aktsyes arop.
> Un keyn farlang iz bay unds mer nit faran
> Un m'oybt on tsu fargesn as men iz a man.
> Oy, Oy.

> [From drinking the wine and eating the soup,
> The desire weakens among us men.
> And there is no more lust among us
> And one begins to forget that one is a man.]
> Oy, Oy.

The Yiddish novelist Benjamin Shlevin wrote in one of his many songs:

> Bromir un vayn un trikn broyt,
> der kleyner ligt geharget toyt.
>
> [Bromide and wine and dry bread,
> The little one lies dead.]

After the collapse of Poland, considerable confusion was caused by the establishment of a Polish Army-in-exile on French soil. Under the terms of a Franco-Polish agreement, Polish Jews volunteering for service with the French Army were to be referred to Polish authorities. Many others were already in the French Army, while those who had volunteered prior to the signing of the agreement but had not yet been called to the colors were re-examined and offered a choice of serving in either army.

Many of the Polish Jews had been living in Paris for so many years that they had practically forgotten the Polish language. More recent arrivals had vivid memories of the antisemitism under which they had suffered. Rumors spread that there had been antisemitic outbreaks in the divisions of the Polish Army in France in which Jewish soldiers had been cursed and beaten. The action of Polish consulate officials in depriving Jews living in Paris of their Polish citizenship, not only before the war but for many months after the invasion of Poland, likewise aggravated the situation. For all these reasons, Polish Jews, quite naturally, preferred to serve with the French forces, even in the Foreign Legion. Many Jews escaped from the Polish army, not to desert but to enlist in the Foreign Legion. Léon Aréga cited the following dialogue of two Jews who had "deserted" from a Polish unit to the Legion:

—Under the flag of the Polish pogromists, never!
—Volunteers for France, deserters for Poland!

Nevertheless, a considerable number of Jews joined the Polish ranks in France. Some indication of their number may be gained from the fact that preparations were made early in 1940 to conduct a passover *seder* for 1,500 Jewish soldiers. (Because of the tense situation at the front this *seder* was never held.) Their ranks were later swelled by Polish Jews from Belgium who had escaped to France after the Hitler invasion.

According to one source, officers were ordered not to include Jewish soldiers among those to be evacuated during the evacuation of the Polish army from France to England. In England the Poles continued their anti-Jewish propaganda. On July 20, 1940, a priest stated in a sermon given at the Polish Church of London that France's collapse had occurred because "France was ruled by Jewish Communists and the Front Populaire headed by the Jew Léon Blum." He praised both de Gaulle and Pétain. In the Polish army units in England Jews were continuously attacked. Readers will recall Franz V. Verfel's tragi-comic account of the relations between a Jew and a Polish officer during the collapse of France.[153]

Kalman Stein recalled:

The new Polish Army fell an easy prey to the anti-Semitic virus. Most of the officers revealed themselves as violent anti-Semites and practiced what they preached. The Government-in-Exile was apparently too weak to institute order and cleanse the Army of elements spreading the venom of hatred.

Thousands of Polish Jews in France volunteered for service with the Polish Army in the very first days of September 1939. Those volunteers were rather reluctantly accepted into the ranks of the Army, for many Poles were afraid lest the Polish Army become too "Jewish." Those among the Jews who were accepted and subsequently called to the colors very often encountered an atmosphere of racial hatred. Though formally they had full rights, they were in most cases excluded from the Officers' Schools and even those admitted were not commissioned. Thus, the situation of the Jewish soldiers in the Polish Army in exile was unfortunate from the very outset.

The writer of these lines was deeply shocked in Paris, at the end of 1939 or the beginning of 1940, when told by a leading French Jew of the following case. Two young Polish Jews who had lived for many years in Palestine left that country of their own free will after the outbreak of the war, in order to enlist in the Polish Army in France. A few weeks after they had been admitted into the Polish ranks, they applied to a well-known French-Jewish organization for help. They declared that, owing to various expressions of anti-Semitism, their position had become unbearable. A short investigation revealed that there was sufficient basis for their complaints. French military authorities eventually permitted their transfer to the French Army [Foreign Legion].

The representatives of Polish Jewry then in Paris took up the matter with the Polish authorities and tried to bring about an improved situation.

Taking a stand against anti-Semitism, the late General Wladyslaw Sikorski issued the following Order of the Day on August 5, 1940:

"The success of our arms and the secure establishment of our national existence require the coordination of our efforts for our common aim.

"In the army, particularly, unity must be firmly established and honest brotherhood of arms must rule, and all squabbles be eliminated.

"My principle is that a Polish soldier now fighting for the common cause has thus given sufficient evidence that he is a Pole, irrespective of his origin and religion.

"I strictly forbid showing to soldiers of Jewish faith any unfriendliness through contemptuous remarks humiliating to human dignity. All such offenses will be severely punished.

"This order is to be read on parade to all soldiers."

General Sikorski's sincerity in this attempt to root out anti-Semitism from the ranks of the Polish Army cannot be doubted. But after a short time, the influence of the above Order of the Day wore off, the more so that words were not followed by deeds. The anti-Semites were not punished, Jews were not commissioned. Small wonder that many of the rabid anti-Semites thought that in spite of the Commander's order they might do as they wished.

On various occasions, Jewish members of the Polish National Council and other Jewish representatives drew the attention of Polish authorities to the tense conditions prevailing in the Polish Army. It was of no avail.

An unfortunate situation developed; unfortunate from the point of view of Poland, whose future depends so much on the goodwill of the world and on the harmonious collaboration of all Poles, without distinction of creed, nationality, or political belief.

The situation became even worse when new units of the Polish Army were formed in the Middle East. The commander of those units, General Anders, published on November 30, 1941 his famous Order of the Day in which he declared that while he understood the anti-Jewish feelings of the Polish soldiers, they must realize that "anti-Semitism is unpalatable to the Anglo-Saxon world."[154]

XV. With Republican Spaniards

Other volunteers from Paris were sent to Barcarès, on the coast near Perpignan. A camp had been set up there before the war for Spaniards of the Republican Army who took refuge in France. Among the Spaniards were many Jews who had been members of the International Brigade. These were mostly Polish Jews, but there were Jews from Central Europe as well.

In Paris there was a branch of the Aid Committee for Former German and Austrian Volunteers in the Spanish Government Army. Before the war this committee was able to help the many volunteers, among them 27 Jews in the camp St. Cyprien, 35 in the camp Argelès, and 29 in Paris and elsewhere.[155]

Spaniards from the Republican Army who had also volunteered were sent to our camps from the training camps in Southeastern France. We were, however, forbidden to fraternize with them, to train with them, even to speak to them. They were isolated in restricted areas. They were treated as criminals. They would sit in groups, singing songs that under the circumstances seemed to us to be very sad. This made us feel sick, but we were being watched and had to be careful. Sometimes the Spaniards used to sing the anthem of the short-lived Spanish Republic *(Himno de Riego)*, but even this song seemed to be sad:

> Serenos y alegres
> Valientes y osados
> Cantemos, soldados
> El Himno a la lid.
> De nuestros acentos
> El orbe se admire
> Y en nosotros mire
> Los hijos del Cid.
> > Soldados: la patria
> > nos llama a la lid;
> > juremos por ella
> > vencer o morir.

El mundo vió nunca
más noble osadía,
más grande el valor,
que aquel que, inflamados,
nos vimos del fuego
excitar a Riego
de Patria el amor.
    Soldados . . .

La trompa guerrera
su secos da al viento,
horror al sediento;
ya Marte, sañudo,
la audacia provoca
y el ingenio invoca
de nuestra nación.
    Soldados . . .

Whenever we could we threw them cigarettes, candy, soap, razor blades, and other things.

Of course, not only Jews "volunteered" for the Legion. There were also Italians, Russians, and Spanish immigrants, among others. Many of them, especially the Italians, bullied the Jewish legionnaires. I remember a violent incident at St.-Maurice-de-Gourdans during which the crude insults of the Italians earned them a beating at the hands of the all-Jewish 10th group of the 39th Company of the 12th Regiment. Only the Spaniards were friendly. But then, their fate was a sad one.

When the time came to form regiments from the various loose training outfits, it seemed that the majority of the recruits were Jewish immigrants and that the regiment to which my outfit was to belong would therefore be composed largely of Jews. This the authorities did not want. Many of us felt that their action was inspired by anti-Jewish motives, that they did not want an almost completely Jewish regiment. Others of us tried to excuse their decision by arguing that it was a tradition of the Foreign Legion not to build a regiment with a majority of people of one nationality. Thus many Jewish recruits were taken from La Valbonne, where my outfit underwent its basic training, and sent to Barcarès, where they were joined by the Spaniards. This was done in a needlessly painful fashion. At La Valbonne where the 12th Regiment was formed, all companies were assembled, Jewish soldiers were called out from the ranks, and most of them were sent away. This left a terrible impression on the remaining Jews.

JEWS AND THE FRENCH FOREIGN LEGION   71

The Jewish volunteers served in the following units: 11th and 12th infantry regiments of alien volunteers; 21st, 22nd and 23rd regiment of march of alien volunteers; 13th half-brigade of the Foreign Legion, consisting of two battalions; 1st, 2nd and 3rd batallions of alien volunteers *(Bataillons de Marche des Pionniers Volontaires Etrangers)*.

At the head of the 12th Regiment was Colonel Besson, a friendly man. We learned from some comrades that many officers had refused to work with the regiment because of the large number of Jews in it. Besson had accepted. In the 22nd and 23rd Regiments which were formed near Perpignan, at least three-quarters of the men were Jewish.

A few hundred Jewish recruits from our company were sent to the 11th Regiment which consisted largely of non-Jews, long-serving legionnaires from Morocco. It was the first regiment of the Legion to be sent to the front. After many hard battles, only a small number of legionnaires survived.

The legionnaires who remained in La Valbonne at the end of the war withdrew, fighting to Lyons; most of them were Jews.

The 13th half-brigade was composed largely of legionnaires from Morocco. About fifty Jewish refugees joined this outfit when it was stationed near La Valbonne. The unit fought in the battle of Narvik and later brought to England. In the interim, France fell before the Nazi onslaught. About twenty Jewish legionnaires remained in England to join de Gaulle's army. The others returned to France by way of Morocco, where they were pitilessly treated despite their valiant service.

The 6th Regiment served in Syria. One battalion consisted of a thousand volunteers, half of whom were Jews who had been shipped from a point near Perpignan. With the exception of the unit that went to Narvik, this regiment was the only one to fight outside France. In all other cases the Jewish volunteers served and fought on French soil.

According to one source, about 100,000 aliens enlisted, of whom 73,000 served in the Foreign Legion, including 28,000 Spaniards.[156]

After the German invasion of Belgium our regiment started to prepare to move to the front line. We received reserve rations and on May 9 we left La Valbonne in "8 horses, 40 men" wagons. On the way, we saw masses of civilian refugees heading in the direction from which we had come. We did not know whom to pity more, the refugees or ourselves. We were hungry and ate our reserve rations which consisted of hard biscuits and conserved meat known as *singe* (monkey). Our train stopped at Ligny in the Department of Meuse and from there we marched to the village of Trepier. Overhead a German plane circled for a long time, a sign that the Germans know of our identity and our arrival. We were attached to the 8th Infantry Division of the 17th Army Corps of the 6th Army.

The discipline was very strict, but we noticed that the attitude of the officers and non-commissioned officers toward men became more humane.

At the front the officers treated the Jewish volunteers as men. Perhaps the common danger of death weakened any anti-Jewish sentiments they might have had. Besides, the Jewish volunteers fought valiantly, a fact the officers frankly admitted. They often promised that after the war those who survived would be looked upon as equals in the eyes of the French and not as aliens, and that families of fallen volunteers would be similarly treated.

Instead of moving directly toward the Belgian border we were transferred to another front, in the Department of Ain where the German army was expected to show itself any day. To the North the department reached Belgium and Northern France, and to the South the rivers Seine and Marne. The land was flat there. During the first World War one of the bloodiest battles took place there on a front known as *Chemin des Damnes* (Road of the Damned).

Was the Legion well-prepared and well-armed? Charles E. Mercier wrote in *Legion of Strangers* that morale in the Legion was low because of the

> refusal of the French to supply the Legion with first-rate arms and equipment. Little new came to it except the khaki uniform of the French Army. Its armament still consisted of rifles, light machine guns and personnel mortars and grenades. Its motorized equipment was antiquated. It still had a regiment of cavalry, armed with sabers and carbines, even though the horse had long since demonstrated ineffective in modern warfare. It had no tanks or half-tracks, no artillery except a few outmoded 75's. Although most legionnaires did not realize it at the time many regular French units also were ill-equipped to oppose the blitzkrieg armored war that Germany would launch.[157]

From my diary:

We are starting to doubt in the veracity of the saying "Impossible is not French." During the furlough we met French soldiers and noticed that they possessed even less enthusiasm than we. We found out from them that the Germans were better equipped than we were. Unlike our have guns, a 1907 model or even older, the Germans were equipped with modern guns, even light machine guns, like the gangsters of Chicago. Some soldiers have difficulties with their guns which jam. How will we be able to move on the front with our heavy clothing and all the equipment? In our company of transmissions the field telephones are outmoded. Surely, the French army must be better equipped. Perhaps they will, at the last minute, issue modern equipment even to the legionnaires. But will we know how to use it?

Is it necessary to give the details of the heroic fighting of both Jewish and non-Jewish volunteers in the Legion? It is well known that the Foreign Legion was sent everywhere. It served in the most dangerous positions on the front where the retreating flank of the French army had to be defended. When General François was called to testify as a witness at the Riom Trial against Léon Blum and his colleagues, he stated that the one thing he had been sure of was the Foreign Legion. The French journalist Jean Monfils, writing in the Vichy-controlled *Paris Soir* of September 10, 1940, gave the following description of the part taken by the Foreign Legion in the battle of Soissons, in which the 12th Regiment fought:

Isolated in a dead city. There is no more contact with the retreating army. The telephone is cut, the bridges destroyed. Alone, hidden in empty houses which they will soon defend . . . The tanks with the swastikas enter Soissons. It seems that Soissons is abandoned. They fight from parlor to dining room, from the stairs to the cellar, in the cellar itself, from the chimney to the opening in the stove, from the left sidewalk of the Place de la République to the right side; and so on all over the entire city, on the Faubourgs, on the Boulevard Jean d'Arc, on the Rue Château Thierry, in the factories, hidden under abandoned machines with revolver in hand. The tanks with the swastikas move over the city, slowly, the machine guns aimed at each door and each window.

It was still not over. There was still an epilogue. The men attacked the guns, broke bottles of gasoline over them and set them on fire . . . The last answer was on the Avenue de la Gare. Legionnaires threw stones from a six-story building upon the first column of the German infantry. Only after the death of its last defenders, the legionnaires, did the French city fall.

The following testimony was given by Charles E. Mercier about the fighting spirit of the Jewish legionnaires:

Even more magnificent was the month-old regiment composed largely of Polish Jews who lacked training and were poorly equipped. On June 15, the day after Paris fell, the regiment flung itself against the Germans near Soissons. In the mounting confusion of the French forces someone ordered it to hold a bridge across the Aisne against the Germans. Using rifles and hand grenades against the heavy German armor, the fledgling legionnaires somehow clung doggedly to the bridge for two days while French forces retreated behind them. Pinched off at last and surrounded, small groups of the untrained men tried to fight their way out. There is no record of any member of the regiment returning to its depot.[158]

Walter Kunitz wrote that "these legionnaires by accident" fought courageously; "they died wholesale." When the Germans broke through at Sedan in May 1940 they were held back by 2,000 legionnaires, volunteers for the duration of the war:

> The doomed battalion stood firm for almost 48 hours and was finally annihilated to the last man. But the delay of 48 hours, caused by the heroic self-sacrifice of these 2000 men, enabled the bulk of the French forces to retreat in order and to reform behind safer positions. That, subsequently, they were not able to stem the Nazi flood does not change the value of the Legion Battalion's heroic performance.[159]

According to various sources this regiment formed in February 1940 was surrounded near Soissons. Only one-third of the men were able to break through and join the general retreat.

The 13th half-brigade of the Legion which fought for the liberation of Narvik, Norway, was wiped out. Of 2,000 legionnaires, only about 150 came back alive, many of them wounded. The rest remained buried in the fjords of the land of the midnight sun.

On June 15, 1940, I was wounded in the chest. Many months later I wrote in a letter to my elderly friends Elias and Rebecca Tcherikower:

> I was wounded near Pont-sur-Yonne, not far from a small bridge that was defended by two machine guns. We were the last legionnaires to cross an open field, trying to reach the bridge. From somewhere to the left of us the Germans opened fire, and we saw a tank coming. It was then that I was wounded. I could not continue toward the bridge, and I fell. The legionnaires passed me by. I knew almost every one of them from the times when we were active in the Communist movement. But I had left the movement; I was a former Communist and I knew that they would not help me. They looked at me and continued to run toward the bridge. Not one of them stopped to help me. I could not see; my eyes were closed. Then Henri was shaking me. He was my sergeant, a career soldier who had spent fifteen years in the Legion. He was not a bad fellow, but a heavy drinker. Once he told me that he had killed his parents and escaped to the Legion. I doubt if it were true, for he told me all kinds of

fantastic stories. Anyway, after crossing the bridge, he looked for me, and when he was told that I was wounded he came back to pick me up. For this he was decorated.

Later, while serving as a paratrooper with the United States 82nd Airborne Division, I learned what really formed the *esprit de corps:* the knowledge that if one were wounded, one would not be left behind. How I admired the willingness of my buddies to take care of a wounded comrade at the cost of endangering their own lives!

After France collapsed in May 1940, a tragic chapter in the history of the French Legion was written. Units of the fourth regiment stationed in Syria fought for Vichy against the allies under General Dentz while many legionnaires fought with General Leclerc on the side of the Allies in the campaign of Lake Tschad. In Morocco, the legionnaires fought against rebellious native tribesmen who had been encouraged by Germany to revolt.

XVI. Demobilized for the Antechambers of Death Camps

The legionnaire Leon Sandlersz of the 45th company stationed in La Valbonne, in civilian life had been a tailor, expressed his doubts of the future in a song:

>Un afile ven svet zikh shojn endikn di krig
>Un mir veln shojyn ale zayn tsrik
>Fremde vet me ints nokh zogn
>Geyt aykh men darf aykh do nisht hobn
>Khotsh geyt zikh zukhn a naye heym.

>[And even when the war will end
>And we all will be back
>Foreigners we will still be called
>Go we don't need you here
>At least go look for a new home.]

The demobilization of volunteers was not always accomplished without incident. At the camp at Septfonds, for example, the legionnaires declared a strike, demanding to be demobilized immediately. They were told that their action would be interpreted as a rebellion and that gendarmes or regular troupes would be sent to the camp. Piraud, commandant of the camp, stated that the Vichy government had ordered not to demobilize the volunteers who were to be sent to labor camps. Piraud finally agreed to demobilize all fathers of five children and those volunteers who could prove that they had some kind of business or employment in civilian life. Finally, however, forced labor camps were organized. *Voilà comment la France nous remercia pour notre engagement voluntaire!* (That's how France thanks us for our voluntary enlistment)—wrote one volunteer.[160]

Indeed, after June 1940, demobilized Jewish soldiers were rarely set free. Instead, they were sent by the French Government of Vichy to labor camps (known as GTE—*Groupements de Travailleurs Etrangers*) and to concentration camps, from which they were deported in August 1942 during the mass deportation of foreign-born Jews. During the discussions preceding the signing of the Franco-German armistice, Gen. Wilhelm von Keitel agreed not to make any demands that would affect foreign-born soldiers serving in the French army. France was free to demobilize them as free men. Nonetheless, most of them were demobilized and interned in labor camps. Demobilization did not necessarily mean freedom to a Jewish legionnaire. According to Walter Kanitz, the Franco-German armistice had claimed the right to ask for the extradition of foreign volunteers. Kanitz wrote that regular legionnaires of German nationality were permitted to break their contract and to return to Germany after a screening by a Nazi commission. Kanitz learned of several instances in which German legionnaires, rejected by the Nazi screening team, had returned to their unit. "They ended up in the penal battalion in Colomb-Béchar and the chances are that they never got away from there alive. This depicts the spirit among the Legion command at that time despite armistice and collaboration with Germans." Moreover, Kanitz makes the following statement:

> However ambiguous Marshall Pétain's position may have been at that time, one thing has to be said in his favor. He did not intend to enforce the extradition clause in the armistice treaty which had been imposed on him and he did his best to protect the volunteers. Fundamentally Pétain was a soldier and it was against his deep-rooted conceptions and feelings of honor to sacrifice these men who had come voluntarily to fight for France. This writer, who was one of the men discharged after the armistice, and who, after that, lived in France until the Allied landing in 1942, does not know of one single case where a man had been handed over to the Nazis, despite numerous requests for extradition.[161]

However, Kanitz was referring to an earlier time when the Legion was fighting in North Africa. In France, Jewish volunteers in the Legion for the duration of the war were delivered to the Germans by the thousands. When it came to Jewish legionnaires, Pétain ignored his "deep-rooted conceptions."

Most of the Jews interned in May 1941 at Pithiviers and Beaune-la-Rolande (in the occupied zone) had been volunteers in the army. At the Pithiviers camp 1,300 out of 1,800 internees were volunteers, including 300 front-line veterans. The French gendarmes guarding the camp were told that the internees were all criminals. Among these "criminals" was a veteran, wounded in both lungs, who at the military hospital had been in the same room as an officer of the guard. One internee asked the reasons for his internment. "Because you loved too much France," he was told. The names of the internees had been taken from the recruiting offices and from the Police Prefecture.[161a]

As a rule, the Vichy authorities discriminated against demobilized Jewish volunteers of the free zone in matters which were exclusively French. In Nice volunteers were refused employment permits. In Marseilles, Lyons and Toulouse the prefects refused to grant them residence permits. In Grenoble two wives of Jewish prisoners of war were refused their military allowance.[162]

A legionnaire who had escaped from a German P. W. camp to the unoccupied zone of France tried to obtain identity papers. He was asked to bring an employment contract to prove that he had found work, a residence permit from the Préfecture, and a residence certificate. Otherwise, he was told, he would be sent to a labor camp.[163]

In July 1942, an internee of the forced labor camp GTE 355 at Coupiac complained that he was "demobilized" but interned. By demobilizing the volunteers before internment, France deprived them of their military status as well as any protection they might have had as prisoners of war.

The legionnaires who were taken prisoner had to suffer many hardships: they were interned in separate barracks (Judenbaraken), they had to wear a yellow star and were forced to do heavy work. Still, these camps were favored over the death camps. Vichy deprived the "demobilized" legionnaires of even the possibility of being treated as prisoners of war. By putting them in camps Vichy France made it impossible for many of the volunteers to go underground.

Wounded and sick volunteers were demobilized as *inaptes* and interned as such. The volunteers' applications for membership in Pétain's Legion, the official organization of army veterans, were rejected.

During the German occupation, service in the French army was constantly cited by the Jewish organization as the reason for opposing arrests, deportations and other measures that were taken against both native and foreign-born veterans and their families. In isolated cases such intervention helped, for not only Frenchmen, but even Germans were sometimes deferential to veterans. Their respect for army service sometimes overrode all other considerations. However, this was not a widespread policy, and in the end, very few volunteers were saved because they were *anciens combattants*. Most who were interned were later deported to death camps.

Everything depended on the particular official in charge. If he were a soldier who had been at the front and knew of the Legion's fine record there, he would treat the Jewish volunteers a little better. But the young Fascist officials who had not been near the front cared nothing for the men who had served their adopted country. They would arrest former Jewish soldiers on the streets and drag them to the police, who, in many cases, would promptly release them.

Joseph Ratz, himself a volunteer, organized the *Fédération des Engagés Volontaires* (Federation of Former Volunteers) which had branches in many cities of the Free Zone. The center was located in the barracks of the 23rd Regiment of the Legion at Montauban. Piraud, former commandant of a demobilization camp of volunteers, gave his permission to organize the Fédération and in many cases intervened on behalf of Jewish volunteers. In Marseilles, for example, four Jewish former volunteers who came to the Préfecture to ask for the legalization of a branch in that city were arrested. They were released only after Piraud's vigorous intervention. However, by October 8, 1942, 782 members of the organization had been deported.[164]

After having been wounded, I was taken by ambulance to a military hospital in Bordeaux and, when the city was included in the occupied zone, I was transferred to the hospital in Carpentras.

I was lucky. When I left the hospital in Carpentras after the armistice, I went to Trets-Fuveau, near Marseilles, where I was demobilized. On September 21, 1940, over 300 German legionnaires who had served in Morocco had already arrived and were waiting to be transferred to the German army. They had come to town singing Nazi songs and promptly began attacking the Jewish volunteers. Earlier, on July 27, 1940, I had been awarded the croix de guerre with a bronze star *(Légionnaire courageux et de sang-froid)*.

Curiously enough, those months in the hospital of Carpentras and later in that city were among the most productive of my life. I made many friends there, and my elderly friends, Elias and Rebecca Tcherikower, came to visit me at the hospital before they had left for the United States. They had left Paris in a hurry, taking with them only the proofs of the book, *The Jews in France*, which contained many of my studies (it was published in 1942 by the YIVO Institute for Jewish Research in New York). I had always been fascinated by the history of the Jews in the Four Communities of Avignon and Comtat Venaissin, and now fate had brought me there, in the most terrible circumstances. However, I did not despair. I spent many days in the famous Carpentras library, and when I left France for the

United States, I carried with me the first drafts of my studies on the Jewish aspect of the annexation of the Papal Province of Avignon and Comtat Venaissin during the French Revolution, Jewish motives in the popular culture of the province, and on the language of the Jews in that part of France. Moreover, while in Carpentras I smuggled out from Paris, with the help of French friends, the archives of the Historical Section of YIVO, those of Sholem Schwartzbard, the Simon Dubnow archives, and the private archives and library of the Tcherikowers. The latter included the archives on the pogroms in the Ukraine. Some of these archives I was able to send immediately to YIVO in New York via Martinique, the others I had to hide. In December 1944 I obtained permission from the U.S. 82nd Airborne Division to go to Marseilles and get the archives. I found them intact, they had been well hidden, and the United States military authorities consented to send them to YIVO in New York.

Now, looking back to those days after thirty years I am amazed at the energy and will power of the young historian which I then was. In spite of the difficulties and uncertainties of that era, this was a truly beautiful time and probably the most exciting period of my life.

As I have already noted, many of the forced labor camps were first intended for soldiers from the Spanish Republican Army and their families who sought refuge in France after Franco's victory. It was because of them that French concentration camps were first established. At first, the improvised camps were merely stretches of sand surrounded by barbed wire. Then barracks were constructed. Later the Spanish refugees shared the camps with the Jews. Thus these two groups shared the same fate. A nun who worked as a social worker in a camp asked a very young Spanish internee:

> "Are you Jewish?"
> He hesitated, "No, sister."
> "Then why are you in a concentration camp?"
> "We are Spanish."[165]

From the outbreak of the War and even earlier, and until the armistice of June 1940, Austrian and German refugees were sent to camps, as were demobilized Jewish legionnaires after the Franco-German armistice. Later, a law of September 27, 1940, and an ordinance of November 28, 1941 decreed that all immigrants, including those who were considered "superfluous" to the national economy, those who were without evident means of support, those who were already in non-labor camps, former volunteers of the army *(prestataires)*, etc., were to be sent to labor camps. These free-zone camps were, to the best of our knowledge, strictly French camps and not, like the Todt camps, under German jurisdiction. If there is proof to the contrary, then it has not been made public.

The GTE camps were organized into seven regional Groupements with headquarters located in: 1) Vic-le-Comte, 2) Toulouse (merged later with No. 7), 3) Montpellier, 4) Marseilles, 5) Lyons, 6) Limoges, 7) Toulouse.

Some documents may give a false impression of the real character of these camps. On March 19, 1942, Gaston Kahn of the First Section of the 5th UGIF Direction in the Southern zone (CAR—*Comité d'Assistance aux Réfugiés*) appealed to foreign-born Jews who had arrived in France after January 1, 1936, to register for such camps. (The UGIF—*Union Générale des Israélites de France* was the French *Judenrat,* forced upon the Jews by the Germans and Vichy.) The appeal was in response to a promise made by the Vichy government that registration for such camps would be carried out in a "social spirit" in collaboration with the UGIF. Thereupon many interned Jews quickly volunteered for the camps, hoping for better treatment, more food, and possible safeguards for themselves and their families. The relief organizations and the alien workers (TE— *Travailleurs Etrangers*) soon discovered that they had been given false promises. Discipline at the camps was very strict, often stricter than in other camps and food was in short supply. Outside the GTE camps, the situation was not much better for the GTE sections (called also "Commandos") and individual workers attached to factories, forest camps, farms, etc. A Jewish internee of the GTE in Beaucaire was sent to work in a laboratory in Nîmes. On his "good" monthly salary of 1,000 fr. he had to support himself, his wife and two small children. The families of the workers seldom received what was promised them in accordance with the decrees of February 22, 1941 and May 31, 1941, and if they did, they were in danger of being interned for receiving it—indeed, a vicious circle.

According to a report of April 1942, there were 10,000 Jews in forced labor camps, including a few hundred children of 15 years or older.

Mass deportation of Jewish workers from the free zone, including former soldiers, began in August 1942 (2,391 were deported on August 23, 1942, and another group on August 29). Prior to that date, the French authorities began separating Jewish from non-Jewish workers and for this purpose special Jewish GTE units, known as the *Palestinian* groups, were created. On May 7, 1942, there were seven such groups which were subject to much stricter discipline than were the other GTE units. In some Palestinian GTE groups, the Jewish internees had to wear special darkgrey suits with blue-and-white insignias on the left arm. The rabbinate refused to cooperate with official efforts to enlist the rabbis' help in screening lists of alien workers for deportation. In October-December 1942 after the deportation, the number of Jewish workers was estimated at 4,000. The French police were given instructions to intern increasing numbers of Jews in forced labor camps in order to facilitate their deportation. In 1944, Vichy conducted a vigorous campaign against "lazy Jews" because not enough of them had voluntarily joined labor camps.[166]

One historian of the French occupation years titled a chapter in his book, *"La passion des engagés volontaires étrangers."*[167]

According to a decree published in the *Journal Officiel* of January 18, 1940, foreigners enjoying the right of asylum in France were obliged to furnish work for the same period that Frenchmen were obliged to serve in the army. Thus political refugees, mostly Austrian and German Jews, who had not volunteered for the Foreign Legion in North Africa and, for some reason, had not yet been interned, were sent to labor camps. After the armistice they were not liberated.

XVII. In North Africa—"This Hostile Place with a Perfumed Name"

Jewish volunteers, mostly refugees from Germany and Austria, were sent to North Africa—*Ce lieu hostile au nom parfumé* (this hostile place with a perfumed name), to quote one author.[168] According to one source, the Jewish communities of Algeria in April 1940 prepared a Passover for 1,500 Jewish legionnaires.[169]

Many refugees who had been interned in camps of France were sent to North Africa and there were coerced into enlisting as regular members of the Foreign Legion. The sergeants and corporals in North Africa were even worse than those in charge of the legionnaires serving in France for the duration of the war. In North Africa most of them were regular legionnaires of German birth who had enlisted before the war for obvious reasons and they did not hide their pro-Nazi, antisemitic feelings. Many of the legionnaires were German spies, or simply Germans who, after the defeat of France, enthusiastically embraced Nazism. Ted Harris described a camp of the Legion, "Then it was Oran, the camp of the Legion, the German sergeants, the Russian corporals."[170]

In April 1941, a group of American correspondents received permission to visit one of the camps in France. They were told that the camps would eventually be closed. However, what they were not told was that this would be accomplished by sending many internees to North Africa and, after the armistice, by delivering even more volunteers to the German labor and death camps in Eastern Europe. In the camps of Argelès and Port Vendres, disorders occurred and escapes were attempted as internees were being embarked for North Africa. Some of them were actually able to escape. A Jewish member of the International Brigade was first interned at Saint-Cyprien and later at Gurs and Vernet. When he discovered that he was to be shipped to North Africa, his wife and friends were able to help him escape. According to an O.S.S. report of August 26, 1942, there were then 800-1,000 internees at Djelfa. They had all fought in Spain "but are not Spanish," i.e. they had belonged to the International Brigade. The report further stated: "They were interned in France, then transferred to

Algeria. They live in bad conditions as regards hygiene and nutrition. From the rare subsidies they receive, the Commanders of the camp deduct whatever they see fit; they do not earn anything."[171]

According to a HICEM report of August 1941, about one thousand internees at the Algerian camp of Djelfa came from Argelès and Vernet. According to Michel Ansky, there were 2,000 Jewish legionnaires in the camps of North Africa. Actually their number was much larger. According to another report of HICEM for June and July 1941, there were 6,000 Jews in three camps of Algeria: there were 1,000 internees from the Vernet and Argelès camps at Djelfa, and 5,000 at the disciplinary camp of Boghari and the Colomb-Béchar camp for demobilized legionnaires. In Morocco there were then 1,300 internees: 900 refugees at the three camps Kasba Tadla, Oued Zem and Azemmour and at Bou Arfa where 400 demobilized legionnaires were interned.[172]

After the Franco-German armistice, the Vichy government claimed that Germany would not permit legionnaires who had signed up for the duration of the war to emigrate for fear they would continue to fight for the Allies. But the refusal to grant to these men exit visas should not have prevented their demobilization.

At first, certain conditions were laid down for the demobilization of the legionnaires in North Africa. They had to have a French identity card valid at the date of mobilization and a guaranteed means of livelihood for at least one year, that is, a contract for employment or 5,000 francs. Later, the amount was raised to 10,000 francs. An American visa was helpful. "Few of the volunteers could meet these conditions. They had hardly any money. The Jews found it almost impossible to obtain work contracts. The identification papers of many had been burned when the German army approached the recruiting center of the Legion near Lyons. Only a very few foreigners got a legal discharge from the African regiments," wrote Printer.[173] Finally, however, neither money nor a visa could obtain a release. As a result, most of the refugees were forced to remain in the Legion. In order to give the impression they were demobilized, the government interned them in labor camps.

"The armistice permitted him to be demobilized, but not to be liberated," Mrs. Frydman wrote on December 19, 1941, from Prades (Pyrénées Orientales), to a Jewish relief organization. She referred to her brother, Aron Tauber, who was interned at the Berrouaghia Camp in Algeria. When the war broke out, he signed up as a volunteer in the

Legion. After the armistice, he was demobilized and immediately interned in Algeria. His sister, a war widow, would send him packages of food. When she asked for his release and permission for him to settle in Pyrénées Orientales, the regional police prefect replied that there were too many foreigners in the department.[174]

One Jewish legionnaire, Julius Wolf of Vienna, was lucky. Somehow he was able to buy his way out of a camp for a bribe of 10,000 francs and leave for the United States after working on the Trans-Sahara for five weeks at 50 centimes a day.[175]

The legionnaire Charles Ser of the 1st march batallion arrived in Beirut, Lebanon, on April 7, 1940. Later he was transferred to a punitive unit of a Syrian prison where the men were awakened at 2:30 A.M. for a daily forced march of 60 kilometers. After three months he was transferred to a forced labor company. His outfit refused to take up arms against the Allies. On September 6, 1941, he arrived in Marseilles, was interned in various forced labor camps and finally, with the help of a sympathetic officer, was demobilized and liberated.[176]

Anthony Delmayne, an English ex-legionnaire, wrote of the fate of those who volunteered for the duration of the war and who found themselves in North Africa after the Franco-German armistice:

> "Few of us had any wish to fight undernourished natives unable to pay their taxes," he said, "when there were so many Nazis waiting to be killed. Many of us had a considerable stake in the war. There were Jews and other refugees from Germany, Czechs and Poles, Italians and many Spanish Republicans who were naïve enough to think that if fascism was destroyed in Germany, democracy would be restored to their own country too. Rumors that Vichy was going to sell us down the river filled these men with dread, and there were riots, mutinies, fights and suicides in the fort; sometimes there were as many as five or six suicides in a day."

The officers constantly called upon the volunteers to "protect" themselves by signing up for the next five years, thus becoming regulars. Many did sign up; those who did not were sent to forced labor camps south of the desert where France was extending the railway beyond Colomb-Béchar.[177]

Twenty per cent of the Zouave Regiment of the 86th North African Division stationed within a radius of 25 kilometers of Tripoli consisted of Jews. The other eighty per cent were Spaniards and Frenchmen from Algeria. On May 13, 1940, two White Russian officers arrived. They were to have the rank of officer but were to exercise no command. The new arrivals had lived in France for the last twenty years and could speak French. Their original home was Tiflis. The arrival of these Russian officers indicated that France had contemplated the possibility of using the French army of the Orient against the oil fields in Baku.[178]

In addition to volunteers in the Foreign Legion there were in Morocco over 3,500 refugees, including the emigrants to the United States and other countries who were taken off from the boats Alsina, Montviso, Wyoming, and other boats near the Basque shore. Among them were about 1,200 Jewish refugees, mostly Austrian and German Jews who had left Belgium after May 10, 1940. They were coerced to join the Foreign Legion, and many were actually interned as "volunteers" for the labor camps. The military authorities of Tunisia decided to intern all Austrian and German refugees. For this purpose an internment camp was established at Le Kef, nearly one hundred miles southwest of Tunis. On April 24, 1940, the first 28 Austrian refugees left Tunis for the camp.[179]

XVIII. Building the Trans-Saharian Railroad

In the spring of 1941, the Vichy government started laying the rails for a Trans-Saharian railroad between the Algerian and Moroccan ports and the port of Dakar. It seemed that the Vichy government was simply carrying out a project which had been in the planning stage since the middle of the nineteenth century. The plan, which was often much discussed, was laid aside for a while, then taken up again when military expeditions established France's influence and political control over large parts of Africa. Several commissions were sent to investigate possible routes. World War I interrupted their work, but the idea was not given up and the explorations were renewed after the war. For a while the idea of a motor service rather than a railroad was regarded as the best answer to France's needs for transportation over the desert. Indeed, a regular motor service was operating between North Africa and French Equatorial Africa. Still, the idea of a railroad was not completely abandoned. In 1928, the French government formed an official commission to study the project. Six years later the Radical Party discussed the proposed railroad at its congress held at Vichy, where the promoters of a Trans-Saharian railroad encountered opposition from advocates of the motor service. The Radicals suspected a link between the steel trust and the Trans-Saharian plan, which had to be given up. The plan was again revived by the Vichy regime.

At the time of France's defeat in 1940, there were a few local railroad lines running from North African ports to the desert. The longest was a narrow gauge line connecting Oran with Colomb-Béchar. In French West Africa a line ran a few hundred miles from Dakar to Koulikoro in the French Sudan. Between Colomb-Béchar and Koulikoro there remained a gap of over a thousand miles of desert.

In the minds of many Frenchmen, the plan of a Trans-Saharian railroad was linked to ideas of France's colonial prestige and development. With the defeat of France the plan became vitally important to her remaining military power in Africa. In March 1941, the construction of a Mediterranean-Nigerian railway system, known as Trans-Saharian, was authorized by a decree signed by Pétain. It provided for the construction of a railroad beginning at Bou Arfa in Morocco, passing through Colomb-Béchar in Algeria, and from there going on to Kenadsa, where an important coal field was located. From Kenadsa the line was to run through Béni-Abbès, through the desert to Adrar and continue to Tassit in the French Sudan. From there it would divide into two branches, to Niamey in French Niger and Segou in the French Sudan, with a link between Segou and Koulikoro.

Of course, Germany was to a large degree behind the plans of the Vichy government. The Trans-Saharian railroad would have made possible the transporting of Sengalese troops through French controlled territories rather than by hazardous sea routes as well as troops from France sent to defend Dakar from an Allied invasion.

This was a fantastic plan. It had been rejected or postponed many times because of the great difficulties: the problem of recruiting people willing to work in the trying Sahara desert, where the heat mounts to 125° during the day and the nights are bitterly cold; where strong winds are blowing and water is scarce.

The Vichy government found construction gangs in the French Foreign Legion and among the "half-legionnaires," the refugees and other aliens who had enlisted for the duration of the war and were now in forced labor camps.

The tracklaying progressed to Béni-Abbès before the English and American troops won the battle for North Africa. The Americans had become concerned over Dakar whose proximity to Brazil made it a convenient port for launching attacks on the Americas.[180]

In the Summer of 1941, Heinrich Pol wrote in *The Nation* that the Trans-Saharian railroad had been planned for a long time as a link between France's possessions in North Africa and her colonies on the West Coast of Equatorial Africa. However, before the war, France was reluctant to invest capital in this gigantic undertaking and workers willing to work in the forbidding desert climate for low wages were scarce. The Vichy government announced that it was finally about to realize the plan and in fact, work was started, with many German technicians working behind the scene. Labor was no problem. Thousands of former volunteers in the Legion were herded into camps, into crowded barracks and tents, and even assigned to areas with no protection at all from the hot sun and cold nights, and forced to work from ten to twelve hours daily. The New York *Times* queried Vichy in order to ascertain the truth about the charges of slave labor on the Trans-Saharian project made by H. Pol. On July 25, 1941; the *Times* published a reply by the governor general of Algeria who described the charges as "exaggerated and absolutely inexact." He added that the discipline imposed upon the "semi-militarized works" as well as the punishments were less severe than those imposed on the legionnaires in the military units. Pol replied that instead of being demobilized the volunteers for the duration of the war were placed in forced labor camps as "half legionnaires," earning fifty centimes (about 2 American cents) a day. Spanish internees with Mexican visas were refused exit visas. An Austrian refuge wrote to his relatives:

> We are starving and worst of all we are full of lice. This is not in the least surprising, since all we have is one shirt and one pair of pants. I have not seen a piece of soap for over four months. Our sleeping quarters are put up in an abandoned airdrome which does not even protect us from rain. I have no socks to wear.

Corporal punishment, deprivation of drinking water and other forms of punishment were inflicted by Legion regulars who were overseers in the labor camps. Pol called for an investigation.[181]

On June 25, 1942, Robert D. Murphy, the American diplomat, wrote to the State Department:

> I discount reports regarding German influence actively at work in the Trans-saharan project. I do so because I know that there was active German interest in the general proposition of completing the Transsaharan, manifest immediately after the Armistice in June, 1940. Then the Germans thought that the war was practically over and were barging ahead with their economic plans involving the development of the scheme which they term EUR-AFRIKA. Then they wanted work on the Transsaharan rushed visualizing, I believe, and overland route to join up with the railhead at Bamako in the French Sudan, thus tapping the resources of French West and Equatorial Africa independently of water communication. I discussed this subject with General Weygand several times. He and others, except a handful of rabid collaborationists, never believed that a railroad through the Sahara would be practical or within the realm of the possible or desirable. Such a railroad would have to plow through well over a thousand miles of uninhabited desert. A railroad of this importance is only practicable, I am told, if it serves a population, but there is no population to be served in the Sahara. The French know perfectly well that the ocean route supplemented by aviation is the answer.

However, work on the project continued. Murphy repeated General Weygand's explanation for this by citing the desire of the French for an easy access to coal deposits:

> Before the war French North Africa imported over 200,000 tons of coal annually from England. Now, of course, the area is deprived of that supply and is also having great difficulty obtaining coal from the continent of Europe. This is added to the fact that liquid fuels, as you know, are practically non-existent. The combination of lack of solid and liquid fuels disrupts and it may well have a disastrous effect on North African life, depriving the authorities of the means of providing for the population. This added to the shortages of medicaments, food, clothing, etc. generally is also one of the reasons that the French authorities have not been in position to provide properly for the workers on the Transsaharan project.

Murphy was invited to visit a few labor camps where he noticed many ameliorations. He was told about Countess Ladislas de Luart and her "fleet of motor vehicles constituting a mobile hospital . . . a staff of doctors and trained nurses" available to administer to needs of the workers confined in these camps. He was even shown "pictures of the ambulance equipment, which includes a modern operating installation."[182] However, this information was contradicted by all other reports. For example, on October 31, 1941, W. Stafford Reid, American Vice Consul at Casablanca, sent to the State Department the following memorandum prepared for Consul General H. Earle Russel, "Re: Trans-Saharian Railroad or More Collaboration Propaganda?":

> The German pressure on Vichy to hasten operations on this important link between the Mediterranean Sea and the Atlantic Ocean has been very pronounced. They are using ex-members of the French Foreign Legion, former members of the Spanish Republican Army, et cetera, to form work gangs across the great stretches of the Sahara Desert. They receive from 2 to 4 francs a day in payment and sleep in shallow dug holes in the sand to secure protection from excessively cold nights and very hot temperatures in the day time. A full report on this railroad and on the conditions of work connected with it has been made by other officers of the American Consulates in North Africa.
>
> Leading officials at Rabat have divulged the following information: There had undoubtedly been considerable conversations between Vichy officials and German representatives before the law of March 22, 1941 was enacted; and the German Government had pressed for the commencement of the railroad. One of these officials stated that according to conversations with one of the German Armistice Commissioner's in Morocco, the Transaharian had been included

for a long time in the German program of the economic adjustment of the world under German control—to be placed in effect after they won the present war. In this program Africa figured as "Unser Afrika" connected with a German-Controlled Europe, and traversed by Transaharian and Tranafrica railroads.

The same informant admitted that the German Armistice Commissions in North Africa had shown considerable interest in the progress of the railroad until recently when their inquiries had been fewer, possibly, he thought, because the realization of their hopes seemed much less likely.

It is reported from various sources that the German Commissions have been insistent from the beginning on the use of demobilized ex-volunteers (Czechs, Poles, Belgians, British, Spanish Republicans, Middle European refugees etc. . . .) as forced labor on this railroad. These men were interned in concentration camps later converted into work camps under the terms of the Armistice Convention which prevented the exit from French Morocco of male Allied nationals of military age. The same informant reported that the German Commissions frequently had insisted that more of these men be taken from the work-camps or other public works on which they were employed, for work on the Transaharian, for the double purpose, according to them, of accelerating work on the railroad and of killing off enemy prisoners by convict labor in a pitiless climate. Demands of this nature were made again by the Commission in March 1942.

Together with this memorandum the Vice-Consul sent the text of the following wall poster in Casablanca in which Vichy boasted of its accomplishment:

Le *Transsaharian* est le débouché indispensable de l'A.O.F. sur la Méditerranée; pourtant la IIIe République en avait discuté pendant 50 ans sans arriver a prendre une décision.
Un seul conseil de Cabinet du Maréchal Pétain, Chef de l'Etat a suffit pour la mise en oeuvre immédiate des traveaux!
[Signed] Colon (Souviens-toi).

[The *Trans-Saharian railroad* is the indispensable outlet of French Occidental Africa to the Mediterranean; nevertheless, the 3rd Republic debated for 50 years on the subject without arriving at a decision.
A single decision of the Cabinet du Maréchal Pétain, Chief of State, has been sufficient to start immediate operations!
[Signed] Colon (Remember).][183]

On May 15, 1942, H. Earle Russel, American Consul General in Casablanca, reported to the State Department:

At the time of writing the Transaharian has not gone further than a few miles

South of Kenadsa . . . Work is progressing in the direction of Taghit (or Tarhit) on the route to Béni-Abbès. It is estimated by the engineers in charge of the construction work that if the present rate of speed can be kept up and the necessary supplies and equipment provided as required, the railroad may reach the Niger in four years time from now, and Sfaïa—90 kilometers South of Colomb-Béchar—before the end of 1943. This estimate is much contested by Public Works experts. Extensive anthracite coal deposits have been discovered at Sfaïa and this area is expected to be the only "paying" station between Kenadsa and the Niger.

The main points on the line will be Taghit, Igli, Béni-Abbès, Adrar, Reggan, Erg Ergatolis, Im-Tassit. It is not certain what direction the railroad may take after reaching Im-Tassit. It may curve Westward to Tosaye and Bamako or cross the Niger to Mossi, or run South to Gao, then through Niamey to join the Dahomey railroad line which would link it with the Atlantic. From Colomb-Béchar to Im-Tassit, the soil is said to be firm, hard and fairly level. Very little construction work is said to be required, consisting mostly of small bridges over ravines, culverts, and built embankments. The engineers report that they expect to be able to lay a track the minimum curve of which will be 500 meters, and its maximum grade 6 milimeters per meter.

The engineer in charge of the construction work and in fact of all operations concerning the Mediterranean-Niger railroad is Monsieur MAITRE-DEVALLON, who, with his second in command Monsieur CHADENSON was specially appointed by the Vichy government to this post, although there was already a Director of the Railroad in Algiers. The latter's position now appears to have become a sinecure. These chiefs are aided by a large personnel of trained French engineers, whose headquarters are at Colomb-Béchar where so far, most of the repairs to machinery have been made. Other engineers accompany the track squads and repair trucks. The engineers report that the major part of the machinery used is of American manufacture . . . It is reported that repair work is heavy owing to the speed of the work; the extreme heat and the shortage of lubricating oil. Major repairs are executed at Colomb-Béchar.

3 scarificators clear the rock from the track, and are followed by 2 scrapers working together. The maximum rate of progress of these scrapers is 5 kilometers per hour, and each can scrape 50 cubic meters per hour. These scrapers are followed by a squad of 150 men who level the track. Embankments are thrown up by the elevating grader at the rate of 10 kilometers per month, and the work of finishing then done by manual labor. Where no ballast is required, the laying of the track follows immediately, and rails are placed and bolted on the sleepers by trained native squads at the rate of 1 kilometer per diem. A large portion of the track has been laid in this manner (it is said, unsatisfactorily). Ballast, where required, has been obtained by blasting rock hills and having the stone brokers by hand—labor which has cost the lives of many of the European demobilized volunteers forced to perform it. Certain stretches of the soil are rocky, requiring pneumatic drilling, and in other areas chalky strata have been encountered which resisted the scrapers and in which trenches had to be dug by

laborers with picks and shovels. As regards structural work, the engineers estimate that over the stretch of 130 kilometers that lie between Kenadza and Béni-Abbès about 320 minor structures, consisting mostly of culverts, small bridges, etc. will be necessary. In the region of Erg Ergatolis, a fair amount of blasting may be necessary.

The report added that the track was laid on badly prepared soil. Visiting engineers considered that track so laid could not support traffic.

The report further included the following information about the men working on the line:

About 6,000 men in all are employed on the Mediterranean-Niger, between 3,000 and 4,000 of which actually are engaged on the work of laying the track and the remainder on works at Colomb-Béchar and Kenadsa. Of the men working on the line, over 1,500 are European volunteers demobilized from the French Army after June 1940. Following the Armistice Convention, the French Authorities in North Africa did not permit the exit of male belligerents of military age. These men were first interned in concentration camps called "lodging camps." Later they were forced to work on the Mediterranean-Niger. The German Armistice Commissions in North Africa have been insistent that as many of these men, particularly those of Polish origin, be used on this work. The majority of these men are Spanish Republicans, the rest Poles, Czechs, Russians, and Central-European nationals who were living as refugees in France in 1939. There are also a small number of Belgians and some British. These men have been drawn from all classes of their respective nations. Some of them were officers of high rank in their own country, many of them are professional men, physicians, college professors, writers and scientists who had responded to France's call for aid in 1939. Regardless of their age or condition these men have been forced to perform penitentiary labor in a climate where the heat in summer runs over 50° Cent. in the shade and the winter temperature drops below zero Cent., particularly at night. The remaining 2,000-odd men are natives, about 600 of which are hired laborers and about 1,200 are demobilized volunteers which the Algerian Government has sent to work on the railroad. All that need be said regarding these natives is that the French Government's present treatment of them is in striking contrast to the offers and promises made to them during the 1939 recruiting campaign when France was strenuously endeavoring to increase her man-power by North African volunteers.

A good deal of just indignation has been expressed in North Africa over France's treatment of these men. Many French military officers of superior rank have expressed their disgust, saying frankly that the maltreatment of these volunteers had been acquiesced in out of sheer servility to the Germans, that by doing so France had stained her honor and built up hatred and vindictiveness against herself in those men's countries, and above all, would hardly be able to obtain either foreign or North African volunteers in any future emergency. They also admit that there will be a heavy reckoning with the North African Natives afterwards.

To counteract these sentiments the railroad organization has published a number of articles, particularly in papers in France which stress the Company's excellent treatment of those men who are described as enthusiastic *volunteer* workers, who are well housed, well fed, well cared for, and whose morale is such that they actually insist on doing overtime! Liberal menus are described, with a daily allowance of 35 liters of water per man, while the attitude of the officers and petty officers in charge of the camp and work squads is described as one of paternal solicitude.

It is regretted that the accounts of eye-witnesses and the interviews which the writer has had with some scores of these men from the Bou Arfa and Colomb-Béchar camps do not bear out these roseate descriptions. The men actually interviewed were ragged, haggard, worn and lean, some of them appeared to have been half-starved and exhausted by hard labor. Most of them were shoeless and wore sandals and hats manufactured by themselves of palm rope. Many of them showed sores from heat blisters and injuries from rocks. They explained that so long as a man was able to stand on his feet he was forced to work, and that the doctors at the camps passed as fit for labor men who were suffering from severe malaria or even broken ribs. They related—and this was confirmed by French officers who had visited Bou-Arfa and Colomb Béchar—that these camps were guarded by native soldiery, Algerians and Senegalese under the orders of petty officers of the Foreign Legion (most of whom were ex-Germans) and that some of these men took a fiendish pleasure in ill-treating their charges. Stories were told of men who had refused to work being locked up for 48 hours without water while others were stripped naked, bound and placed in pits covered only by a tent-sheet until they submitted. While the heat in these pits (in which they could not lie down) was intense during the day the cold at night was so extreme that one man (said to have been formerly a Vice-Admiral in the Spanish Republican Navy) became crippled with arthritis. All these men admitted that their guards frequently beat them. The Poles and Spaniards suffered most. On the stretch between Bou-Arfa and Kenadsa a good deal of ballast had to be provided, and each man working on that line was forced to break 0 cubic meter 60 [?] of stone per day in the summer heat, and without sun helmets or glasses. Food, they said, was poor and insufficient, sometimes four men would be given a loaf of bread and a box of sardines to share amongst them. Shelters are reported to consist of small army tents which provided insufficient protection against either heat or cold. Clothing served out consists of one shirt, one pair of trousers and one blanket (when available) per man. Defaulters have their blankets taken from them, and are placed in barbed wire enclosures within which they have to lie on the ground, without covering (See photograph. This photograph was taken at Bou-Arfa, in January 1942, when the temperature was 5° below zero (Cent.). Note the Pole in the foreground chafing his hands and the Arab huddled in his garments at the right). Attention also is invited to photograph showing a series of dugouts inside another barbed wire enclosure. These dugouts are low covered trenches very much resembling bakers' ovens, which are used as punishment cells for men who refuse to work. The condemned men are forced to lie flat in them until they submit. If they hold out too long, they may be deprived of their water ration.

In this respect it is interesting to note in an article written by one of the Company's engineers that he and other French civilian engineers working on the line were housed in insulated trailers equipped with refrigerators "as otherwise life would be impossible for us."

Russel further reported on the projected train services, water problem, supplies, and other obstacles:

> Upon the completion of the line to the Niger (which, according to their project, is expected to be accomplished by 1947) the Company expect to place on the rails powerful Diesel stream lined locomotives with a speed of 100 kilometers per hour capable of hauling 3,000 tons, passenger coaches and freight cars (all covered) to be insulated against the extreme temperatures. Each train (at present two per week in each direction is considered sufficient as a maximum) will be self-contained and will be equipped like an ocean-going vessel for a cruising radius of several thousand kilometers, to take care of possible break-downs in the desert. These trains, as projected at present, should cover the distance from Colomb-Béchar to Gao in 24 hours.
>
> The project, it will be noted, calls for the use of only Diesel locomotives. It has been expressly laid down by the experts that no steam equipment may be used in the Sahara, for the obvious reasons that the water problem is most acute in these regions. In fact, concurrently with the railroad, it will be necessary to build a line of wells, tanks, irrigation channels, etc., to provide for the needs of the trains, passengers and personnel. The main water-points on the line will be at Colomb-Béchar, Kenadsa (which is supplied with 500 cubic meters of water per diem from a conduit connecting it with the Béchar River at Colomb-Béchar) and Sfaïa. The water available at the points between Kenadsa and the Niger district is scanty, heavily mineralised with a strong magnesium content which makes it unfit for use in machinery, and almost unfit for human consumption.
>
> Actually a project is under consideration for the extension and improvement of Colomb-Béchar which is expected to acquire a new importance as the chief terminus of the line. Designs submitted by the leading architects of North Africa call for the construction of an imposing station, a palace-hotel built in Neo Saharian style, public parks and gardens, municipal electric plant (there is none in the city at present), market gardens for the supply of vegetables and fruit, and the general conversion of the township into a tourist center. Very little importance will be given to the other stations in the Sahara, which will be merely freight loading points.

The directors frankly admit that there is no prospect of the Mediterranean-Niger becoming a paying prospect for many years. Its ultimate remunerativeness will depend on the intensive exploitation of the Niger basin, of the Kenadsa coalfields, and of the coal deposits believed to lie around Sfaïa and Reggan. In the meantime, the directors stress the value of the civilizing influence that France will bring to the 6 or 8 million inhabitants of the Sahara through the creation of the Mediterranean-Niger railroad, by connecting them with the outside world and bringing them an increase in their hydraulic resources. Military experts have stated that the strategic importance of the railroad is sufficient to justify its cost but admit that its usefulness in a future World War could be cancelled by an extension in the cruising radius of bombing planes.

Certain parties in North Africa consider that the Mediterranean-Niger may never be completed, or at any rate, cannot be completed as projected. Their arguments may briefly be summarized as follows:

Reference is made to the statement of the Company's engineers to the effect that the railroad might be completed in four years' time, provided the present rate of speed could be maintained and the necessary supplies and equipment furnished as required. In this connection it may be stated that officials of the French Moroccan Transportation Office have reported the Transaharian engineers barely have enough lubricating oil to last them three months and that what they have is of poor quality; and have not enough rails, sleepers or other material to lay 100 kilometers of track; also, that most of the rails now being used are old rails from condemned tracks in France and Algeria and shortly may require replacement. Experts who recently visited the railroad have stated that in their opinion efficiency and security were being sacrificed to speed, in a desire to advertise the rapidity of the construction work, and that a good part of the track now being laid would have to be laid again. In fact, one described the manner of the construction as "sheer bluff." Another major obstacle, which cannot be denied by the Company, is the paucity of water supplies. Up to the present, only a few of the projected well-borings have been made in this direction.

As already indicated, most of the construction work is now being done by prisoners of war. Obviously this source of labor supply can only be a temporary one, and must cease with the war, or whenever a major political change should take place in North Africa that would permit the liberation of the prisoners. Then the hiring of labor to replace these men would become an almost insoluble problem and wages would be a burdensome charge on the Company's budget.

In its law of March 22, 1941, the French Government estimated that the total cost of the Mediterranean-Niger would be 5,000,000,000 francs—indicating, at the same time, that this estimate was based on costs current in April *1940*. Experts consider that the completion of the railroad would require a far larger sum, for the following reasons: (1) they consider the basis of this estimate (i.e., 1940 prices) as unsound, and that all machinery and material required after 1942 will have to be purchased at prices far above costs in 1940. These purchases would have to be fairly extensive since the material and equipment now available are insufficient to provide for the construction of more than a fraction of the track. (2) The present labor supply must shortly be replaced by a costly hired force. (3) Negotiations with foreign governments, French colonies and protectorates and other railroad companies (particularly in the Niger basin) may call for considerable future expenditures, which have not been provided for. These parties further state that the present Vichy Government is unable to reserve the 5,000,000,000 francs estimated by it as necessary for this work, and that the first consideration of whatever French Government succeeds it will, or should be, the restoration of a ruined France, rather than indulgence in costly and unremunerative colonial projects.

For these reasons, these parties consider not only that the Mediterranean-Niger will not be built in ten years' time, but that the chances of its ever being completed are doubtful.[184]

On September 18, 1942, Felix Cole, American Consul General in Algiers, reported to the State Department that according to reliable sources

It appears from this that there are about 14,000 workmen employed on the actual building of the railroad, of whom 8,000 are Moroccan and Kabylian natives, the rest Europeans. The Europeans are all aliens who are existing under what amounts to peonage or chain gang conditions, most of them being either Spanish civilian refugees or refugees from Germany who volunteered for the French army and were discharged at the Armistice, or former soldiers of the French Foreign Legion whose contracts have expired.

The Trans-Saharian Railway Company and the coal mines at Kenadsa which belonged to it, both Government owned, had four main centers: (1) *Colomb-Béchar* (450 miles from Oran, the proposed terminus of the Trans-Saharian); (2) *Kenadsa* (16 miles from Colomb-Béchar); (3) *Bidon II* (4½ miles from Colomb-Béchar) and (4) *Gao* (in French Sudan, the opposite proposed terminus of the Trans-Saharian).

(1) At *Colomb-Béchar,* which was the general depot for the railway constructions, there were 4,500 workmen: 3,000 were Moroccan laborers and 1,500 European aliens. The former, who were civilians, were paid at the rate of Frs. 30 per day. The latter were Spaniards, Poles, Czech, Russians, etc. who had served their period in the Foreign Legion; they were still under military control and received Frs. 10 per day with board and lodging. About 100 were specialists and received Frs. 60 to 100 per day without board and lodging.

(2) *Kenadsa* was the center of the coal mines. There were about 6,000

workmen: 5,000 Kabyle natives and 1,000 Europeans belonging to the Cie. des Militaires Travailleurs, i.e., aliens, almost all Jews, demobilized from the French army which they joined voluntarily for the duration of the war. They were still under military control and discipline. The Kabyles worked in the mines and the Europeans were the architects, engineers, designers, doctors, overseers, accountants, etc. The Kabyles received Frs. 25-30 per day and the Europeans Frs. 10 per day with board and lodging. There were wells from which water was allowed to be drawn only 2 hours daily. About 350 tons of coal were extracted daily. The coal was used for the Algerian railways. The Kabyles, who are white skinned, North Algerian mountaineers, worked badly; they were badly fed and lodged. They were bitter at the false promises made to them. Many tried to desert but were soon caught. About 10-20 died daily.

(3) At *Bidon II,* 4½ miles from Colomb-Béchar, there were also coal mines. Three thousand Spanish civilian refugees from the Spanish civil war worked there in the mines. They were not under military control and received Frs. 100 a day, because they were civilians and not ex-soldiers. After paying for their board they were little if any better off than the other aliens at Colomb-Béchar and Kenadsa. Moreover, although not under military control they were not free to leave the region of the mine which was, in effect, a concentration camp.

(4) The center at *Gao* was about two years old. About six months earlier there were 700 workmen under military control, mostly soldiers from the Foreign Legion who had served their period. Foreigners were not allowed at Gao.

At *Bidon V* in the center of the Sahara there was a store of 15,000 liters of water. There were only about three dozen French people working on the mines and the railway men, managers and directors. There was much waste, theft and graft. For instance, officials built private villas with the railway's cement.[184a]

Who was responsible for all this? The Germans? Murphy wrote in his above-mentioned report of June 25, 1942:

> During my recent trip to Rabat I made inquiry in this connection of some of the competent officials. I was told in *strictest confidence* by the Director of Public Security that conditions in these camps are far from satisfactory. He said that part of this is due to lack of means at the disposal of the authorities but that most of it is attributable to lack of organization, negligence and indifference of the French authorities. He pooh-poohed German influence saying that was nothing

but an alibi and that the responsibility for lack of sanitation, atrociously bad living conditions, bad food, etc. lies directly with the French. From what I also learn from other sources in Morocco I believe that his statement is accurate.

This official told me, for example, that the French Moroccan police authorities had just arrested fifty-two men in the Bou Arfa camps who were given solitary confinement under charges of having formed "communist cells" in the Bou Arfa work camps. I told the official that I was not certain what was meant by "communist cells" but that it is surprising the men, confined to the camps and obliged to work under the deplorable conditions which I am told have prevailed, would not as a minimum form "anarchist cells." He agreed that it was only normal that any man would be justified in violent reaction against such treatment. This official had admitted that many of the men were intellectuals, office workers, former Government employees of different nationalities, particularly Spanish, and that a considerable percentage were not physically trained or fitted for hard manual labor under adverse conditions. Hundreds of them had been living in North African towns where they had sought refuge principally for political reasons, and most of them had no visible means of support. The French authorities feared that if allowed their liberty the refugees would be forced by economic reason if no other into all sorts of activity, political and otherwise, which would make them a menace to the public security. Therefore, they were rounded up and placed in these work camps where they could not create trouble and disorder, but where they could accomplish something useful. The official said that that was the basic theory back of the French action.[185]

However, most internees in the forced labor camps did not have to be "rounded up and placed in these work camps for the simple reason that they were not free. These were half-legionnaires, already interned in the camps."

The World Jewish Congress in New York received the following report about the Moroccan camps:

The sinister account of these Moroccan camps is well known in America. Although situated in a healthy region, the camps were denuded of all comfort—beds were mats of earth, this in a region where there are enormous differences in temperature between day and night; the food was insufficient; and the discipline more severe than in the camps of the Foreign Legion, which is no small item. The camps were headed by officers who had become savage after many years of living in the Moroccan Bled. Punishments were frequent and left nothing to be desired if compared with those given in German camps. The following information comes from "specialists" in concentration camps (there are many, alas) who were initiated in Dachau, escaped to France, joined up with the Foreign Legion for the duration of the war, were demobilized in

Morocco and were finally sent to the labor camps.

A model punishment was the "tomb," which consisted in placing the victim in a kind of tomb dug by himself. He had to stay there several days, eating there and satisfying his natural needs. He was forced to stay in a horizontal position, and this was enforced by stationing an armed Moroccan or Senegalese sentry on the rim of the "tomb." The punished remained thus for several days, under the brilliant daytime sun and the freezing nights. Naturally some died, although the figures quoted by "La Voix d'Amérique" from an article in "Life" (a few thousand dead) are exaggerated. Another punishment very much in favor was "the lion's cage," which consisted in putting the delinquent in a ditch where he had to remain for several days. It was so barbarous and incredible, that, when the foregoing was told to American officers in November 1942, they didn't want to believe it and spoke of "atrocity propaganda." The French officers in charge of these camps were the refuse of the Army and among them, Maj. Janssens became notorious.[185a]

XIX. "A Most Atrocious Camp"

The fate of the Spaniards from the concentration camps who volunteered for the French Foreign Legion was as miserable as that of the Jewish volunteers. On November 24, 1942, Leslie O. Heath, Delegate of the American Friends Service Committee wrote in a report from Casablanca:

> The Spanish are nearly all refugees from Republican Spain, and were rounded up into these camps by the French. The others are political refugees from the Axis powers, or were interned by the French as a result of military operations. Many of the men were in France at the outbreak of the war in 1939 and volunteered with the French armies. With the fall of France they were sent to North Africa and as a reward for their voluntary service in the defense of France they have been interned in these camps, many at forced labor under rather atrocious conditions, which still unfortunately persist in some cases.[186]

A report sent from Algeria to the World Jewish Congress also noted that the fate of the Spanish Republicans in the camps "was worse than that of the interned Jews. As Marxists they were treated with the utmost severity and there were many revolts in the camps."

In April 1943, A. D. Printer, a former legionnaire for the "duration" who emigrated to the United States recalled:

> The Legion was not an easy place to serve in. The old legionnaires, who fought only for the pay, resented the newcomers, who fought for an ideal. Often they bullied them but never when their intended victims were Spanish soldiers who had seen as much action as they and who knew how to hit back. Even from their fellow volunteers the Spaniards met suspicion. Most of the others, having been residents or refugees in France, spoke the language and understood the people. The only French contacts the Spaniards had had before they came to the Legion were with the Gardes Mobiles or the Senegalese in the concentration camps at Gurs and Le Vernet. In order not to be lonely, they formed "cells," which were against the spirit of the Legion and which isolated them still more. For the officers and for the non-coms, the Spanish legionnaires were a nuisance. They did not fit in. They had been members of a popular army; now they were subjected to the ironclad discipline of a mercenary unit. They brought with them their typical Spanish individualism. They brought, too, their great sense of personal dignity, which was constantly trampled upon in the units where

German sergeants and veteran French colonials had formed the outlaws of Europe into soldiers. Most of the left-wing extremists had preferred to remain in the concentration camps. Those who joined the Legion were loyal young soldiers of the Republic, professionals of the Spanish army, a few intellectuals and tradesmen. But to the officers of the Legion, brilliant young reactionaries from Saint Cyr and Saumur or old troopers without any political convictions at all, every Spaniard was either a Communist or an anarchist, to be handled with the same affection as a box of dynamite. This attitude changed when the officers began to appreciate the soldierly qualities of the men, and later the Spaniards were chosen for the hardest tasks. These young Spanish volunteers were famous for their skill as machine-gunners and for their marching ability. They were not, as a rule, good shots with light arms, lacking the phlegm that is essential. They loved the feel of steel in their hands—their great pocket knives and the four-edged bayonets of the French army.

In the spring of 1941 the Vichy government sent thirty new men to the camps of Colomb-Béchar and Kenadsa. They pretended to be deserters from the German army and navy in France. These men were met from the very beginning with distrust and were later found to be a fifth column planted in the camps by order of the Armistice Commission. The affair caused a great uproar. For the first time the *travailleurs,* mostly Jews and Spanish loyalists, dared to act. As a result the "deserters" were combed out and transported to an oasis farther south. There they later started a little revolt of their own and finally asked to be brought before the Armistice Commission—very peculiar behavior for soldiers who were supposed to have committed the greatest military crime.

In the general breakdown of morale the Spaniards were in by far the worst situation. They had no families, they received no letters, no outside organization took care of them, and many of them were in constant danger of being put in the *compagnie de discipline des travailleurs,* a parallel institution to the famous *discipline* of Colomb-Béchar. Into the *discipline des travailleurs* came not only the men who broke the rules or worked too slowly but also those who were simply suspected of being opposed to the spirit of Vichy. Into the discipline came also the men who had been guilty of serving in the International Brigades of Spain. That they had later volunteered and fought for France had not washed them clean. After this *compagnie de discipline* was formed, it was sent to Khersas, a lost oasis deep in the south which soon became a Devil's Island of the Sahara, viciously ruled by Corsican and German sergeants. Here the men did not even have tents. They had to scrape holes in the sand to sleep in, the famous *tombeaux* of the Legion, just long enough for a man to stretch out in. They had no shelter from the pitiless sun during the siesta hours of the day and no protection from the bitter cold of the desert nights. In the evening after work was finished they were not allowed to talk together or to play cards. They had to hand over their sandals to the *Goums* before nightfall lest somebody be crazy enough to run out into the desert.

Anyone who passed through this company came out a broken man. Even in the regular working companies nearly everybody became affected after a time

—nearly everybody except the Spaniards. They built up a very intelligent collective self-defense. Like everybody else, they grabbed and stole whatever they could get outside the camps, but they shared their booty with all. They fought anybody who attacked their rights, superiors or fellow soldiers, but they never quarreled among themselves. They were the only ones in the camps who found the strength to sing and to joke, and if once in a while they found enough wine, they showed the rest of the men the noble art of getting drunk in a decent and quiet way.

When the German Armistice Commission came to North Africa, the French were forced to reduce the effectives of their garrisons. Thousands of legionnaires were ostensibly discharged but were in reality formed into new military units and sent to the southern part of Algeria and Morocco to work on roads and on the trans-Saharian railway. The men had all the disadvantages of being soldiers and none of the advantages. They wore soldiers' uniforms, but they were treated as if they were men condemned to hard labor. They worked from eight to ten hours a day in heat that at noon would rise to 140°. Until the spring of 1941 their pay was only half a franc a day, half a cent as the franc was then valued against the dollar—about a fifth of what they had to pay for a package of cigarettes. They slept in tattered tents that offered little protection against sand storms or rain. Seventeen men shared a tent built for ten. Their clothes swarmed with lice, and boils spread from one to another as they lay crowded together on their rags. In most of the camps water was scarce—hardly enough for drinking and cooking. The men didn't wash for weeks. There was not enough food. The men killed and ate everything alive around them, from dogs to lizards, from stray donkeys to the rare gazelles they could catch. They dug holes in the roads so that camels coming from the South with the date caravans would break their legs in the traps and the beasts could then be bought from the Arabs for their almost worthless meat.

There were revolts. Everybody, overseers and men, became desperate and slightly crazy after a while. The famous *cafard* rode the camps. In some units the officers were so terrified that they asked for *Goums*, Arab guards, to watch their tents at night, and hardly dared move among the men without arms. The ironical part was that the men were not prisoners but apparently just soldiers. There was no barbed wire around the camps. But there were hundreds and hundreds of miles of sand, of hot, burning death, around them to prevent escape.

When I left Africa in December, 1941, four companies were at work around Colomb-Béchar, each containing from 200 to 300 men. About a third of these men were Spaniards. The four companies all belonged to the 1st Regiment of the Foreign Legion in Algeria. Two more companies of the same regiment were farther north in Ain Sefra and Saida. Across the Moroccan border the labor units of the three Moroccan regiments worked under similar conditions. Besides these men in uniform, thousands of Spanish civilians worked on the trans-Saharian railway and in the coal mines of Kenadsa. They were paid, but their pay was outrageously small.

Today the foreign volunteers are in a paradoxical situation. They were formally discharged in October 1940. But at the beginning of the war they had signed a contract for the duration. Now the war has started anew in Africa, and according to the regulations of the French army they are *rémobilisables*—subject to be called from the reserves for new service. It is doubtful, however, whether they will be allowed to leave the camps of the south. A general has the right to decide how he will use a soldier, whether as a fighter or a worker on a military project.

These men are good soldiers by any standard; they are especially well trained for African warfare, they are, besides, soldiers who fought and are still fighting for an idea. And with Spanish stubbornness they will stick to their convictions. It is to be hoped that impending changes in Africa will allow these veterans of the war for democracy to take their place again in the ranks of the Allies and to exchange the pickax, which was forced into their hands, for the gun which they once chose.[187]

On November 7, 1942, the eve of the Allied landing in North Africa, Leslie O. Heath, delegate of the American Friends Service Committee (AFSC) to North Africa, submitted a report on the camps to his organization. It was based mostly on separate reports on each camp visited during the preceding summer by Dr. Edouard Wyss-Dunant, delegate for North Africa from the International Red Cross at Geneva. These reports covered nearly all camps where there were foreign internees, although there was one camp, Missour, in Morocco, not visited because of its inaccessibility ("lack of transportation"). There were a number of other internment camps in North Africa exclusively for French prisoners, many of whom were believed to be there for political reasons. At that time very little was known about these camps.

In Morocco alone there were fourteen camps and at least five more in Algeria. In Morocco, these camps were, in some cases, several hundred miles apart. There were apparently about four thousand people interned in Morocco and at least two thousand five hundred more in Algeria. To this figure has been added the known increase as a result of the arrival of English internees. The largest percentage of internees were Spanish with at least 3,000 in Morocco and Algeria alone. Exit visas from Morocco and Algeria were refused so that there was no opportunity for any appreciable number of these people to improve their condition by leaving for the New World.

As far as was known then, there were only a few women and children in the camps in Morocco, and they were all in one camp, Sidi-el-Ayachi, about fifty miles down the coast from Casablanca. Not counting the British arrivals, there were about fifty children under sixteen years of age, most of them Spanish and approximately 75 women. The British were under the auspices of the United States Consulate.

After making allowances (the war, the blockade, the lack of foodstuffs, etc.) Dr. Wyss-Dunant's conclusion was that the conditions in certain camps were "simply atrocious and should be tolerated nowhere." As a result of his efforts, one camp was abolished and the North Europeans interned in a camp that was particularly hot were transferred to another where the climatic conditions were more like those to which they were accustomed. Dr. Wyss-Dunant also requested the abolition of "a most atrocious camp," Berguent, whose population was exclusively Jewish. His recommendations were not only disregarded, but there were reports that plans were underway for moving this camp to an even more intolerable location. Dr. Wyss-Dunant was to make further representations in Rabat in an effort to have this camp abolished before winter.

The International Red Cross representative had visited the camp of Berguent on July 29, 1942. The camp, under the supervision of the Department of Industrial Production, was organized as Groupent de Travailleurs Etrangers No. 4. He reported:

> There is not enough water since it must be brought twice a day on camel back from Berguent, a distance of five kilometers. The men can bathe once a week in the pool at Berguent. Six internees sent to the disciplinary section of Bou Arfa. As morale is bad, voluntary discipline disintegrates and penalties rain down without producing any real effect. Other men have been sent to Berguent prison. The Camp Commandant is a former legionnaire with an inflexible disposition. The internees prefer sleeping in the open to sleeping in the shelters. They always lack water. They complain that the ill are tended only when their temperature goes above 38 c. They are badly shod. A certain number of internees declared unfit by the reform (revision) commission were nevertheless kept in camp. Work on the roadbed is not suitable for them since they consist for the most part of tradesmen, intellectuals, accountants or artisans.
> Conclusion—We have petitioned government headquarters for the discontinuance of this camp.

Missour, the camp which was not visited was, according to the information reaching the AFSC representative, populated principally by Spaniards and was "bad—perhaps as bad as Berguent."

Of all the nationalities interned, the Spanish were, according to Heath, perhaps the worst off, as there was no government to look out for them and no committee supplied with adequate funds to give aid even to the most needy.

In general, Heath wrote, conditions in these camps have deteriorated since Dr. Wyss-Dunant's visit in the summer. This was very definitely the case at Sidi-el-Ayachi, where the food was certainly poorer. Acetylene formerly used there for lighting no longer existed; the supply of calcium carbide for producing acetylene was depleted.

With the sudden arrival at Sidi-el-Ayachi of the British who were destitute, blankets were taken from some of the long-term residents of the camp, and "very properly" given to the British; however, they were not replaced. The local Jewish Committee succeeded in purchasing a few native blankets at a very high price to help relieve the situation.

The internees were frequently not given proper attention and consideration until they were very ill, when it was perhaps too late. "I am continually amazed to find not that there are many cases of illness, but that the camps are not entirely decimated by outbreaks of malaria, dysentery and other epidemic diseases," wrote Heath. In many camps there were practically no medical supplies. The lack of sulpha drugs was also most serious. Madame du Luart, Heath reported, has indeed endeavored to supply hospital service to some of the camps, but because of the lack of gasoline and medical supplies, he did not know "how effective it can be."

The AFSC representative further reported:

Anti-Jewish sentiment in North Africa is regrettably on the increase, and of course is also evident in the camps. Berguent is an example where approximately 90% of the men are ex-volunteers from the French Army. They are ill clad and subjected to the most severe rigors of heat and cold with wholly inadequate shelter and are without comforts of any kind. Recently when one of them was offered a job as a baker at Rabat the authorities refused to let him take it as he was a Jew. A very influential and well-known Frenchman intervened on behalf of this man on the basis that this man had volunteered and fought for France; but the plea was refused and the boy had to return to the camp.

Up until recently Sidi-el-Ayachi had been apparently free from any anti-Jewish bias; but a short time ago when the local Jewish Committee entered a mild protest with the camp management against the lower quality of the food, they were threatened with the statement that all the Jews would be sent to Berguent unless protests ceased. The English upon their arrival were told to keep away from the rest of the residents, who were described as "Jews and Bolsheviks." A separate school for the English children is planned as well as a separate cantine.[188]

At the camp of Djelfa in Algeria, called a Center of Supervised Residence under the Supervision of Public Security, an internee who lighted a fire in order to cook some food or was "warming up at night" was punished by fifteen days in a cell. The internees, to avoid starvation, had to look for supplementary food, they captured and ate wild dogs and rats. Caboche, the commandant, punished a well-known Jewish physician with 17 days' imprisonment at the Caffarelli fortress for having written in a letter to his family that "Europe was starving under German domination." By the end of 1941, the administration of the Djelfa camp (described by the representative of the International Red Cross as "a remarkable camp") decided to organize a special group of "Jews and suspected." Jews were punished for being Jewish and anti-Nazi. About one hundred internees, among them thirty Jews, were sent to the disciplinary camp at Hadjerat M'Guil.[189]

In 1942, Rudolf Selke described the following punishment administered at Ain el Ourak, a disciplinary camp of the Trans-Saharan inferno, located 15 kilometers from Arfa:

> There are not sepulchers of saints, nor remains of pre-historic civilization. Ain-el-Ourak is the disciplinary camp of the Trans-Saharan, and these graves are the ditches where the culprits are placed. The graves are the length of a man and only some 15 inches deep. The culprit must lie down in a grave, and the ditch is covered. A goumier (Moroccan soldier in the French service) is posted beside him, with a high pile of heavy stones in front of him. As soon as the victim raises his head from the grave, the goumier throws a stone at him. He lies there, thus covered, not one day, nor two days, but as long as two weeks, tortured by heat and cold, by insects and by the sand, which permeates everywhere. During the rainy season he is permitted to sit up when the water covers his face. Few avoid being stoned to death. "Camp sickness" at Ain el Ourak means a fractured skull.

Selke wrote that the men of Vichy intoxicated themselves with the words, "greatness of the Empire." The symbol of this greatness was the Trans-Saharan railroad which was to join the Mediterranean to the Niger across the African desert. He, too, wrote that it was an old project but, somehow, the Third Republic never liked it. The problem of labor made the project impossible but for Vichy France labor was no problem. Foreign legionnaires who volunteered to fight for France were at the disposal of the Office of Industrial Production at Rabat which was in charge of the project. Col. Hoffenheimer and Capt. Kiesele, two Frenchmen, were in charge of the office, but the German Control Commission was the real power behind the operation. The legionnaires were forced to work ten hours a day, breaking hard stones made of quartz. Their pay was 1.25 francs per cubic meter. Ten hours a day was the minimum required, the alternative to which was punishment. At Berguent the men pushed heavy carts loaded with stones to distant points; the minimum requirement was to push twenty-five carts. Long time legionnaires, mostly Germans, were the overseers. Bou Arfa was then a village containing a few miserable huts. The workers did not live there. They were divided into small groups and stationed along the road. During the day the heat was unbearable; at night they suffered from the cold. They were devoured by vermin and mosquitoes. The April sandstorms and terrible downpours carried away the tents which consisted of no more than rags. Many internees contracted fever, suffered from dysentery, diarrhea and plaudism. They were without treatment.[190]

According to an O.S.S. report of August 26, 1943, the fourth company of foreign workers in the coal mines of Kenadsa "was in way of being transformed in December 1941 and was to become 'a company of Jews and suspects.'" According to the same report the sixth company of foreign alien workers at Hadjerat M'Guil was a "compagnie de discipline et d'isolement." One hundred to one hundred and fifty men lived there "under inhuman conditions." They were kept under guard and had to work hard for 50 centimes (or half a franc) a day.[190a]

In August 1942, the following report about the conditions at the camp Ain el Ourak in Morocco reached the Office of Strategic Services (O.S.S.) in Washington:

> The camp at Ain-el-Ourak is located approximately 80 kilometers from Bou-Arfa and is part of the "Groupement des Travailleurs Etrangers." It is under the direction of the Commander of the "Groupements de Bou-Arfa" and of the "Direction des Communications de la Production Industrielle et du Travail" at Rabat. The majority of the persons interned are Spanish workmen and former soldiers of the Foreign Legion (enlisted for a period of five years), and, finally, approximately twelve former volunteers taken on for the duration of the war. In summary, this concerns 100 men sent 6-14 months ago, to Ain-el-Ourak by order of their group chiefs (French officers). Having come from various work camps in Morocco, they were transported to Bou-Arfa, from there to this disciplinary camp; non-important acts of incorrectitude were the reasons of such punishment.
>
> The camp at Ain-el-Ourak is under the command of six former under officers of the Foreign Legion (having had more than 16 years of active service and being of German origin). It is guarded and supervised by a detachment of "goumiers" (troup of native Arabs from the southern territories), numbering

about 60. These "goumiers" stop the entrance of strangers in the camp and attempts of escape of the men being "disciplined." They guard the camp with a bayonnet on their rifles, their guns loaded, and are instructed to make use of their guns should an attempt to escape be made.

The inmates of the camp live in small brick houses, rectangular, and constructed in a row and mounted with cupolas; they have an aspect of Arabian tombs; they hold 10 to 12 persons, i.e. the inmates find place only if they gather up their legs and place themselves in double row. Their beds consist of braided rafis which they must make themselves as well as the bricks necessary for the construction of their houses which they themselves must build. Work is obligatory and only those who have over 39 degrees temperature are exempted. The new inmates arriving for disciplinary purposes are, at their arrival spoken to by the captain of the camp whom one must call "Mon Adjudant" and who informs them briefly that they are there for "disciplinary" purposes and that here they no longer have any rights.

Nourishment is insufficient, breakfast is composed of a sort of soup equal to warm water colored by red pepper having a taste of onions. At 9 o'clock there is a rest period of 10 minutes and some figs of the worst quality are eaten. Lunch is composed again of soup and some sort of vegetables with a great deal of water and one or two tiny pieces of meat. Two hundred grams of bread per day is allotted. Towards 6 o'clock there is again soup and vegetables as at lunch. The bad quality and insufficient quantity of the food cause serious illnesses. There is a male nurse in the camp who is also an inmate of the camp but he has neither the right nor the possibility of helping the sick; the doctor at Bou-Arfa passes one time each week.

The clothing of the inmates is insufficient and is composed of military as well as civilian wearing apparel. The blankets placed at their disposal are also insufficient.

For the least reason the overseers pronounce as punishment 8 days of "tomb." The punished person must remain 8 days and 8 nights in a tomb and gets nothing but bread and water. A tomb is a hole dug in the ground, 2 meters long, 50 centimeters large, 30-35 cm. deep. There are two rows of such tombs one meter apart. The tombs occupied are, during the day, covered by a blanket kept down by heavy stones. The prisoner covers himself with this blanket during the night. During the summer it is intolerably hot in the daytime while the nights are disagreeably cold. During the winter the prisoners suffer day and night from cold. One has not the right to talk or smoke and one gets water and 200 grs. bread each day. It is permitted to leave the tombs only three times a day for five minutes. Those who dare only to raise their heads expose themselves to a rain of stones thrown by the Arabs who are on guard or to be kicked, or blows from rifles. Once it was raining continuously day and night and the prisoners had to remain in water up to their heads and could not leave their tombs until noon. As a consequence, some of the prisoners caught a fever—other illnesses do not count. At another time, two Spaniards escaped. Their escape was discovered only some hours later. As a punishment 16 of their comrades were sent to the tombs. In running towards the tombs they were mishandled by the "goumiers" who inflicted rifle blows. Those who dared to sigh or groan were beaten with rifles and kicked even in the tombs.

Some of the work done by the inmates is supervised by the "goumiers"; the inmates must march in a row and are pushed forward by rifles. Those who dare to cry against such treatment and complain to the overseer are immediately punished by being thrown into the tombs. It is not permitted to leave the place where one sleeps after dinner, i.e. after 6 p.m. until 5 a.m. The inmates remain in the dark, tortured by hunger and cold, thinking of their families and only the ardent desire to see their dear ones gives them the strength to bear this misfortune.

They have done nothing wrong, they are neither criminals nor bandits but they are kept in the disciplinary camp to intimidate their comrades in the regular work camp and to force them thus to finish the construction of the trans-Saharan railway.[190b]

At Berguent the construction yards were located four kilometers from the camps. The internees had to march from and to the camps four times a day. The shelters consisted of *cagnas* in the ground and covered with mats made of esparto-grass. In English *cagnard* means a tramp's sleeping-place under the bridge, but at Berguent there was not even the bridge to protect the men from the rain. When it rained, the *cagnards* were flooded and the men had to seek refuge in the rain. Each man was given only one liter of water per day. At Bou Arfa the internees had to produce from two to four times as much as the Arab workers, who deserted after receiving the first pay. A few officers protested against such treatment of volunteers for the defense of France. On March 9, 1942, Colonel Lorillard, who served forty years in the army, mostly in the Foreign Legion, wrote to General Noguès that aliens who remained at home continued to live a normal life while volunteers were treated like pariahs.[190c]

The name of the camp El Ourak was later changed to Foum de Flah and was a disciplinary camp. The representative of the International Red Cross visited the camp on July 30, 1942, and reported:

> We brought to the attention of the Camp Commander that several men have endured this very arduous life for five or six months, all of which is contrary to the provisions of the Geneva Convention. We were struck by one case in particular, that of a hopeless negativist whose punishments are increased in proportion to the growth and progress of his disorder. The resident general's attention has been called to this case.[191]

Some men of the 6th company of foreign workers dared to protest against the harsh working conditions. In order to discourage any further protest the entire company of 150 men became a disciplinary group and was sent to Kerras in the middle of the Sahara. From May to November of 1942 nine men died: Bienstock was tortured and died in the hospital; Moreno was strangled; Marshall weakened and died; Yaraba de Castillo, tuberculate and rachitic, died as a result of overwork and hunger; Nassariaz was tortured to death; Alvarez Ferrier and Kyzonois were beaten to death; Poras and an unnamed foreign worker were assassinated. The internees were constantly punished. Their meals consisted of soup and a slice of bread. They had no shoes and no water to wash themselves. The camp was full of parasites. Those punished with imprisonment had no right to go out in order to relieve themselves; instead they were forced to use at night for this purpose the bowl from which they ate during the day. As special punishment internees were locked up for eight days in a cell. Every day they were hit with bludgeons; for food they received two quarts of salted water and a slice of bread every second day. An Italian named Taba, an anti-Fascist and volunteer for the duration of the war, was handed over to the Italian Fascist authorities. Later, after the Allied invasion, the internees furnished the names of those responsible for these acts. Lt. Santucci, commandant of the camp, ordered to kill internees; Adjutant Finidori, personally killed internees; Mosca, adjutant of the milice, gave an order to fire at the internees; Riepp, auxiliary guardian, a long-time legionnaire of German origin, personally killed four internees.

On June 1, 1943, the office of the World Jewish Congress in New York published the following "Eye-Witness Report" prepared in November 1942 on Atrocities Committed Against Foreign Volunteers at the Berguent (Bou Arfa) Camp:

> Brennmann: He tried to escape from Berguent. Lt. Jansen sent him to the disciplinary camp and declared him a mutineer. Jansen had appointed him group leader. In this capacity he had refused to drive his men. Jansen declared he would not tolerate any undue friendliness. Brennmann was in "tombeau" without food for twenty-five to thirty days. Emaciated to a skeleton, he was sent to the infirmary at Bou Arfa where he died after a short period.
>
> Fischl Ehrlich: Lt. Jansen sent him to the disciplinary camp because of undue solidarity. Starvation and beatings by native soldiers, administered with their rifle butts, completely broke him and led him to cut his arteries. He is laid up in the Bou Arfa infirmary.
>
> Gruen: He often had fever as a result of a heart condition and due to malaria from which he suffered. This prevented him from attending to his daily "task"

of two cubic meters, and thus he was sent to the disciplinary camp by Lt. Jansen. Starvation caused skin eruptions on his arms and one arm may have to be amputated. He is now in the infirmary at Bou Arfa.

Kleinkopf: He protested in a friendly manner to the Chief Quartermaster about the further curb of the bread rations. Lt. Jansen threw him into the disciplinary camp. He was put in "tombeau" and refused to take "food," which consisted of three hundred grams of bread and water, nothing else whatsoever. He was kept there for twenty-five to thirty days, together with others. Then he died. The others were sent to the hospital at Bou Arfa.

Muster: Muster was remanded to the disciplinary camp by Lt. Jansen because of an act of solidarity. As a result of starvation, he developed water on the knees. He is still laid up in the infirmary at Bou Arfa.

Selo: Selo attempted to flee from Morocco and was sent to the disciplinary camp at Ain el Ourak, approximately in the middle of November 1941. He was forced into "tombeau" where his feet were frozen and both his legs were amputated at the knees. As his wounds are still infected, he is still at the *Civil* in Oujda.

"Tombeau" is a cave in the ground shovelled out in the size of a body. In this hole, one must stretch out. It is uncovered. One must lie still without the slightest movement. The guard sees to that, throwing stones at the instance of even the merest motion. He may also beat you with the butt of his rifle. The native soldier is also authorized to shoot. This was often done in the cases of Spaniards. In the case of Selo, it rained so hard that the rain froze him to the ground. This measure has been ordered by the Production Industrielle, located at Rabat. Its director general is a certain Vivier, its secretaries are Domschique Kiesele, da la Pleine, Commanders Janney and Marty, Captain Avelar of the "2me Bureau."

Upon Liberation of Morocco by the United States Army! Rosenthal, Austrian:

On November 10th, 11th or 12th he was stabbed in the back with the rifle butt by Chief Sergeant Habicht. He protested and was sent to the disciplinary camp by Lt. Jansen.[192]

Maurice Vanino-Wanikoff described the following punishments of the internees: attached to the stake, without any cover over the head, and during the entire day; the bastinado, a cage for animals; and, of course, the torment of the *tombeaux*, a hole in the ground no larger than 1.80 meters x 0.60 meters where the victims were forced to remain not less than eight days—some were punished with twenty-five days. They had to remain completely motionless, or were beaten. At daytime they were lying there in the heat and when it rained in the cold bath. According to regulation the men in the *tombeaux* had to be given soup and vegetables three times a day, instead they were given bread and water only once a day. Very, very few men were able to function normally after such punishment. Very often their arms or legs had to be amputated. Men died, or became insane. Wanikoff concluded his description with these words:

> Demain sur nos "tombeaux" les
> blès seront plus beaux . . .
>
> [tomorrow on our *tombeaux* (graves)
> the wheat will be more beautiful . . .]

However, although it sounds very poetic and noble, one may doubt if this was the last thought of those volunteers who had passed through the hell of the *tombeaux*. One may rather imagine that the last words of these volunteers for the defense of France was a vehement curse for the system of the Legion.[192a]

On October 9, 1942, six internees (Maier Birkenwald, Alexandre Culebras, Lewin, Schmul Lerner, Joseph Rocha, Dr. Ephraim Scharf) at the camp Sidi-el-Ayachi complained to the Quakers that a discharge commission at Oued Zem declared them unfit for work at a labor camp. However, the regional controller obtained a reversal of the commission's decisions.[193]

On November 7, 1942, the number of internees was estimated by the French authorities at 3,357 in 15 Moroccan camps (Berguent, Bou Arfa, 2 Colomb-Béchar camps, Djérada, El Ayachi, Foum de Flah, Im Fout, Menabba, Mengoub, Missour, Moulay-Bou-Azza, Oued Akreuch, Oued Zem, and Settat), and 2,185 in 5 Algerian camps (Berrouaghia, Boghari, Colomb-Béchar, Djelfa, and Kenadsa).[194]

One cannot speak of the fate of volunteer legionnaires in North Africa without mentioning the outstanding role played by the agencies in trying to alleviate the legionnaires' suffering. The American Friends Service Committee was magnificent. Count Emeryk Hutten-Czapski headed a Polish agency which had some limited funds available to aid Polish internees. Czapski has been quite successful in persuading the authorities to permit his people to leave the camp for jobs which he has found for them provided the people were not Jewish. There was also a Norwegian representative with funds to distribute to his people but in numerous cases his difficulty also was in finding supplies as well. The Czechs, too, had a representative with funds at his disposal. The Spanish had a representative but he had no money for his people in the camps. Marin-Chencerelle, of the International Migration Service, was doing splendid work, operating with the Region Civile. She spent several days a week in a camp, becoming thoroughly acquainted with the conditions that existed there. She made these visits alone, with the poorest transportation facilities imaginable. Working in this way under these circumstances required not only remarkable physical endurance but magnificent courage and devotion.[195]

The Comité Juif d'Aide et d'Assistance (Jewish Committee for Relief and Assistance) of Algeria tried to alleviate the sufferings of the internees. Elie Gozlan of the Committee visited the camps bringing food and clothing whenever possible, in spite of the sufferings the North African Jews themselves had to undergo. Jacques Oettinger and other representatives of HICEM, a Jewish migration agency, accomplished miracles. According to the AFSC representative, Mrs. Helen Nelly Cazes de Benatar of the AJDC also did "splendid work."[196] One would like to give some details of her activities. However, there is no material available about AJDC activities in North Africa or, if it hadn't been destroyed and was still available, it was not made available to the author.

We noted above that many old ex-legionnaires worked in the labor camps. They, too, suffered from the new French spirit. A "very old Moroccan" complained in a letter to the *Presse Marocaine* that men who had served 5, 10 or 15 years in the Legion, men who were applauded as heros when France was in need of their services, men of "the heroic Legion," were refused employment. *Ces lions sont devenus des bêtes puantes!* ("These lions became stinking animals!") *L'Echo d'Alger* told the story of a former legionnaire who was wounded in World War I. In 1939 he enlisted again. Even so he was still a foreigner and as such could not find employment.[197]

Old time legionnaires who had left the Legion for service in the German army were in charge of Jewish internees in the forced labor camps of Tunisia. These were brutal murderers who made use of their knowledge of the French language in order to further refine their brutality.[198]

XX. North Africa Liberated—Internees Punished for Hoisting the American Flag

The American assault forces began landings in North Africa on November 8, 1942, and the French resistance in Algiers ceased later that same day. Oran surrendered on November 10, and on November 11, the French forces in the Casablanca area capitulated. The TORCH operation was thus successfully terminated. Algerian resistance consisted almost entirely of Jews. They led the insurrection of Algiers which neutralized the city while the Americans landed their forces.

President Roosevelt declared: "I have requested the liberation of all persons in Northern Africa who had been imprisoned because they opposed the efforts of the Nazis to dominate the world and I have asked for the abrogation of all laws and decrees inspired by Nazi government or Nazi ideologies." The *Jewish Frontier* commented: "These are good words to hear."[199]

On November 10, 1942, Admiral Jean François Darlan ordered to deck all public institutions with Allied and French flags. However, the commandants of the forced labor camps did not think that the order also applied to them. During the night of November 11-12, 1942, an American flag was hoisted on the main mast of the Kenadsa camp. The "alien workers" *(Travailleurs Etrangers—TE)*, as the internees were officially called, were accused as perpetrators of this "provocation." On Thursday, November 12, at 8 A.M. the American flag was removed during a demonstration of "force and patriotism." Many alien workers were arrested for having protested against this act. During a noon-time assembly the internees refused to listen to the camp commander in the presence of armed Algerian guards. One internee named Schnek told the camp commander: "We were treated by you as 'dirty foreigners' and we will not forget it. Churchill and Roosevelt came to North Africa in order to continue the war and bring liberty to the oppressed." Friedrich Schnek, a former solicitor-general of Vienna, added: *Nous ne sommes plus des T.E., nous somme des messieurs* ("We are not anymore foreign workers, we are gentlemen.") Schnek was not arrested because the administration was afraid this would provoke a strike at the coal mine. An unofficial report stated that Schnek was neither a revolutionary nor a professional troublemaker. He was a bourgeois-minded jurist of Vienna in charge of preparing indictments of criminals.[200]

During the American invasion of Algeria the discipline at the Colomb-Béchar camp was doubly reinforced. At the camp of Saida the internees were locked up in cells of the prison for an entire week.[201]

On the day of the Allied landing in North Africa Caboche, commandant of the Djelfa camp, placed machine guns around the camp pointed at the roads on which the Allied forces would be traveling. The internees were officially advised that no demands for liberation would be met. As late as March 1943 an inter-Allied commission visited the camp and thanks to the firm and courageous position taken by a British major named Brister, a group of internees, among them 65 Jews, was able to leave the camp for the British Pioneer Groups.[202]

On November 24, 1942, Leslie O. Heath, delegate of the American Friends Service Committee to North Africa, wrote:

> The coming of the Americans has naturally increased the hope of these men that deliverance is immediately at hand and they have become restive. Most of the English have already been released from the camps and the rest soon will be. The Poles constitute no problem as they will be taken care of immediately by the Polish government. The same will undoubtedly hold true for the Czechs. Many of the Poles and Czechs will join the military forces, and there are American and other visas available for many of the others for migration, just as soon as transportation is available. By the terms of the arrangement between the French government and Mexico most of the Spanish could emigrate to Mexico once transportation is available. This leaves then merely the anti-Nazi ex-Germans and Austrians, although many of them could be absorbed into a civilian corps attached to the U.S. Army, as many of these men have special skill, being professional men, engineers and trained workmen. There have been some attempts by French officials to force some of these men again to "volunteer" in the French Foreign Legion. With their past experience it is unlikely that any will do so and there is grave danger that further attempts by the French to force them will provoke serious incidents. All of these circumstances and the long period of internment without adequate food, clothing or medical attention brings about a tension which may be the cause of serious trouble; but by prompt action now it is believed such trouble may be avoided with great woe for all—internees, French and Americans. What would appear to be the simplest solution—namely to give them all their freedom immediately—probably would cause confusion worse confounded as they would all flock to Casablanca and the larger towns which are in no position to receive them all at once due to already over-crowded conditions.

Heath suggested to "notify the [internees at the] camps at once to keep quiet—that they are receiving prompt attention but that patience will be required on their part pending working out details."[203]

The *New Republic* wrote in November 1942:

> In French North Africa, there are some 330,000 native Jews, and the American occupation will doubtless release them from the Nuremberg laws imposed on them by orders from Vichy. But there has been no word as yet about the many Frenchmen arrested for supporting the United Nations; at the beginning of November they were still being confined in Algiers and Oran. Neither has there been any word about the many thousands of Spanish Republicans, Czechs, Austrians and Poles who were building a railroad across the Sahara. Most of them are former soldiers who fought for our side—forgotten heroes who were being treated worse than slaves; who were starved, beaten, half-frozen by night and burned by day; and who at any sign of complaint might be punished, sometimes by being buried in the sand up to their necks and left for hours in the African sun. How well we treat them will be regarded as a test of our good intentions. When our advance guards reach the slave camps in the desert, we want to hear that they are being set free, given food and clothing and sent to rest camps in the mountains. Today, most of them are only the burned shells of the men they used to be; but after a few weeks of recuperation, they would be ready to continue fighting for a free Europe.[204]

However, it took at least five months, from November to April of 1943 before the Allied promise to liberate the anti-Fascist prisoners and internees began to be fulfilled. Who was responsible for this delay? The French authorities of liberated North Africa or the Allies who did not dare to order immediate liberation? Or both?

The *New Republic* of February 1, 1943, wrote that the United States government—and no other—was morally accountable for every man who died from mistreatment or filth-born diseases. "We can either have them released immediately, or else acknowledge ourselves as the accomplices and protectors of the Fascists who are still betraying France."[205] René Pierre Gosset, a Gaullist, wrote:

> Gaullist, communists, unfortunate penniless foreigners and those ill-fated men kept in prison lost hope day by day. On November 8th they had believed that the prison doors would be flung wide open. Today they heard talk about their files being examined one by one—some fifty or sixty thousand files!—and of the impossibility of finding accommodation. At a press conference held in London General de Gaulle suggested a solution to this problem: "I would suggest, if my advice was sought, that the examination of the files be made by

throwing them in the fire." Two and a half months after the landings, the Allies had not had the doors of camps and prisons open.[206]

Giuttone Zannutelli correctly wrote in the *New Republic* that the North African Fascist was not an instrument of American politics, but rather the United States government was an instrument of these Fascists.[207]

On February 15, 1943, after the Allied invasion of North Africa, *La Dépêche Algérienne* proudly wrote of the fact that the Foreign Legion had participated in a military parade together with Allied units. It said that the Legion had been a refuge for men who had escaped from Fascism and Nazism. By then, however, these men, who had been seeking a chance to fight for France, had still not been freed from the forced labor camps of North Africa.

Jewish volunteers marching at Place de la Bastille in Paris, Aug. 1, 1914, with a banner reading, "Long Live France. Brother Jews! Let us fight for France, our beloved, generous and hospitable fatherland." *Below:* Inscription on the banner.

VIVE LA FRANCE!
FRÈRES JUIFS!
Allons nous Combattre pour la France, pour notre bienaimée patrie, GÉNÉREUSE & HOSPITALIÈRE

ברודער יודען!
לאמיד געהן קעמפפען
פאר פראנקרייך אונזער
געליבטע פאטערלאנד

CAMARADES JUIFS
Groupe de volontaires Juifs Russo-Roumains du 18ᵉ

La France, pays de la Liberté, de l'Egalité, de la Fraternité,

La France qui, la première de toutes les nations, nous a reconnu, à nous juifs, les Droits de l'Homme et du Citoyen, ce cher pays, où nous trouvons, nous et nos familles, refuge, protection et bonheur,

Actuellement la France est en état de guerre. Qu'allons-nous faire pour prouver à notre seconde patrie notre amour et notre attachement ?

Allons-nous, pendant que le peuple français se lève comme un seul homme pour défendre la Patrie nous croiser les bras. Non! Car si nous ne sommes pas encore Français de droit, nous le sommes de cœur et d'âme, et, notre devoir le plus sacré, est de nous mettre de suite à la disposition de cette belle et noble nation, afin de participer à sa défense.

Camarades, c'est le moment de payer notre tribut de reconnaissance au pays qui nous hospitalise.

Tous en cœur, la main dans la main, au service de la France.
       VIVE LA FRANCE!!

Les adhésions d'engagement volontaire sont reçues tous les jours, Café WEISSMANN, 82, Rue Marcadet.
         LE COMITE.

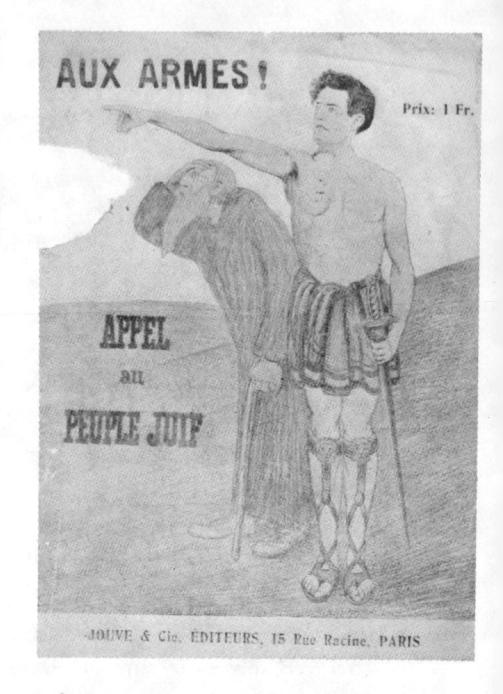

Left: Appeal by the group of Russian and Rumanian Jewish volunteers to enlist for the defense of France. August 1914 (Harvard). *Right:* Cover of a pamphlet calling upon Jews to enlist for the defense of France.

Left: France to pogromist Russia: "Only you can be my protective angel!" *(The Big Stick,* Sept. 11, 1914). *Below:* A group of Jewish immigrants in Tours during World War I, among them some in the uniform of legionnaires and a baby dressed in a Cossack uniform. Photographed in front of a poster decorated with the flags of the allied nations and the inscription, "Campagne 1914 Vive l'Alliance" (YIVO); and receipt for a donation to the Society for Aid to Civilian Immigrant Prisoners, i.e., civilian internees, during World War I (Harvard).

From top: A group of Jewish legionnaires during World War I, photographed at Tours (YIVO). Edmond Fleg, Franco-Jewish poet of Alsatian origin, who served as a volunteer in the army *(L' Univers Israélite).* Psenin (left) and Rothberg, two Jewish labor activists and volunteers during World War I (YIVO).

Left: Photograph of a Jewish volunteer with the inscription, "Engaé pour la gamelle," as a protest against the slanderous remarks that Jews enlisted in the Legion for the food (Schwartzbard). *Below, from right to left*: the legionnaire Levy-Aaron Litwak, killed in action at Carency; Yom Kippur (Day of Atonement), 1914, the 46-year-old Isidore Unterman, a volunteer in the Legion for the duration of the war, praying at a training camp near Bayonne.

Jewish legionnaires in the trenches, 1915 (Schwarztbard).

The ruins of Carency after the battle in 1915 (L'Illustration).

Above: Letter written by Maurice Sloutchewsky before his execution for having taken part in the mutiny of Jewish volunteers in the Foreign Legion, Dec. 14, 1915. On Dec. 15 a legionnaire on leave mailed the letter to the union of capmakers and marked on the envelope: "Sloutchewsky his last letter" (author's collection). *Below:* When the revolutionary emigré Vladimir Bourtzev went back to Russia to volunteer for the defense of his country, he was deported to Siberia (cartoon in *The Big Stick,* Feb. 12, 1915).

Qu'ils s'engagent ou qu'ils partent!

Nous avons demandé vendredi à la Chambre de bien vouloir accepter une addition à l'ordre du jour concernant les interpellations ayant trait à la meilleure utilisation des...

que je parle des Juifs et c'est M. Moutet qui m'y oblige.
Ce n'est point tout de même une raison, parce qu'il y a beaucoup...

LE SERVICE OBLIGATOIRE POUR TOUS

Obligation politique et morale

Les Juifs russes de France et d'An- | d'Angleterre, nous appliquons nos

L'Espionnage

Depuis que nous sommes en guerre, nous avons appris par de multiples et terribles épreuves avec quelle maîtrise les Allemands ont organisé leur service d'espionnage. Ils en ont inondé les pays neutres et c'est grâce à ce réseau de communications ténébreuses qu'ils accomplissent leurs mauvais coups. Ce sont des espions qui ont dénoncé aux sous-marins de la Méditerranée le pas-

de chez nous? Il est donc conforme à la prudence la plus élémentaire de tout naturalisé pour un conspirateur guerre secrète contre nous et de l'e ser impitoyablement. Pendant des maines et des mois nous avons pro dé à notre défense militaire des A des Munitions, des Canons. C'était dit. Je demande aux pouvoirs publ permission d'ajouter une addition triple appel et de réclamer d'eu Balai!

JULES DELAFOSS
député du Calv

Les Juifs, sac au dos!

Le projet de loi portant obligation du se vice militaire pour les sujets des nations alliées réfugiés chez nous va renforcer n effectifs
Bien qu'à Paris, en effet, on compte ur quarantaine de mille Juifs russes qui seror touchés par la nouvelle loi, des gaillards qu

DÉBUSQUONS-LES!

La propagande boche se poursuit dans Paris par circulaires et tracts. Elle n'y produit en rien l'effet espéré parce que mal faite, et parce que ses auteurs n'ont pas encore compris les sentiments profonds des Français après deux ans de guerre. Les mensonges allemands sont tellement ridicules et si grossièrement inventés que les appels venus de Berlin ou de la *Gazetta*

LA Sécurité de Paris

Il s'agit ici non de la sécurité de Paris vis-à-vis des armées allemandes, sécurité définitivement assurée par la victoire de la Marne et de l'Yser. Il s'agit de la sécurité de Paris vis-à-vis des influences boches qui y sont demourées malgré la guerre et des éléments de troubles dont pourraient disposer ces influences boches, si jamais la surveillance se relâchait. Je n'ai pas ici la prétention de faire la leçon aux autorités compétentes, qui ont assuré à la grande ville, depuis le début de la guerre, une tranquillité parfaite. Je...

Above: Headlines in the French press against Russian-Jewish immigrants, 1915–16. *Below:* A censored article in defense of the immigrants in the bulletin *Je dis tout*, Aug. 1915.

LES ÉTRANGERS A PARIS.

M. Henri Galli publie un article contre la présence à Paris d'un grand nombre d'étrangers. Cet article contre la liberté des étrangers, il le publie dans LA LIBERTÉ. Il y a de ces contrastes. M. Henri Galli signale particulièrement les individus qui se prétendent russes et il demande quelles sont les puissantes interventions qui ont tenu en échec les mesures prises à l'encontre de ces Russes.
Et M. Galli termine son réquisitoire en ces termes :

" La police militaire et les autres — car il y en a plusieurs qui ne s'entendent pas toujours — poursuivent sans relâche enquêtes et recherches; mais combien leur tâche est difficile dans le maquis où peuvent facilement se dissimuler les malfaiteurs et les agents de l'ennemi ! "

Le Vice-Président de la LIGUE DES PATRIOTES est aussi député du IVe Arrondissement. Nous avons dit quelles raisons particulières ce député avait à pourchasser toute une partie de la population de son arrondissement qui ne constitue pas pour lui une clientèle électorale. En réalité, ces étrangers contre lesquels s'acharne M. Galli sont, pour la plupart, des Juifs Russes qui se sont pliés à toutes les formalités, si nombreuses qu'elles soient, édictées tant par le Ministre de l'Intérieur que par le Gouverneur Militaire de Paris. La plupart de ces Juifs Russes que leur santé ne met pas en état de porter les armes sont apparentés aux engagés volontaires russes qui firent l'admiration de M. Gustave Hervé, lors de ces combats meurtriers où leurs légions furent littéralement décimées.

SUPPRIMÉ PAR LA CENSURE

Les Juifs Russes qui soulèvent l'indignation intéressée de M. Henri Galli n'ont rien de commun avec les Boches. Leurs frères, leurs fils ou leurs neveux ont donné leur sang pour la France. Que M. Henri Galli nomme ceux qu'il suspecte. Si sa suspicion est fondée, qu'on agisse. Il y a sans doute dans la masse quelques brebis galeuses. Mais il est injuste d'accuser en bloc " les étrangers de Paris ", il est également injuste de jeter le discrédit sur plusieurs milliers d'individus qui aiment profondément et sincèrement notre pays.

JACQUES LANDAU.

(Visé par la Censure)

Headlines in liberal and French labor newspapers in defense of Russian-Jewish immigrants, 1915–16.

Above: Rabbi Abraham Back, chaplain of the Moroccan Division, with a group of North African Jewish soldiers during World War I. *Below left:* a group of North African Jewish soldiers during a visit to the synagogue of Rambervilliers, Vosges. *Below right:* Postcard with a reproduction of a painting showing Rabbi Abraham Bloch, a chaplain, giving the last rites to a wounded Catholic soldier (Aug. 1914). Moments later the rabbi was himself killed. In spite of this and many similar symbolic acts of the *Union Sacré*, the antisemitic campaign continued (YIVO).

LE GRAND RABBIN AUMONIER ABRAHAM BLOCH
Dans une ambulance bombardée par les Allemands, Il apporte a un catholique agonisant le crucifix que celui-ci réclame: un instant après, le Rabbin est tué par un obus.
Août 1914.

The Foreign Jews Protection Committee against Deportation to Russia and Compulsion.

Representing 120 Organisations.

דער פֿערטײדיגונגס קאָמיטעט פֿון די אױסלענדישע אידען געגען צוריק
שיקונג קײן רוסלאַנד און געצװאוּנגענע מיליטערדינסט.

All Communications to be addressed to
ABRAHAM BEZALEL,
Hon. Sec.,
6. COMMERCIAL ROAD, E.

London, August 18th, 1916.

Dear Sir,

I beg to draw your attention to the following letter I have just received written in French from one of our affiliated bodies.

Trusting you will use your influence to alleviate their sufferings,

I remain, yours faithfully,

Hon. Sec.

Russian-Jewish (French Refugees) Protection Committee.

All communications to be addressed to the Hon. Secretary G. BERNARD, 58, Whitechapel Road, E.

LONDRES, le 15 AOUT, 1916.

Cher Monsieur,

J'ai l'honneur de porter à votre connaissance que nous sommes un comité executive élu à l'unanimité par une assemblée tenue à New King's Hall, Commercial Road, E., le 1 Août 1916, et dont l'assistance compacte se composait des juifs russes venant de France pour se refugier en Angleterre.

Par la présente nous vous prions de prendre en consideration notre cas special, et de vouloir bien attirer l'attention du gouvernement anglais en notre faveur afin d'arriver à solutionner notre cause, dans le sens de la Justice et de l'Equité.

Les elements qui constituent notre groupe sont les produits des faits suivants :

Au mois de Septembre 1914, alors que Paris etait menacée par l'invasion allemande, et que le gouvernement français se retirait à Bordeaux, on procédait à l'évacuation partielle de Paris, la population parisienne affolée se jetait dans des directions aussi nombreuses que differentes courant àl'avanture, avec le seul but de s'eloigner de la fournaise dont chacun croyait inevitable. Une grande partie de la population juive a eté entrainée dans ce courant, et des milliers de nos correligionnaires se sont dispersés et disseminés un peu partout, une partie ayant echouée en Angleterre.

D'autre part, il est des voyageurs de commerce ou simplement des gens qui sont venus ici pour des affaires de famille et avec l'intention de ne sejourner ici que quelques semaines et qui se voient obligés de rester ici DEPUIS PLUS DE 15 MOIS sans pouvoir obtenir un passeport, soit pour rentrer en France soit pour aller ailleurs.

Voilà les circonstances qui nous ont emmenés en Angleterre.

Or, depuis la dernière campagne qui a eu son echo auprès du gouvernement anglais et qui a costerné toute la population de juifs russes par l'alternative : ou de servir ce pays ou d'être deportés en Russie. Nous nous etonnons amèrement qu'aucune voix jusqu'aujourd'hui ne s'etait levée pour demander SI A NOUS AUSSI cette alternative serait posée, à nous qui n'avions jamais l'intentions de fixer notre residence en Angleterre et qui avons laissé nos occupations, nos commerces, nos meubles et même nos habits en France avec l'espoir d'y retourner dès qu'il nous serait possible.

Nous nous etonnons amerement qu'aucune voix ne s'etait levée pour demander au gouvernement anglais d'agir envers nous comme a agi le gouvernement français, c'est à dire DE NOUS LAISER PARTIR LIBREMENT.

A ce sujet, permettez moi, de vous rappeler qu'en Juillet 1915 une agitation pareille soulevee par les partis antisemites et nationalistes de France, ayant pour but d'enregimenter de force les juifs russes ou de les deporter en Russie, a complètement echouée, et le gouvernement français, fidèle à ses traditions de Liberte, de Justice et d'Asile, a continue de ne pas inquieter les nôtres qui sont restes en France et a permis de quitter le territoire à tous ceux qui en ont fait la demande.

Voilà pourquoi nous nous adressons à vous, qui representez 120 groupements differents et qui avez pour mission de defendre tous les juifs russes en general, et nous vous demandons de porter notre voix auprès du gouvernement anglais et lui dire, en notre nom, que si on nous considère maintenant comme des hôtes indesirables et si on pretend maintenat que nous profitons du desastre europeen pour enlever le travail aux citoyens anglais qui font leur devoir pour leur patrie, que le gouvernement ait l'obligeance de vouloir bien nous ouvrir la porte de l'Angleterre et nous laisser partir pour un pays neutre...

C'est la seule faveur que nous demandons, et nous esperons que vous ne refuserez pas de prendre notre cause, pour en faire triompher l'esprit de Justice.

Veuillez, cher Monsieur, agreer nos très sincères salutations,

Pp. le Comite (Signe:)   G. BERNARD,
Hon. Sec.

Leaflet of the London Foreign Jews Protection Committee against Deportation to Russia and Compulsion, containing a letter by the Russian-Jewish (French Refugees) Protection Committee, Aug. 15, 1916 (Harvard).

Bulletin of the General Committee of the Russian Colony in Paris about the Franco-Russian agreement of July 28—Aug. 10, 1917 on the military status of Russian citizens in France (Harvard).

Cover of the first issue of the bulletin of Jewish volunteers, May 9, 1919.

From top: (1) Former Jewish volunteers at the Hôtel des Invalides celebrate the anniversary of the mass enlistment of Jews, 1921 *(L'Univers Israélite).* (2) A group of Jewish veterans of World War I and their families during a visit to Carency. (3) Representatives of the Association of Jewish Veterans at a ceremonial igniting of the flame at the Tomb of the Unknown Soldier. Paris, Sept. 25, 1946 (YIVO).

In the offices of a Paris Jewish organization in 1939, volunteers enlisting for the defense of France.

A group of Jewish volunteers at the Foreign Legion camp at Barcarès during World War II (Le Combattant Juif).

Top: **General view of La Valbonne (Rhône), a training center for volunteers in the Legion.** *Center:* **St. Maurice-de-Gourdans, another training center.** *Bottom:* **Montluel, a near-by village often visited by Jewish legionnaires (YIVO).**

Top: Passover at Barcarès, 1940 (L'Univers Israelite). *Bottom:* Passover at La Valbonne (YIVO). *Right:* Rabbi Rene Hirschler, chaplain of the Foreign Legion; he was deported to a death camp.

Left: A group of Jewish legionnaires at La Valbonne. In the front row, left: Sgt. Henri, who saved the author's life. *Right:* The author (right) with a friend. *Below:* The author (first row, center) with a group of friends of the Jewish Socialist Bund during training at La Valbonne, Jan. 7, 1940.

The drummers of the Legion during World War II.

A group of Czech and Spanish legionnaires in North Africa.

Top: The choral and dramatic group formed by the internees, mostly former volunteers, in the concentration camp Beaunne-la-Rolande, Dec. 3, 1941. *Center:* Committee of the "Palestinian" forced-labor camp at Mauriac. *Right:* The camp Pithiviers, where many former volunteers were interned. From there they were transferred to the camp at Drancy for deportation to death camps (YIVO).

From top: Note by the commandant of the Pithiviers camp punishing the Jewish veterans. June 27, 1941 (*Le Combattant Juif*). Leaflet distributed by the Committee of Jewish widows, wives and mothers of Jewish Prisoners of War. Paris, Oct. 1942 (*Dos vort fun vidershtand un zig,* Paris, 1949).

False demobilization papers furnished by a Jewish underground organization (YIVO).

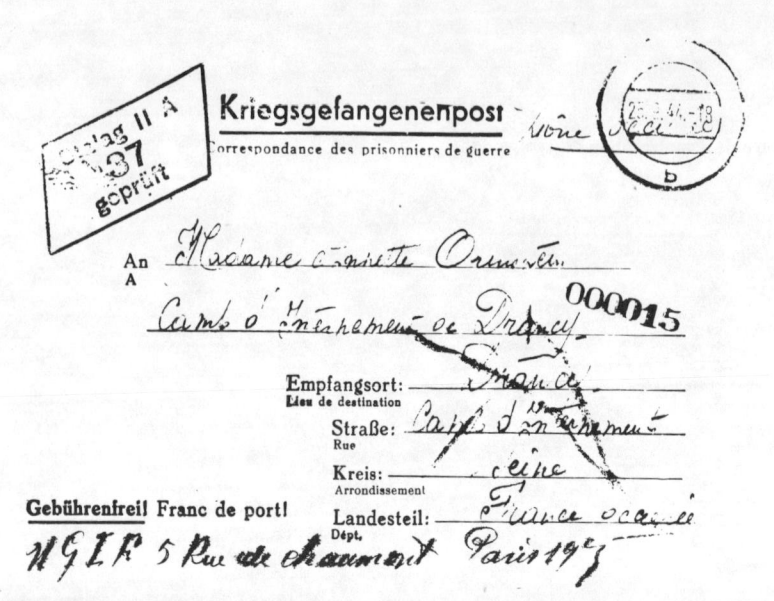

Top: Letter from Fredy Orinstein, a Jewish prisoner of war in M-Stammlager II A, at Neubrandenburg i. Mechl., addressed to his wife Annette, at the Drancy deportation camp. Sept. 1944. The letter was not delivered because she had been deported (YIVO). *Center:* A group of French soldiers in the German P.O.W. camp Stalag IV B at Muelhberg. In the center of the first row: The dentist Lt. N. Chatt with the yellow star. *Right:* A Jewish legionnaire in a German P.O.W. camp with the yellow star (*Le Combattant Juif*).

VI° ARMÉE
XVII° CORPS D'ARMÉE
VIII° DIVISION D'INFANTERIE

XII° RÉGIMENT ETRANGER D'INFANTERIE

CITATION
à
L'ORDRE DU RÉGIMENT
-o-o-o-o-o-o-

(Extrait de l'Ordre du Régiment N° 16)

F R Y D M A N Szajko. légionnaire 2° classe du 12° R.E.I

" Légionnaire courageux et de sang-froid. A assuré son
  service de télégraphiste dans une équipe de construction
" et de réparation de lignes avec bravoure, entrainant ses
" camarades sous la mitraillade et le bombardement ennemi
" A été blessé le 15 Juin 1940, au cours du repli derrière
" l'Yonne ".

P.C. St Amand, le 27 Juillet 1940
Le Lt-Colonel BESSON Cdt le
12° Régiment Etranger d'Infanterie.

From left to right: (1) The author as a legionnaire. (2) The author, during his convalescence, photographed in front of the old Jewish cemetery at Carpentras. (3) Citation of the author.

From top: (1) Former volunteers for the defense of France leveling a dune for the construction of the Trans-Saharian railroad at Colomb-Béchar. (2) Shoveling the sand into baskets, which were carried down by hand. The temperature was 120 in the shade. (3) Former volunteers, now prisoners in a barbed-wire enclosure (NA, RG 59).

Photographs of forced-labor camps in North Africa where Jewish and other legionnaires were forced to build the Trans-Saharian railroad. *From top:* (1) Stone-breaking squads near Bou Arfa. (2) Tents covering punishment trenches into which internees were placed. (3) Underground punishment cells. The men had to lie flat in heat or cold (NA, RG 59).

Ex-volunteers for the defense of France forced to construct the Trans-Saharian railroad. *From left to right:* (1) Carrying sand and rocks in baskets. (2) Leveling a hill of rock and sand by blasting and pick and shovels. (NA, RG 59). (3) Gravel roadbed leveled by internees *(Life).*

Entrance into a mine at Kenadsa, where ex-volunteers were employed as forced laborers, and the barracks for engineers and guards (NA, RG 84).

SECOURS POPULAIRE ALGERIEN
IL FAUT LIBERER
tous les emprisonnés et surveillés antifascistes

Par ordre d'Hitler, Vichy avait transformé notre belle Algérie en un vaste camp de concentration et de souffrance

MAISON-CARREE, LAMBESE, BERROUAGHIA, BOSSUET- DJENIEN BOU-REZG, COLOMB-BECHAR, KENADZA, AIN-SEFRA, OUARGLA-

et tant d'autres villes et villages étaient et, malheureusement sont encore les lieux de détention de milliers d'antifascistes et resteront les symboles d'un régime de barbarie et de cruauté.

Non sans beaucoup d'hésitation et de retard quelques unes des victimes de la répression des gouvernements réactionnaires et fascistes français sont maintenant libérées. Les 27 députés communistes français qui étaient à Maison-Carrée, 8 des 9 femmes détenues politiques dans cette même prison, la plupart des emprisonnés de nationalité française ont été libérés de même quelques français et musulmans des camps ont été rendus à la vie libre.

Mais il reste encore beaucoup d'antihitlériens et d'antifascistes dans les prisons et les camps de séjour surveillé: français, musulmans, étrangers dont un grand nombre sont les héroïques combattants des Brigades Internationales et les soldats de l'armée républicaine espagnole.

Ces hommes sont l'objet des brimades et de mauvais traitements de la part de:

du tortionnaire EL RIKKO, commandant le camp de Djenien-Bou-Rezg, qui a confisqué à son profit des objets et des vivres appartenant à des détenus;

du Sadique CABOCHE, commandant le camp de DJELFA, qui a pu cravacher jusqu'au sang les combattants espagnols et ceux des BRIGADES INTERNATIONALES;

de SANTUCCI, commandant la 6ème Compagnie de Travailleurs Etrangers à Bedjerat M'Sul, qui a pu donner l'ordre de frapper des volontaires de la guerre de 1939-1940 de les torturer jusqu'à ce que mort s'en suive, ainsi que d'autres garde-chiourmes qui ont commis des atrocités semblables dans tous les autres lieux d'internement.

Dans les prisons il y a, il est vrai, le régime politique depuis le début de Mars, mais si le traitement est moins dur, l'alimentation n'est guère améliorée: 50 grammes de légumes et 1/4 de vin de plus par jour; c'est nettement insuffisant.

Le typhus sévit et menace les prisonniers comme les

FÉDÉRATION DES AMICALES
DES ANCIENS ENGAGÉS VOLONTAIRES
ÉTRANGERS

SIÈGE :
28, Avenue du Maréchal Pétain - LIMOGES
Téléphone 35-72

STATUTS

Bureau: 47 Rue de Strasbourg
CASABLANCA
T I. A 14-61 et A 13-52
Permanence Mardi et Vendredi
de 18 à 20 heures

From left: (1) Leaflet of Secours Populaire Algerien on the situation in the camps after the liberation (LBI). (2) By-laws of the Association of Former Alien Volunteers with the stamp of the Casablanca branch. (3) Former legionnaires constructing the railroad (*Le Combattant Juif*).

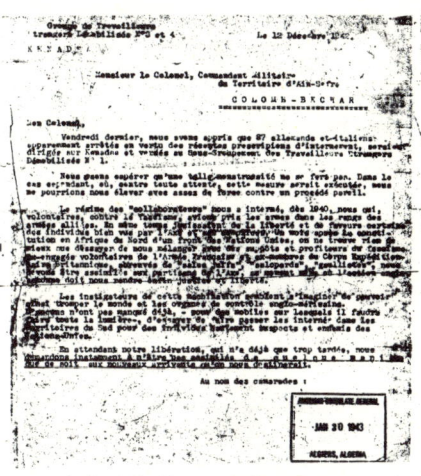

> My God sir,
>
> How can you expect us to believe that America is fighting a war for the liberation of freedom loving people when ANTI-FASCIST PRISONERS ARE STILL BEING HELD IN NORTH AFRICA.
>
> I think this is shocking and something should be done at once to alleviate the condition.
>
> Very truly yours,
>
> E Hannes
> 617 W 170 St
> NYC

From left: (1) One of the many protests sent to President Franklin D. Roosevelt about the treatment of the anti-Fascists in the North African camps, Jan. 28, 1943 (NA, RG 59). (2) Report by a group of internees in an Algerian forced-labor camp on the treatment of ex-volunteers, March 3, 1943 (AFSC). (3) Protest by the internees in the camp at Kenadsa against the internment of Germans and Italian Fascists at their camp, Dec. 12, 1942 (AFSC).

From top: (1) Letter by an internee in the camp at Djelfa on the behavior of the Polish consul in Algeria (LBI). (2) Announcement on forced labor in the camp at Sidi-el-Ayachi, Morocco. (3) A funeral in the camp at Sidi-el-Ayachi (YIVO).

XXI. Suffering and Death After the Liberation

M. Alexandre, chief of the Colomb-Béchar camp appealed to the internees to remain disciplined and work "intensely for the common cause."[208] Construction of the Trans-Saharian railroad was not stopped after the Allied landing in North Africa, nor were the half-legionnaires free to leave the camps.

French promoters of the railroad were disappointed at what they considered to be the failure of the Americans and British to understand the importance of the project. Almost no material had been coming since the American landing in November 1942 and rolling stock and locomotives were already wearing out.

The journalist Kenneth G. Crawford obtained permission to visit some of the North African camps. He wrote that this was made possible because Robert Murphy, President Roosevelt's personal representative to North Africa, came to the conclusion that in order to deny stories that he himself was standing over political prisoners in the Sahara "with a black-snake whip in his hand and blood in his eye" he had to permit correspondents to visit the camps. Crawford was the only one who benefitted from this decision. At the time of his visit, representatives of the Joint Commission on Political Prisoners were also making the rounds of these camps, and so the situation of the prisoners was somewhat ameliorated. Crawford's first visit in the beginning of 1943 was to the Bou Arfa camp. He wrote that the French had never quite understood American anxiety about political prisoners and that the forced labor camps of North Africa were a source of shame for the whole Western world. It had taken weeks of patient explanation to make the managers of the Compagnie Méditerranée-Niger understand why it would be necessary to hire Arab workers to replace the prisoners. He added:

> The railroad's managers insisted, moreover, that their project was a noble one and that its good end justified questionable means. A railroad across the desert, tapping the fabulous valley of the Niger, they said, would be a boon to all the peoples of western Europe. An almost fanatical faith in their enterprise mitigated any self-reproach for their employment policies.[209]

There is no doubt that the resolution to continue work on the Trans-Saharan railroad was at least partly responsible for guarding the former legionnaires in the camp.

On February 11, 1943, Leslie O. Heath wrote in a report of the "Concentration Camps" in Morocco that the situation had "deteriorated seriously in the past two months." With the arrival of the Americans all the internees expected to be released by them immediately. The American policy had been "not to interfere with the political situation here and it has been considered by the American Command that the camps and their conduct was exclusively a French affair." In essence, the French were continuing all of their past camp policies. Forced labor and the disciplinary camps were existing "virtually under the shadow of the American flag." Most of the anti-Jewish laws remained in force in Morocco; needless to say, this same atmosphere pervaded the camps.

Heath further reported that a number of the internees had escaped from the camps and had come to Casablanca still believing that the Americans would protect them and give them work. The official American point of view was that citizens of Axis countries, regardless of their individual records, could not be employed by the U.S. Forces. Rabat had gone even further by declaring that the camps were filled with fifth columnists and Communists. These men, not finding American protection, had been picked up by the French police and punished or were forced to join the Corps Franc, or still wander around hoping to find some kind of employment before they were discovered and punished. The French had stated that they would release all internees who would leave the country. All the English had been released and had left and many of the Poles had also gone. But the Polish Consul was unable to secure the release of the Polish Jews from Sidi-el-Ayachi and guarantee food and lodging for them until they found jobs or left the country.

The offer was refused to internees of "Axis origin." According to Heath this matter was then referred in writing to Col. Pugh of the Civil Affairs Division of the U.S. Army. Heath had a list of internees from the U.S. Intelligence Service and Col. Pugh wrote that the U.S. Army had no objection to the release of these people under the conditions stated above. The French in Rabat to whom the matter was again referred in writing, refused to give permission for the release of these internees. Attempts to secure the release of individuals to whom jobs had been offered had either failed or been successful only after great difficulty or long delay. People who previously received permission to take jobs outside the camps had their permission revoked.

Heath wrote that with the U.S. Army disinclined to employ the people of Axis origin, regardless of individual records, French industry would probably be inclined to follow suit and that prospects for those people were anything but encouraging.

By internees of "Axis origin" he meant, of course, Jewish refugees from Austria and Germany as well as those from countries under German occupation. Thus, these internees, who had been first persecuted by Germany and Vichy France, were, after the Allied invasion of North Africa, victimized by the Allied policies as well.

Heath recalled the program of November 24, 1942, suggested by voluntary agencies trying to help the internees.

As already noted, it was then decided to notify the camps at once "to keep quiet, that they are receiving prompt attention but that patience will be required on their part pending working out details." By January 18, 1943, Heath noted, the camps had been notified and were "reasonably quiet under the circumstances, but they are fast losing patience."

On November 24, 1942, it was recommended that the internees of Berguent—a punitive camp for Jews—be closed because of its inhuman condition and that the internees be distributed among the other camps. Dr. Wyss-Dunant, delegate of the International Red Cross to North Africa had recommended closing this camp in the summer of 1942. The French authorities, however, had continued this camp in defiance of his recommendations. By January 18, 1943, some of the men at Berguent had joined the French Foreign Legion and the Corps Franc, some (those not of Axis origin) had been allowed to join the Allied Forces in England and some had been removed to Bou Arfa.

On November 24, 1942, it was recommended that all the Poles and Czechs be removed as soon as possible. By January 18, 1943, the Czechs had left but the Polish Consul was, as noted above, been unable to secure the release of Polish Jews from Sidi-el-Ayachi.

On the same day, it was recommended that if the French authorities were unable to furnish adequate food supplies while the internees were still required to remain in the camps, then the Americans might raise the quality and quantity of the food to a reasonable standard. This had again been called to the attention of the American authorities. However, because the French authorities insisted that all supplies enter Morocco through the various business agencies, this made it increasingly difficult for the U.S. Army to donate any supplies to the voluntary agencies serving the camps. The same demand was made by the French with regard to clothing for the internees while they still had to remain in the camps.

On November 24, 1942, it was suggested that a list be prepared of all internees not likely to join the armed forces or likely to emigrate in the near future so that places could be found for them either as civilians employed by the U.S. Army or by French industry in Morocco. By January 18, 1943, progress in this direction seemed impossible, although lists of men from Im Fout, Berguent, and Casablanca and vicinity had been furnished to the American authorities.

Likewise, little was done with the suggestion that the administration of internees be turned over to the civil administration or some private voluntary organization such as the American Friends Service Committee.[210]

On June 14, 1943, Hugh S. Fullerton, Assistant Chief of the Division of European Affairs at the Department of State, forwarded to Miss Madge F. Trow of Wellesley (Mass.) a report dated May 19, 1943, and issued by the Joint Anti-Fascist Refugee Committee at 425 Fourth Avenue, New York City. The man who gave this report asked that his name be omitted.

Before leaving North Africa on March 30, 1943, the author of the report met a member of the Joint Commission on Political Prisoners and Refugees. With regard to the internees, he said that there was "not very much hope for their release." The Spanish Republicans could not be released by the Joint Commission because they did not want any trouble with Franco and his consuls in North Africa. The report continued:

> The people in the work companies are for the most part foreign legionnaires and "volunteers" for the French work companies. They work for public and private enterprises and they have worked on the construction of the Trans-Saharan Railroad. They are interned in camps and are regarded as mobilized. They are so-called members of the "produccion industrial." They are under the control of a government bureau. The management of the work companies lends the workers to official and private enterprises, and receives 45 francs for each worker from which they nourish, shelter and pay the worker. The nourishment consists of 240 grams of bread and a soup twice a day and sometimes meat, plus a pint of coffee made of date pits without sugar. Shelter in the camp on the Trans-Saharan Railroad consisted of barracks while in the worst camp at Berguent it was only holes dug in the ground. From the 45 francs received per man—the workers were paid 1 franc 25 centimes. The special workers such as the chef or the quartermaster receive 2 francs 50 centimes. The

people in these work camps are really working at slave labor. They have no rights to leave the camps.

The Americans were asked to intervene on behalf of these cases but they answered that it would not be possible for these workers are an internal problem of the French, for the French consider them as mobilized and refuse to demobilize them and therefore the United States cannot mix in the internal affairs of North Africa. Not even the Quakers have been permitted to visit these camps.

"How many of the camps have been abolished?" Berguent is the only camp that I know has been abolished. This was done before the American occupation by the French Red Cross. A woman delegate of the French Red Cross asked for permission to go to Berguent and the effect of her visit was the abolishment of the camp. The internees in Camp Berguent were sent to Bou-Arfa.

"How do the Spanish Republicans escaping from the camps live?" All those escaping from the camps head for one goal—Casablanca. There they rely on the help of the Spanish population. If a Spanish Republican obtains work with the American forces he cannot be returned to the camp from which he escaped.

"How many Spanish Republicans are in Casablanca?" I cannot say. It is very difficult for many of them are living there illegally.

When I was in Casablanca in January, 1942, one of my friends was caught by the police and put in prison for escaping from a concentration camp. He told me a very interesting story. When he was in the civil prison at Casablanca, a high functionary of the Confederacion Nacional de Trabajo of Spain (National Workers Confederation) was brought in for escaping from a concentration camp. He was caught by the Casablanca police. In general, the punishment for escaping is six months imprisonment. This man was sentenced to prison, he served 8 months and then was turned over to Franco and we learned later that he had been executed.

"How many anti-fascist refugees are there in North Africa?" Although there are thousands it is impossible to give an exact figure of the number of refugees in North Africa for the French authorities are always shifting the refugees around from one camp to another, from one labor battalion to another.

In a concentration camp, I recall hearing of President Roosevelt's request for our liberation on November 17, 1942 on the radio. I remember hearing broadcasts from London stating that all of the concentration camps had been abolished but here we were still behind barbed wire.

"How many refugees have been released?" Up to March 30, 1943, when I left North Africa, only 100 refugees (Jewish) out of the total number of refugees in North Africa had been released.

"Has there been any change in the prison personnel?" Absolutely no change whatsoever. You still have the same old collaborationist police, the same administration in Casablanca and in Morocco. You have Nogues, the well-known Vichyite Governor General in Morocco and that is sufficient for all of his people are in power.

After the occupation, the situation became a little better for the French authorities in the camps feared they would be discharged or purged. But as no changes in personnel took place and none of the guards were removed, they continued in their old ways. In Bou-Arfa, there was a rebellion. The leaders of the mutiny were put in solitary confinement and several of them died.

American newspapers are not available in North Africa. The only way to obtain one is to borrow one from an American officer and his newspaper is always one month late.

Pamphlets and material brought over by the Office of War Information for distribution in North Africa were not circulated for the OWI feared the Giraud forces. De Gaullists are illegal in Morocco. Many were put in prison after the American occupation and received brutal treatment.

During the last few months, Axis spies and criminals were removed from the prisons in which they were being held and were thrown into the concentration camps with the anti-fascist refugees. This was done purposely by the French authorities to confuse the situation and thereby hinder the release of the real anti-fascists. In the camps, however, the Axis prisoners were singled out to receive better treatment than the anti-fascist prisoners because the prison guards are their friends.

"How soon do you think the refugees will leave for Mexico?" Mexico? . . . there was no talk anywhere of any Spanish Republicans being taken to Mexico before I left North Africa. However, when I was in your office last week, I was told that the United States State Department announced that a large number of Spanish Republicans would be coming. It seems to me that this Committee is responsible to the Spanish refugees for making this promise come true.

Two months before the American occupation, an English ship carrying German and Italian prisoners as well as English citizens was wrecked off the coast of North Africa. It carried about 700 English citizens and about 500 prisoners. The survivors were picked up by a French destroyer. They were to have been taken to Dakar but only reached Casablanca. The French authorities released the Axis prisoners and sent them back to Germany and Italy and put the English into concentration camps.

The trade union movement in North Africa is still completely underground.

"What was the effect on anti-fascist refugees when they knew the American forces had landed?" The refugees were all exhilarated and excited by the knowledge that the American forces had landed. However, as I have already said, there was no change in the personnel of the guards and the treatment in the camps did not improve.

In the camps where I was, one of the anti-fascist prisoners believing that with the Americans in North Africa the fascist regime was over, tore down from the walls of the concentration camps a large picture of Pétain and threw the pieces to the winds in the yard. That afternoon, the camp Commander told him that he would receive his visa by going into the village with him and the Adjutant. The Czechoslovak anti-fascist smelled a rat and refused to go but was forced into a buggy with the Camp Commander and the guard.

However, he managed to escape from the buggy and while running away was shot through the ankle and the head. The Commander and his Adjutant seeing the man fall took it for granted he was dead but he managed to crawl back to the camp. He was placed in solitary confinement but as I was the camp doctor I was allowed to see him. He told me that he knew the Camp Commander and his Adjutant were planning to liquidate him and, therefore, he made his escape. The camp Commander years before had been in the French army but had been demoted and was made camp Commander. Shortly after the "incident" of the shooting of the Czechoslovak in the camp, the Commander was called to French headquarters and was appointed military Commander in charge of all concentration camps in that section.

The story that I have just told tonight is part of my experience of the North African concentration camp system. My personal opinion is that conditions have not changed and that the American people must work harder than ever to accomplish the release of the Spanish Republicans and the other anti-fascist refugees in North Africa.[211]

On November 11, 1942, an internee at the Djelfa camp sent the following note to a worker of the American Friends Service Committee:

Dear Friend, I beg you to have copied and corrected as you wish this report in order that it may be presented to the Allied and French Authorities by such means as are at your disposal. All that the said report contains is exact. We know that the wireless has spoken on the subject of our liberation but the management of the camp do not wish to know anything. The Polish are as badly treated as the others. The Jews are persecuted. I think that you will make a report and that in the near future it will be seen. Why do you write nothing? The bearer of this letter will, perhaps, also tell you what he knows, and if, before this letter gets through, our lot changes I think the report may still serve you. Au revoir.

Following is the report on "The Conditions of the Internees at the Djelfa Camp":

The condition of the internees, numbering about 870, has not changed since the liberation of Algeria from German protection. *Quite to the contrary in fact they have got worse.* However, the internees want only one thing—to serve the cause of the Allies. Many amongst them belong to the United Nations, Poles, Czechs, Russians and Belgians, etc., and all the others are able easily to show that the only reason for their internment was their activity against the Axis forces.

1. *470 Internees,* Spanish, old soldiers who fought in the Spanish Republican Army who have been interned for nearly four years. They have fought under the orders of their legal government in defending the country against internal revolution and the intervention of the Axis against foreign invasion of

the country.

2. *275 volunteers* of the International Brigade of the Spanish Republican Army who have fought under the orders of the legal government and who have been interned, persecuted and mocked at for four years. Amongst these are *111 Poles, 91 under the jurisdiction of U.S.S.R., 35 Germans, 11 Czechs, 9 Roumanians, 8 Austrians,* and *10 Hungarians.*

3. In total 745 old soldiers of the Spanish Republican Army, 85/100 of the internees from Djelfa Camp. People who, in spite of everything have kept intact their morale, the spirit of sacrifice and love for their people. And that in spite of the inhuman regime to which they were submitted.

4. 122 other internees called officials [collaborators] are really victims of the anti-semitic, racial and political repression. Only a very small section of this category deserve the title Official of the Sureté. Even today the Jews are victims of an attitude deliberately anti-semitic and of racial distinction on the part of the administration. There are 10 Spanish residents of Algiers who have been interned because of their activities in helping Spanish refugees—their fellow-countrymen.

There are 43 Spaniards (among the old Spanish soldiers) who resided in Algiers before their internment and who have ties, both family and econonic, in the country.

There are 12 Spaniards and many others who are in possession of visas for Mexico and the U.S.A., etc. There are more than 100 Russian citizens who should have returned in 1940 but were prevented from going by the change in Africa.

5. *Correspondence.* The camp management prevent the *sending of letters* to Allied governments and institutions as well as to their families and friends. It is sufficient that a letter treats even indirectly with the problem of liberation for it to be returned or spoiled.

6. *Bullying.* The internees are victims of a regime of repression deliberately more marked since the Allied troops liberated Algeria. One retains the impression that the internees are exasperated [driven to exasperation] in order to be able to justify, if events make it necessary, the notoriously inhuman regime of the past.

The report added that about 50 internees at Djelfa were suffering from serious diseases, about 50 were over 50 years of age and 20 were infirm or war invalids. The internees suffered from epidemics; "the infirmary is lodged in ceilingless cabin," etc.[212]

During a Parliamentary debate in the House of Commons which took place on March 24, 1943, it was stated that at Djelfa, prisoners were sent to the "dungeons" at Fort Cavacelli and often horsewhipped naked, in front of other prisoners.[213]

The report of May 19, 1943, thus described the conditions at Djelfa:

I will tell you first about the situation of the Spanish Republicans and about 300 members of the International Brigade in the Camp of Djelfa. Camp Djelfa, in immigration circles, is considered as the worst concentration camp that ever existed in North Africa. Djelfa is a camp for political internees. It is a counterpart of the camp of Vernet in France. The most "dangerous" people from the camp of Vernet were deported to Camp Djelfa in North Africa. Djelfa is situated on the terminus of the Algerian railroad that goes from the coast to the interior. It is situated in the Middle Atlas mountains and near the Sahara.

In Djelfa, besides the 600 Spanish Republicans and about 300 members of the International Brigade, there are some 30 or 40 emigres from Germany and Austria. The camp is about 100 kilometers away from the nearest village. It is forbidden for the internees to go to the town. The camp is surrounded with three rows of barbed wire and a machine gun is posted at every corner of the camp attended by a sentry. The Commander of the camp is a French officer who has been Commander of Camp Barcares, one of the camps for Spanish Republicans and International Brigaders in France. He is a sadist who uses narcotics and is a drunkard. I left this camp in October, 1941. Every morning he would put about 8, 10 or 12 internees in prison for no reason whatsoever. First, they are severely beaten. The prison consists of a cell built out of cement with a little window at the corner of the cell and with a cement block that was supposed to be the bed. It is forbidden to take blankets or overcoats into the cell. Many of the people put in this jail have asked me to give you a picture of the cell for most of the members of the International Brigade and many of the Spanish Republicans have been in this prison for days, some of them for a month or more.

A group of 12 members of the International Brigade, among them a doctor, were imprisoned for thirty days for having made fire in the camp for making coffee from toasted date pits. The food is rationed. We received daily about 240 grams (3 ounces) of Arab bread and half a pint of coffee made of toasted date pits. For dinner and supper we had soup made of water and carrots or turnips. Sometimes we received a little piece of meat.

All of the internees in Djelfa are really starving. They have lost about 30 pounds each and are very weak and therefore are very susceptible to disease. In 1941, 18 persons were ill from tuberculosis. There also was a typhoid epidemic with a loss of 16 lives. There is a big barrack in this camp that serves as an infirmary. It consists of a room with 40 beds and a consulting room. When the epidemic started, the big sick room was soon filled and we had to leave the other patients in the tents. Twelve people occupied a tent. The sick had to live with the other internees. We once received about 50 cans of unsugared condensed milk. The diet for typhoid is a cup of hot milk every two hours. The box of 50 cans of milk was used up in a day and a half. We had a very difficult problem with nutrition for the sick. We tried to get all the potatoes from the kitchen for them. The Commander prohibited giving all of the potatoes. The only nourishment for the sick was potatoes cooked without salt. We never received medicines from the French authorities. We sometimes received medicines from relief organizations.

The internees lack shoes. The Spanish Republicans and the International Brigaders left Spain with poor clothing and it was never replaced during the time that they were in France. They came to Djelfa without any clothing. In the summer they wore sandals made from alfalfa. The sandals created wounds on the feet and wounds are not very quickly healed in the Sahara. They easily became infected. In winter, there is about three feet of snow in the camp.

The French Commander of this camp put some of the internees in prison every morning. This was a daily feature of the camp. Beatings were also meted out daily. This is the situation in Camp Djelfa.[214]

Kenneth G. Crawford's guide at Bou Arfa was a Spaniard named José Campos Peral, once the editor of *Lucha,* a left republican newspaper in Almeria which supported the government against the Franco rebels. When Franco won, Peral fled to Oran where he was interned at Cherchell. In June 1940, he was sent into the desert with otmers from Cherchel to work on the railroad.

At first Peral was paid one franc, or ten centimes a day. Later, when the French became self-conscious about the attention their forced labor camps were attracting throughout the world, his pay was raised to 20 francs a day. In February 1943, after the Americans had started investigating the affairs of the internees, Peral's pay was boosted to 70 francs a day, from which 25 francs were deducted for food.

> The French had even invented the fiction that internees remaining in the camps were now free men working under legitimate contract, after the manner of contract workers in metropolitan France. Technical freedom in Bou Arfa was meaningless. The camp is surrounded by razorbacks which could be scaled only with difficulty and even if one got out of the bowl it would be hundreds of miles through the desert to civilization. Desert Arabs knew they would be rewarded for returning escaped prisoners dead or alive. Unless they could get passage on the railroad, which was impossible without the consent of its officials, the free men on Bou Arfa could do nothing about their freedom.

The buildings of the camp were separated by wide streets of desert gravel. Through these streets walked or rode native troopers in Arab dress with rifles slung over their shoulders, "a large and sinister-looking force if its purpose was merely to police the affairs of a community of free men." Crawford saw the kitchen, where "a stew compounded principally of fresh cabbage and water" was simmering in crude cast-iron kettles. Many months after the Allied landing "a picture of Marshall Pétain was still the principal backbar decoration" in the *Foyer des Travailleurs.*[215]

The camp of Kenadsa supplied forced labor for the local low grade coal mines (these mines were one of the excuses for building the Trans-Saharian railroad). At the Kenadsa camp Crawford met W. H. B. Simons, son of Dr. Hellmuth Simons, the eminent German-Jewish authority on tropical diseases. Young Simons and his father had been interned at Marseilles in the fall of 1939 on their way to the United States where the elder Simons, after studying tropical diseases at the Pasteur Institute in Paris, had been offered a chair at a Pennsylvania university. The boy had enlisted in the Foreign Legion, had gone to Sidi-bel-Abbès and was then sent to a forced labor camp. Another of the Kenadsa inmates was Louis de Teran who had been arrested in Algiers shortly after the Americans arrived, presumably because he was suspected of pre-invasion services to Robert Murphy. A group of Spanish orchard workers who were arrested in Oran for drinking wine and demonstrating in celebration of the Allied landing also found themselves at Kenadsa.[216]

On December 12, 1942, the 3rd and 4th *Groupe de Travailleurs Etrangers Démobilises—GTED* (Group of Alien Demobilized Workers) at the Kenadsa camp protested against the camp receiving 87 Germans and Italians who were recently arrested. They started a protest addressed to the commanding officer of the territory of Ain Sefra at Colomb-Béchar:

> We dare to hope that such a monstrosity will not happen. However, in case that, against all expectations, such measure will be carried out, we must protest against such procedure. The regime of "collaborators" interned us, since 1940, us, who, volunteers, against Fascism, took the arms in the ranks of the allied nations. At the same time, certain individuals enjoy their liberty and favors of the Axis and their accomplices. One month after the constitution in Northern Africa of a front of the Allied Nations, one find nothing better to do than to try to mix us with henchmen and profiteers of Fascism. Ex-volunteers of the French Army and ex-members of the British Expeditionary Force insulted as "dirty Jews," "sluts," "Gaullists," we will have to be assimilated to the partisans of the Axis at a moment when the Anglo-Saxon action will at least render to us justice and liberty.
>
> The instigators of this plot imagine that in this way they will be able to deceive the world and the Anglo-American authorities. Not one had already tried, for reasons to be investigated, to try to present the internees as highly suspected individuals and enemies of the Allied Nations.
>
> While waiting for our liberty, which is already too much delayed, we ask immediately not to be assimilated *in any way* with the new arrivals.[217]

According to a report of the American Friends Service Committee the internees of GTE No. 2 (at Kenadsa), GTE No. 2 (at Colomb-Béchar), and GTE No. 6 (at Hadjerat M'Guil, near Béni-Ounif) complained in January 1943 that

> Any attempt to reach Anglo-Saxon forces was callously hindered . . . Neither the Americans nor the English wanted foreign labor or soldiers (although various comrades already have invitations from U.S. authorities) . . . Heaps of letters have been written to British and American authorities to ask them to come and to take us collectively over; but no positive answer has arrived yet, and we ignore the reason of this mishap. In the meantime, vexations continue. Camp officers told the Corps Francs Commissions that "these dirty Jews and Boches ought to be severely interned."[218]

In January 1943, the internees of Kenadsa were able to smuggle out the following appeal "For the English and American Authorities":

> We refugees of the Hitlerian fashisme—belonging to the so-called 3° and 4° foreign demobilised workers Companys, are nearly all interned by the order of Vichy (Darlan et Pétain). The fourth group is officially called the Company of doubtful elements (Compagnie des douteux). Most of us have families and friends in Great Britain and in the U.S.A.
> All of us are ex-volunteers for the duration of the war or members of the A.M.B.C. (R.E.F.). The big majority of us are Jews.
> Vichy's manners are going on here. Up to date we have been treated as dirty communists, dirty Jews; now they are trying to treat us as "Boches." The authorities which we are depending on, do their utmost to prevent us from communicating directly with the American and British liberators. Our numerous letters and wires to the English and American authorities, posted these last days, have been intercepted.
> All of us, we want to put our forces in the service of English and Americans. In contrast you will perfectly understand that after an internment of two years and a half, the interest of being enlisted in any sort of French formation (exception made for the troups of the General de Gaulle) is rather small amongst us.
> A special report will be sent on murders and mansloughters, committed on unfortunate comrades of ours, interned in the so-called "group of discipline."
> We are about 2,000 men (Kenadsa, Colomb-Béchar, Bou Arfa, Saida).[219]

The internees of Kenadsa sent the following letter to the Allied forces signed by H. Hartmut Weil and G. Rothenstein:

> Gentlemen,
> We are very sorry for bothering you with this letter. But we do not know any other way to contact you safely.

DO YOU KNOW
THAT THERE ARE MORE THAN 600 VICHY INTERNED FOREIGNERS IN THE REGION OF COLOMB-BÉCHAR (without the Spanish refugees)?

They come from almost all European nations; there are Poles amongst them, Czechs, Rumanians, Hungarians, Belgians, Spaniards (that were war-volunteers in 1939) and many Austrian and German refugees (Jews or political enemies of Hitler's regime, amongst them various outstanding personalities, newspapermen, attorneys, engineers, former Saar officials). Almost all of them contracted a military engagement in one of the Allied Armies in 1939 (the majority in the French Army, a minority in the AMPC of the British Expeditionary Forces). After the armistice they were interned by the Vichy authorities and sent here.

THAT OUR INTERNMENT HAS BEEN HARD?

We could not count with the protection by any consul or by reprisals from friendly nations. We were absolutely at the mercy of our staff that was composed of former N.C.O.'s (remainders of the pre-fascist "Black Reichswehr" that had to emigrate to France and eventually served in the Foreign Legion without losing their character); Italians, constantly drunk White Russians and various brands of socially uninteresting Frenchmen (that tried to profit at our expense) or Frenchmen of the foreigner-hater type. Corruption was incredible (many "officers" and members of the staff had to be dismissed for theft, lack of personal integrity and so on, and some have appeared in front of military-courts, the scandals having grown too big!) The lodgings are partly indescribable (such as those at Kenadsa!). The clothes we obtained were rotten. The hygiene was worse than at the times of the cavemen. We were absolutely in the hands of these men, had no legal protection, no right to defend ourselves against accusations of the "disciplinary transfer" to the "camp for repression" at Hadjerat M'Guil, near Béni-Ounif. There real murders have been committed on helpless prisoners (quite a lot of them, as witnesses state, either by undernourishment and its consequences or by beating men to pieces).

THAT OUR "GUARDIANS" DO EVERYTHING IN THEIR POWER TO PREVENT US FROM COMMUNICATING WITH THE ANGLO-SAXONS OR THE GENUINE GAULLISTS?

Our letters and wires to American, English and Gaullist authorities or representatives are intercepted at Béchar; also some we sent to our families. Nobody is allowed to go to Algiers or Oran, at present. The men of the "staff" know why they do this, of course. They want by all means to prevent you from re-examining the immediate past in the spirit of President Roosevelt's declarations about the punishments against Fascists that have tortured their adversaires and about the liberation of political prisoners. They try to shake off their past as officials of a Fascist regime, to wash off their crimes against helpless interned, to stay at the head of an organization that has been so profitable for them. They try, by isolating us, to be the only ones to speak about us to the High

Authorities, thus being able to discredit us, the genuine "Gaullistes," for being "Boches" or "revolutionaries." They shall try to manoevure in the following way: To "offer" to us an engagement in some corps that looks like the Foreign Legion, and to await the refusal that will come (as we have suffered enough amongst the mercenaries), in order to be able once more to consider us—without asking the Anglo-Saxons—as "interned men," "enemies," they themselves staying with us as our "staff," our "guardians."

THAT ALMOST ALL OF US WANT TO ENLIST UNDER ANGLO-SAXON COMMAND?

Most people have their families, their relatives or close acquaintances in England or America (and know how decently these refugees have always been treated). France, on the other hand, has never treated us in the expected way. The broken words of honor cannot be counted (and hundreds of witnesses are here to give their testimony). We've been sort of forced into Foreign Legion units (instead of normal units) where we have suffered a lot from the mercenaries and the Nazi staff. Later, in the concentration-camps, we have been severely injured in our personal honor. In any case—and in spite of all individual friendships everybody of us has with some Frenchmen—we cannot get past a feeling of distrust against the French authorities. And especially at the present moment while men like DARLAN and CHATEL who have been severely anti-British and anti-foreigner are still at power after having simply changed their shirt, thus taking the wind out of the sails of decent Gaullists who have fought during years with the United Nations.

THAT WE ARE BREATHLESSLY AWAITING THE ARRIVAL OF AN ANGLO-SAXON COMMISSION TO EXAMINE OUR SITUATION?

We have already written many letters to Algiers, to the American authorities, to British representatives, to Gaullists, to a famous lawyer: Without an answer, our letters having visibly been intercepted at Béchar. We have wired to all friends and to our parents; but only one or two replies have come to the most "harmless" and personal wires. Our situation is still bad. We're still in the hands of those who, under the orders of Vichy and the German Armistice Commission, kept us here as prisoners. PLEASE DO NOT FORGET US!! We all of us want to contribute in one way or the other, as soldiers or workers, to the victory of the UNITED NATIONS!![220]

An "Account on several cases of murder and serious ill-treatment in the French concentration camps" was sent from Kenadsa by Friedrich Schnek of Vienna, a volunteer legionnaire who had been sent to North Africa and interned after the Franco-German armistice. According to his report, Hadjerat M'Guil was a disciplinary camp ("center of repression") and internees were sent there for political reasons. He described the case of Gerhard Lewinstein, a German-Jewish refugee who had volunteered for service in 1939 and who found himself in the Foreign Legion. Occasionally he complained of the treatment in the Legion and was, as a result, sent to the "Compagnie de Discipline" of the Foreign Legion. After the Armistice, he was also sent to the "Groupe de Discipline" at Colomb-Béchar. His death came about in the following manner: One day he was ordered to the railway station to unload sacks of sugar. One of these sacks was torn and sugar fell to the ground. Lewinstein took some of this sugar and ate it. The supervisor, Dotti, put him into jail. From then on, he was compelled to fetch his food in the kitchen "en pas gymnastique" (double time). When he arrived at the jail (200 meters from the cookhouse), his meal had spilled. Besides that, the food was salted in such a way by Dotti and another man named Dauphin that it was practically impossible for Lewinstein to swallow the hot water and beetles it consisted of. Dotti, it may be added, constantly mistreated Lewinstein and forced him to perform the hardest tasks. These tasks consisted mainly of transporting stone blocks of 25 to 40 kilograms. After a few days of imprisonment, Lewinŝtein was incredibly weak, resembled a corpse and could only crouch, until finally he was no longer able to reach the toilet where he had to be carried by two of his comrades (Liffmann and Max Wolff). At last, the sanitary man urged the commander to nourish Lewinstein properly and to leave him alone. Eventually, Lewinstein was fed mostly fat meat from the N.C.O. mess. But after one week of starvation, Lewinstein was utterly incapable of digesting such heavy meals. He vomited instantly. By chance, two days before Lewinstein's death, a doctor from Ain-Sefra visited the camp and saw him. The doctor ordered his evacuation to the Oran Hospital at once. Yet the order was not followed and two days later Lewinstein was dead. The medical examination concluded that "faiblesse générale" (general weakness) was the cause of his death.[221]

According to Schnek's report the Chief Adjutant Finidori of Kenadsa had a dog who was given meals from the N.C.O. mess on a plate. On several occasions hungry internees threw themselves at the meals served to the dog. The internee Nazarian was so hungry that on several occasions he caught snakes, cooked them and ate them. He soon died.[222]

Kenneth G. Crawford thus described the death of an internee named Moreno at M'Guil before the American landing. The commandant named Mosca, addressing his soldiers the day of Moreno's arrival, was quoted as saying, "Look at him well. This is Moreno. He is a criminal who has been violent." Then to Moreno: "You have come here to perish. We have been told that you must die." The next day Dourmanoff, another official of the camp, said to Moreno, "Take a good look at the graveyard. In four or five days you will be lying under the ground here." In the next few days Moreno was systematically tortured and became almost unrecognizable. He was commanded to run long distances loaded down with water or with wood. During these times he was commanded to throw himself on the ground and to get up again. When he spilled water he was struck with iron bars and wooden clubs. When he fell to the ground unconscious, he was thrown into a cold cell naked to the waist. Upon regaining consciousness he was fed a sickening solution of pepper, salt and paprika in hot water. His eyes became glazed and he took on the appearance of an idiot. On September 25, 1942, he was ordered to the mortuary to await his own death. He died that night and was quickly buried. A medical officer issued a certificate of death from heart disease. Affidavits covering eight other similar deaths were submitted to the American authorities resulting in a demand for a thorough investigation and prompt punishment of the perpetrators of these outrages. But what became of the investigation Crawford could never learn.[223]

A group of internees of G.T.E. No. 3 at the Camp of Kenadsa sent out the following report:

On March 3, 1943, the internees again protested the preparations being made for a new prison. The internee Henry Posner, an ex-volunteer legionnaire, told the Chief of the GTE who was named Letor: "We don't need a prison, we will leave soon, and besides, there are now people who protect us." In reply, Letor began insulting the internees, using coarse, indecent language and reproaching them for having enlisted to fight against the Germans and Italians, etc.[224]

A report smuggled out by about 100 internees at Ain el Ourak, a disciplinary camp of forced labor, located approximately 80 kilometers from Bou Arfa, served as basis for the report sent in August 1942 to the O.S.S. in Washington.[225]

On February 24, 1943, as a result of many protests, the French authorities prohibited the practice of punishment called *tombeau* at the labor camps. This terrible punishment was replaced by imprisonment. It should be noted that this punishment had been abolished before the war but it continued to be practiced in the forced labor camps.[226]

On November 26, 1942, Otto Jacobsen of the 9th group of foreign workers (Travailleurs Etrangers) at the Camp Im Fout wrote to Madame Courtin, Chairman of the Comité d'Aide aux Engagés Volontaires Etrangers dans l'Armée Française (Committee to Aid the Foreign Volunteers in the French Army) at 93 rue Coli in Casablanca:

> I hope you received my last letter of November 19th. I take the liberty to give you now the following facts: some days ago we were informed that we could volunteer at the Foreign Legion. *Nobody* here moved. This could have been foreseen, and our superiors should have known that the Engagés Volontaires have no trust in the Foreign Legion. The non-commissioned officers of the Legion were Germans in practically all cases, and they were ready for everything except to fight against Hitler's Germany. They proved that by their behaviour against us. Following their expression we volunteered only "for the dish." In the working camps we met the same non-commissioned officers. We hardly ever were considered as volunteers but much more as a kind of war prisoners or white slaves. Many of our comrades were so exasperated by this treatment that they preferred to go back to Germany.
>
> To-day the Captain of our camp made us a little speech telling us that it was projected to form an armed company, some kind of a free corps, with him as Captain and our surveyors as lieutenant and sergeants. Our surveyors are, excepted one, all Germans. Since we know them for more than a year as well as the behaviour of our superiors, nobody has any trust to them, and the answer of our comrades was unanimous and clear refusal.
>
> Furthermore nobody knows who is at the origin of this plan, and we do not believe that is has been authorized by the competent authorities. Our refusal does not mean that we are not willing to fight against nazism. Most of us have proved and already before the war by their urgent wish to volunteer in the French Army. Now it has become in the first place a question of the appropriated formations where we could serve.
>
> Allow me, Madame, to tell you that we are here very nervous and upset, and that it would be highly desirable to give us some clear information on our situation. There are many rumours of all kind. We would be very grateful if you could give us continual informations about the developments concerning us.[227]

On February 28, 1943, David S. Hartley and Kendall Kimberland visited the camp of alien workers (Camp de Travailleurs Etrangers) No. 12 where the internees worked for the Production Industrielle. The camp was located 2 kilometers from Settat, in the midst of a rather densely wooded area. It was on the site of a reforestation area, which was begun 17 years earlier with Arab labor. Consequently, the woods were enough to give considerable shade to the camp itself which was located on a small hill. The trees were originally planted in order to help retain the moisture from the rain. There were some 85 residents in the camp representing two groups, ex-legionnaires who had signed up for the duration of the war and old-time ex-legionnaires. There were also a half-dozen Frenchmen whose status was not definitely known, but who were said to be there because they were unemployed. The majority of the men were of German origin with a smattering of Italians, Austrians, Spaniards and Russians. The camp was under the direction of a lieutenant, apparently of Polish origin, and several under-officers who all lived in the town of Settat and commuted to the camp by car.

The camp consisted of three barracks capable of sleeping 30 men each. The barracks were constructed of stone, with mud instead of cement used for joining. The roofs consisted of many branches laid parallel with the ridge with a thin covering of cement or mud. One of the major complaints was the fact that the roofs afforded inadequate protection against rain. In one case a man had stretched an extra blanket above his bed as shelter against the rain. The men said that after a rainy spell they were allowed a day off from work in order to dry their bed clothing. The interior of each barrack had a row of beds along each side with the heads to the wall. Each bed was merely four cement blocks on which rested two poles. Between these poles was stretched any kind of material from reeds to chicken-wire with pine boughs or straw for softening. For covers the men had one full size blanket and one half-size blanket with additional supplies available in case of sickness. The floors of these buildings was earth. The cooking was done in a shed which resembled the barracks, but was much more roughly built and less conveniently located. The men received their food in front of the cooking shed in two shifts and sat around in a small circle eating on ·stones. All water had to be carried from the spring about 300 metres from the main barracks, and all drinking water had to be carried in a horsedrawn tank made from an old 60 gallon oil drum and a couple of wheels. There was an arrangement near the spring for washing clothes that was made of concrete. There the men tried to beat out the dirt, little soap being available. There were some men in the camp, according to one informant, who did not wish to leave if they were freed. These men were largely old-time legionnaires of 15 or more years standing or French pensionnaires, whose motivation waś, in some cases, to escape family responsibility. Some of these men received 600 francs a month, and one whose offspring were numerous was reported to have received as much as 2,800 francs. For reasons known only to the French administrators of these labor camps men who volunteered to defend France were classified as slave laborers together with these old-time ex-legionnaires under the supervision of legionnaires still in the service.[228]

Camp Oued-Akreuch was visited by Hartley on March 16, 1943. It was located near a quarry "with all of its dust and grime." The camp was made up of some 50 Europeans who were then in the camp and some 150 detached men of Central European and Spanish origin. These men were farmed out under contracts varying from three months to a year to private employers, and it was reported that there was a daily premium paid to the government in Rabat for each man. The men lived in buildings that looked more like a place for animals than people. One of the men called them "Schweinestall." They were rudely constructed of stone and sun-dried bricks put together with mud. The bricks were made without straw, and hence lasted for only a short time in that weather. The buildings were long and low, divided into stalls along each side, each stall housing two men. The beds were made of reeds or perhaps wire stretched between two poles. There was no light except from the door at one end and a small window at the opposite end. The floors of these buildings were a step or two below ground level. The cookhouse was similar to the other buildings, and, in spite of the weather the men were forced to eat outside. Although there was a quarry nearby there was no work available for these men, and, as a consequence, they were paid only 1.25 francs a day. At this rate the men were able to buy one packet of cigarettes every four days. The problem of clothing was the same as in all the other camps. There was no way of getting extra clothes; consequently, most men had only one set without changes. Here, all men had one idea in mind, and that was freedom. "Most all of them would like to work for the Americans, and are simply waiting until some arrangements can be made for that," Hartley reported.[229]

Kurt Caro, former chief editor of *Berliner Volkszeitung* and later of the *Pariser Tageszeitung*, volunteered for the duration of the war. He was demobilized in October 1940 and was immediately interned in the forced labor camp of Colomb-Béchar. After the Allied landing he was freed in May 1943 and was employed by the Psychological Warfare Branch of the American Army and later at the *Alger Républicain*. On December 27, 1943, he was again interned at the *Centre de Séjour Surveillé* (Center of Surveilled Residence) of Mechata without any explanation by order of the French Commanding General of the Division of Alger.[230]

On March 22, 1943, T. Stern of Marinha Grande, Portugal, wrote to Robert Murphy:

My cousin, Henry Coehen, 22, Italien naturalised, are now in one concentration camp in North Africa near Rabat for thes following reasons: My cousin is a

JEW and he is born in Turkey, and later adopted the Italien nationality just after de 2nd [First] World ware [War], and he came to Italy he was living until the present ware begun. When Italie adopted the anti-simitsme, he was forced to left [leave] Italie with his parents and enter in France. Immediately when Italie declared the ware to France, so [in order to] safe [save] his parents from the concentration camp in France he entered as volontaire in the French Army [Foreign Legion] and paid to France by this way the price for the liberty of his parents.

When France collapsed, the Vichy Government send him to North Africa in one concentration camp as a jew, and forget that this people served this country.

When thes Americens enter in North Africa he was free but shortly after he was put again in the concentration campe as a JEW again and now he are still in the concentration camp, ill, without any money, without any cloth and bad of morality after havin supported all this injustices why he are one jew.

When France colapsed, the Vichy Government delivered his parents to the Italien Government and his old father mother was put in one concentration camp, why he [they] are jews . . He [his] younger brother has been shortly after crached by one Italian military truck.

I request you to no allow this injustice, why thes[e] jews of the whole world have the only hope in the United States of America and it not policy of the United Sates to adopt the anti-semitisme.[231]

On February 21, 1943, Hartley, Leslie O. Heath and Kendall G. Kimberland visited the camp Sidi-el-Ayachi, a fairly humane camp situated outside the town of Azemour. At that time the camp was directed by a new "understanding" artillery officer of the French army who was anxious that the internees be freed so that he could return to army duty. The camp was a place for women and children and men who were unable to work because of age or sickness. Just the same, there were a number of men there, particularly Spaniards who seemed able and anxious to work, although technically on the sick list. At that time there were about 125 men, women and children in the camp. Among the men, the majority were Spaniards, although there were a number of internees of other nationalities as well. The women comprised many nationalities. Within the walls were 6 or 7 long barracks-like buildings, some of which were not partitioned, serving as dormitories for the single people or social halls. Others were divided into rooms about 10 feet wide, enough for two people with crude beds and meager baggage and equipment. One of the buildings had a room which had been set aside as a school containing a few bare tables and benches. It was made attractive in spite of its surroundings, by a foot-wide blue band around the room on which a former internee, a Russian, had painted white silhouettes of squirrels, rabbits, elephants, etc. "Emigration is probably the only escape for many of these people although some of the women will doubtless gain their freedom when their husbands, in other camps, are freed," the report concluded.[232]

XXII. Join the Foreign Legion or Go to Prison

After the liberation of North Africa Leslie O. Heath, delegate of the American Friends Service Committee reported on the camps:

> There have been some attempts by French officials to force some of these men again to "volunteer" in the French Foreign Legion. With their past experience it is unlikely that any will do so and there is grave danger that further attempts by the French to force them will provoke serious incidents.[233]

On February 3, 1943, Heath again reported:

> The French attempted to force the internees into the Foreign Legion under threat that all who did not "volunteer" would be denounced to the Americans as Fascists. After having volunteered in the Legion at the outbreak of the war and then, with the fall of France, to be rewarded by two years of forced labor naturally did not create good will and these attempts to force them back into the Legion again were greatly resented and were the cause of several incidents. A Frenchman internationally well known, and an internationally known neutral citizen had both advised the French authorities in Rabat that such a policy would almost certainly cause widespread trouble; but nevertheless the Foreign Legion recruiting campaign has been continued, though it has produced few recruits.[234]

A similar report was made by Jacques Oettinger of HICEM, a Jewish migration agency. For a time volunteers were accepted for a new French military unit, the Corps Franc. Heath reported in his report of February 3 noted above that the Corps Franc was set up under Admiral Henri Honoré Giraud, to recruit men regardless of nationality or race. Col. Cau was in command of this venture in Morocco and was said to be a good man. A number of god Frenchmen have joined this organization as well as a few men who have left the camps. It appeared, however, that Col. Cau had not been given permission by the French authorities of Rabat to visit the camps in order to make a direct appeal for volunteers. In view of past experiences, many internees viewed the Corps Franc with suspicion. Indeed, on February 10, 1943, the French military authorities announced at all forced labor camps that no more volunteers would be accepted. Those wanting to enlist could only sign up for the Legion.[235]

On April 27, 1943, Giraud announced that alien internees who were nationals of countries who had consular representatives in French Africa, would be at the disposal of their respective representatives, the latter having the responsibility of insuring repatriation or support. All other alien political internees in North Africa except for nationals of Axis Powers, would be liberated, on the condition that a) they volunteer either for the Foreign Legion, the Corps Franc d'Afrique or the British Pioneer Corps; b) depart for a foreign country which would accept their immigration; c) sign contracts with a public or private enterprise in French Africa acceptable to the Commander in Chief. If not accepted freely, these contracts would be proposed to the internees by the Service of Algerian Economy or by the management of Public Works, Communications and Labor in Morocco. A right of priority was granted to ex-soldiers of the Foreign Legion. In any case, alien internees would be submitted to civilian requisition in the spirit of the decree of April 12, 1939.[236]

According to a report of March 10, 1943, to the U.S. Department of State "the majority of the Central European refugees" expressed a willingness to join the British Pioneer Corps. However, most Spaniards refused to serve not only in the Foreign Legion but also in the British Pioneer Corps as well; they expressed a desire to emigrate to Mexico or await events in Spain or work where they pleased in North Africa. The Allied Authorities were not happy with the Spaniards' attitude which they ascribed to the influence of "political" leaders.[237] Some ex-internees worked for the United States army, but as employees of the Compagnie Méditeranée-Niger—the same company for which they were working as slave labor—to construct barracks and hangars for the United States Air Corps at slave wages.[238]

Arthur Negroni, an Italian, had lived in France since the age of 8. At the outbreak of the war he volunteered for service but refused to join the Legion. Later he signed up to fight in the Garibaldi Legion, was demobilized in Toulouse and in December 1943 came to French Morocco via Spain to fight for the Allies. In Casablanca he was told he could either serve in the Foreign Legion or go to prison. He chose prison.[239] At Kenadsa one officer said, "I shall not leave Kenadsa until the last Jew has been sent to the army," i.e. the regular French Foreign Legion.[240]

Claude Ganz, a German-Jewish refugee and ex-legionnaire (a volunteer), arrived from Spain on June 13, 1943, and enlisted in the French Air Force of North Africa. After having served for a time with the 151st Transport Company of the Air Force camp at Blida, he was sent to the Foreign Legion at Sidi-bel-Abbès and forced to enlist as a legionnaire. On November 19, 1943, Thomas Pym Cope, Regional Chief of the United States Civil Affairs Office wrote to Paul W. Gordon, Acting Chief of Mission, that Ganz had been sent to the Foreign Legion "in a manner which does not seem to be entirely just." Jacques Oettinger, a Jewish migration worker at Casablanca, had seen documents proving that Ganz had signed up for the French Air Force and not the Legion.[241]

Gerard and Hans Schmidt were German refugees who left Germany in 1937 and 1939 respectively, because of their anti-Nazi convictions. They went to France where they joined their father who, having rendered notable services to France in the early twenties and having suffered as a result under the Nazi regime, had left Germany in 1935. Both brothers volunteered for the Legion in October 1939 serving there from January to September 1940 and from March to September 1940, respectively, when they both were "honorably discharged." Even so they were required to remain in "labor camps" in French Morocco until July 1941 and April 1941. They made application for immigration to the United States as early as October 1940. These applications were renewed in 1943, having been supported by the American Friends Service Committee and by both H. Earle Russell, American Consul General in Casablanca, and Edwin C. Wilson, Representative of the United States in Algiers. Since November 16, 1942, both Gerard and Hans had been working for American organizations. In spite of their service to France, these two young men were considered as "enemy aliens" by the French authorities who had taken the position that these subjects must either rejoin the Foreign Legion or be interned. The question was raised in October 1943, but since both subjects were trying to emigrate to the United States, the French Commissariat for Foreign Affairs agreed to grant the request of Robert D. Murphy, the American Representative that the Schmidts continue working with the American organizations until their departure for the United States; no time limit was set. Later, however, the matter was reopened by the French, for whom it was understood to have become a "cause célèbre" because of its reflection on French sovereignty. The French had, in effect, said that the brothers must choose by May 15, 1944 between reinternment and the Foreign Legion. In order to ameliorate the situation and, at the same time, protect the brothers from having to elect either solution offered by the French, Kendal G. Kimberland of the AFSC requested on May 5, 1944 that permission be obtained for the Schmidts to be inducted into the U.S. Army.[242]

Hans Ornstein, a German-Jewish refugee, first came to the Civil Affairs Office of the U.S. Army on September 30, 1943, at which time he described in detail to Eric W. Johnson the harsh treatment he had received during his stay at the disciplinary camp of Hadjerat M'Guil. He was tortured so that he finally, under duress, "accepted" an engagement in the Foreign Legion in order to prevent his being killed. His story sounded "interesting" and Johnson asked him to write it down for him in detail, which Ornstein did. This deposition was sent to the French authorities on October 6 (Dr. Marcel Carret, Chief Adjoint to the Cabinet du Dr. Abadie, Lycée Fromentin, Algiers). Dr. Carret replied on October 20 saying that he had transmitted the dossier to the appropriate office.

About a month earlier the newspapers had reported that many of the officers of Camp Hadjerat M'Guil, having been guilty of atrocities, had been arrested and punished. However, this proved to be of no benefit to Hans Ornstein who came again into Johnson's office on February 10, 1944 to say that he was still in the Legion. Ornstein's position was that his enlistment in the Legion was not valid since it was acceded to under duress. He wished to leave the Legion to do one of two things, either to join the British Pioneer Corps or to go to Palestine where his sister was living. He was in good health and fit for military service. He had studied engineering for two years and was an experienced technician in all aspects of automobile mechanics. His occupation with the Legion was that of driving and maintaining armored vehicles.[243]

Many of those who refused to sign up for the Legion were sent—after the Allies landed in North Africa—to the prison camp of Ain el Ourak. In the beginning of April 1943, about 900 internees of German and Austrian origin in six labor camps went on a two-week hunger strike. They declined to see representatives of the American Red Cross who came to the camps with food. Soon 280 Jews of Rumanian and Hungarian origin joined the hunger strike. The strike ended after one week as a result of an announcement that the internees would be liberated on condition that they would emigrate from North Africa within six months.[244]

Even Frenchmen and refugees from Spain "had to sign up for the Foreign Legion," but once in Africa, they were able sometimes to find alternate service.[245]

What was the attitude of the non-Vichy, Free French forces of General de Gaulle in London, towards volunteers assigned to the Legion? According to a HICEM report from Lisbon, former legionnaires who had escaped from France to Spain were not accepted, "because of purely administrative reasons" in the regular Free French Armed Forces. They were given a choice between joining the Foreign Legion in Syria via Equatorial Africa or remaining in a Spanish camp.[246]

We mentioned earlier that Polish internees were often liberated but, according to the Polish authorities in exile, the French would not allow to include Polish Jews among them. However, the Polish authorities also discriminated against members of the International Brigade of the Spanish Republican Army, especially if they were Jews. In September 1943, eight Polish refugees were liberated from Gibraltar by the Polish authorities for "humanitarian reasons." They were given the opportunity of joining the Polish forces in England, but the authorities asked them to sign special papers which were not requested of other Poles. The men thought the reason for this was because they fought in the International Brigade, that they were Communists, or Jewish. After their refusal to sign these papers, they were sent to North Africa. The men preferred to join the Russian instead of the Polish army and stated that if this were impossible they would immediately volunteer for the British Pioneer Corps.[247]

When Count Czapski, the head of the Polish Red Cross, visited the Djelfa camp, his first question addressed to Poles was, "Are you Polish or Jewish?" To Jews he said that the Poles did not need them.[248]

In a report dated January 15, 1943, Robert D. Murphy informed the State Department of Count Czapski's tour of inspection at Djelfa where 850 men were then interned. Almost all of those included in this group were members of the International Brigade which had moved into France after the conclusion of the Civil War in Spain in February 1939. This group of internees included 23 different nationalities. The count stated that he was particularly concerned about the 148 internees who stated that they were Polish nationals for about one-half of these were Jewish. After speaking with each internee individually Count Czapski stated that it was his considered opinion that only a few of them would be able to fully establish their claim to Polish nationality and be eligible for service with the Army of Poland.[249]

Fritz Holschuler left Poland in 1938 for France where he immediately joined the Foreign Legion; he was demobilized on December 29, 1943. Holschuler was "not recognized by the Polish Consulate because he is Jewish and because of his Legion service."[250] Crawford reported the case of a young Polish-Jewish doctor named Heller who was interned at Kenadsa. He had served in the International Brigade in the Spanish war and had come to Kenadsa with other Loyalist prisoners. By now the part of Poland from which he had originally come was claimed by the Russians and he was a man without a country. Polish consular officials had agreed to repatriate some of the Polish internees, but had passed over Heller, either because his claim to Polish citizenship had become questionable or because he was Jewish.[251]

XXIII. "The World Will Never Understand"

The Allies did not have any clear-cut ideas as to what to do with the interned former legionnaires and the Frenchmen were not eager to liberate them. Printer complained that while the political prisoners in North Africa were gradually being released,

> One group, however, has been neglected—the men who fought as volunteers in the French Foreign Legion and who now work in the labor battalions of the Sahara. Other groups have had a voice abroad to speak for them—the stateless Jews near Casablanca, the Spanish Loyalist civilians in the work camps, the Fighting French political prisoners, and the Communists. Many of these are reported to have been freed. But the foreign volunteers who had rushed to join the French army in September, 1939, still sweat in the African desert. These *groupes de démobilisés étrangers* are made up chiefly of Central European Jews and Spanish Loyalists.[252]

Likewise, the *New Statesman and Nation* of London, published the following editorial:

> The Giraud regime in North Africa has pledged itself to release political prisoners who do not deserve internment. We recommend to their notice the case of the prisoners of Djelfa. There are 470 Spaniards, veterans of the Republican army, already interned for four years; 275 members of the International Brigade, the largest group Russian, and about 100 North African residents, imprisoned because they tried to help the refugees, or because they are Jews. Some of the men actually have visas for Mexico, which they have been prevented from using. The food is reported to be inadequate, there is no sanitation, the hospital in an open yard, there is no medicine for constant epidemics nor even for dysentery or phthisis. There is much bullying, and some of the prisoners who try to smuggle in food for the sick are put into "abominable" cells. Apart from 50 who are over 55 years old, and some 100 who are physically unfit, the veterans all want to serve in the Allied armies, but not, naturally, under the French, who, as these men say in a letter of appeal to General Eisenhower, have "for long years humiliated, starved and tortured them." They have appealed to the head of the Allied services and to General Eisenhower, personally offering their services. The suffering of these men has always been a blot on the fame of France; they were sacrificed to the spite of Franco's Spain, and later to the Fascism of the North African governors. They

have fought for democracy, that is for our cause, and suffered a slow martyrdom of captivity for it. Now that we have the responsibility for their fate (for none can doubt that if we choose to insist, they will be released) are we to add active connivance to our former sin of neglect? It is by our treatment of men such as these that our truth to our avowed faith will be judged.[253]

In the United States and Great Britain public opinion demanded that Spanish Loyalists be freed from the concentration camps in North Africa. The *New Republic* recalled:

We Americans share a large measure of responsibility for the fate which has befallen these men, and which will befall many others like them. The representatives of Dr. Frank Kingdon's Emergency Rescue Committee did their best to save them, but they received almost no help from the American Foreign Service officers in France, and the problem of getting the Spaniards out of France illegally was so complicated that without such help they were unable to save any but the most daring of them. Secretary Hull now boasts that from the beginning our policy toward Vichy was designed to pave the way for the occupation of French North Africa which he knew was coming. If that is so, we deliberately betrayed to almost certain death the men who led the first great battle against the very fascism we ourselves are now fighting. Or if we did not do it deliberately, we did it by inadvertence and indifference, which is as bad. From the beginning these men looked to America to save them. America left them to their fate.[254]

Individuals, labor unions and other organizations wrote to President Roosevelt, the State Department and other officials protesting against permitting the French to keep the Spanish Loyalists and Jews in concentration camps. E. Hyslop of Haddonfield wrote: "Natives in North Africa, the anti-Nazi French and especially the Loyalist and Jewish refugees are bound to distrust our rhetorical assurances of intent to carry the Four Freedoms to all the world." Dalton Trumbo of Culver City (California) wrote:

The world may grow to understand and accept the dubious political alliances made under the stern necessity of war. But the world will never understand and will never forgive the existence of concentration camps under the protection of the American Army, in which are imprisoned men and women who were fighting the forces of Mussolini and Hitler long before we ourselves entered the struggle.

E. Hannes of New York City asked:

My Good Sir, how can you expect us to believe that America is fighting for the liberation of freedom-loving people when anti-Fascist prisoners are still being held in North Africa?

Robert G. Halsley of New York City wrote:

It is this strange religious bias against all forms of democracy that defies even the orders of the Commander in Chief in its rabid hate of anti-facists that prevents these war prisoners of the Axis being immediately freed upon the landing of the Stars of Stripes on the shores of Algeria. In spite of the fact that General Eisenhower was put under political pressure to hobnob and congratulate French traitors and murderers like Darlan, it is unthinkable that this meets with the approval of a capable general such as he is.

At a meeting of the National Maritime Union a resolution was adopted to call upon the State Department to recall Bullitt and Robert D. Murphy from North Africa and free all anti-Fascists. The Secretary of State replied to all such appeals by stating that a Joint Commission consisting of America, British and French representatives was created in order to deal with the entire prisoner and refugee problem and that the United States government "is using every effort to bring about as prompt a release of prisoners and refugees as the military situation will permit."[255]

On December 5, 1942, S. Weinberger, formerly a volunteer at the Spanish International Brigade, wrote to the Commanding General of the Allied Forces in North Africa that thousands of Spaniards

would wish to fight in the ranks of the Allies in order to help to exterminate our common enemy. We do not want to enlist in the French Army, the commandment of which is the very one that, for four long years, has humiliated, starved and tortured us. Moreover we cannot trust a commandment that gave the signal to Franco-German "collaboration" after the Armistice . . . You may have under your orders thousands of picked and experienced who will fight fiercely for liberty. Not to accept them, would mean to lose them for the sacred cause of the Allied Nations.[256]

In addition to the volunteers, there were about 3,000 Spanish refugees who had signed up for five years with the regular Foreign Legion in March-May 1939 and in 1944 were at the end of their service. By March 15, 1944, 450 had been discharged. Practically none had reengaged, although a good deal of pressure was put on them to do so.[257]

On March 24, 1943, David Hartley of the American Friends Service Committee wrote that by interventions, by finding work with the Americans or other employers, his organization was helpful to the internees, but little was being done for the Spaniards. Some had escaped and the AFSC was trying to help them to avoid being picked up by the police. While some camps got smaller, others grew. One of the groups that the AFSC had been unable to help were the people who were too old or not strong enough to do the heavy work which the Americans offered.[258]

In April 1943 there were roughly 400 men from the camps working for the Americans in Casablanca. In a report of April 5, 1943, Hartley wrote to the AFSC in Philadelphia:

> Public Opinion has already been stirred enough so that the camp situation will clear in time. The most pressing problem is that of immigration. When the Americans leave, it looks now as if the situation would revert to its former state, and unless steps are taken to get these people out, it is very likely that they will be put back into camps. Those people who want to leave and show some promise of adapting to a new situation should go. This means mainly visas and that is no easy problem.
>
> One of the things that was most difficult for me to understand is the waiting on the part of many refugees to return to their homeland. There are some who feel that their future and responsibility lies at home. This is likely to become a more numerous group as things develop in Europe. We must recognize that there are some we will have to support until they are free to return.
>
> There are others who, like the White Russians after the last war, will never be able to return but who will never give up the hope. I feel that possibly some of the Spanish here are in this category.
>
> Since the problem of camps is the result of refusal of the French to make any original efforts at incorporating this excess labor into the economy of the country, I feel that perhaps it is one of our functions to get these people settled in their professions or in professions that have not been completely exploited (in the French sense) here.[259]

In January 1943 the British announced that an Allied commission was to be set up in Algiers to study the cases of the Spanish, ex-Germans, ex-Austrians and others still in concentration camps in North Africa. In this connection, Leslie O. Heath wrote to Robert M. Murphy in Algiers on January 5, 1943 that very little progress had been made toward accomplishing the release of internees in Morocco. "Unofficially," Heath wrote, "the Americans are prepared to employ people from the camps, if I can persuade the French to release them for such work. There is an extreme labor shortage here, and with such a reservoir of labor as there is in the camps, it seems to me incredible that some arrangement cannot be worked out to make use of these people."[260]

Madame Benatar of the American Joint Distribution Committee (AJDC) had from time to time made up lists of men who were checked by G2 and the local officials and freed to work as long as she could guarantee lodging. At first this had been organized on a small scale with the men housed in several apartments leased for this purpose. Later they were accommodated in an old amusement park which Mme. Benatar kept at Ain-Sebaa near Casablanca (where a group of refugee children stayed). The park had several good sized dance halls. With straw mattresses on the floor, the freed internees were comparatively comfortable until they received employment.[261]

XXIV. The Joint Commission on Political Prisoners and Refugees

As a result of the many complaints and protests, a Joint Commission on Political Prisoners and Refugees in French North Africa was set up in Algiers on January 6, 1943 by order of the Commander-in-Chief of the Allied Forces in North Africa.

At a preliminary meeting held on January 11, 1943 with Murphy in the chair, the United States Counsul General and the British Consul General were appointed Joint Chairmen of the Commission. Subsequent meetings were held on January 29, February 2 and 19. In addition, at each of these meetings there were present, in addition to the Joint Chairmen, representatives of Allied Force Headquarters, the Office of Civil Affairs, the French High Commissariat and the Psychological Warfare Department. A Secretary (Maj. A. R. Cheatham) was appointed with an office in the United States Consulate General.

The personnel of the Commission consisted of Samuel Hamilton Willey (United States Consul General), J. Eric M. Carvell (British Consul General), Col. H. Richmont (Judge Advocate of the Allied Force Headquarters), J. Holbrook Chapman (Office of Civil Affairs), Lt. Col. S. S. Hill-Dillon (G-2, Allied Force Headquarters), two French representatives (Colonel Ronin and M. Poniatowski) and Eric W. Johnson, representative of the American Friends Service Committee.

A field party was appointed to tour the camps holding foreign workers and political internees (other than Axis sympathizers). It consisted of Maj. D. Coster (U.S. Air Force), Maj. K. G. Younger (G-2, Allied Force Hdqs.), Major de la Chenelière (French High Commissariat) and Edouard Conod (International Red Cross).

In addition, the following people attended the meetings as consultants: David S. Hartley, Leslie O. Heath, and Kendall G. Kimberland (American Friends Service Committee), Capt. Paul F. Warburg (Office of Civil Affairs), Fred K. Hoehler (Foreign Relief and Rehabilitation), Dr. Edouard Wyss-Durant and Roger Vust (International Red Cross), Richard F. Allen (American Red Cross), Lt. Col. C. H. Bonestell (Engineers of the Allied Force Hdqs.) and others.[262]

On January 27, 1943, Consul General Willey reported to Washington that the preliminary meetings of the Commission had clearly demonstrated "the wide scope of this investigation and potential complications which may arise." The British were showing "unusual interest in this investigation and the British Consul General was having specially selected men sent to represent him on visits to camps." M. Makins of the British Foreign Office devoted a considerable amount of his time to bringing pressure on American officials to get the work of the Commission under way. At the meeting of January 8, British representative Harold MacMillan stated that in view of British public opinion, it was essential to let it be known that the problem was being dealt with objectively. In his view, the fact that a joint American-British-French Commission had been set up and was shortly to begin work would be enough to silence critics in England pending the report which should be written immediately.[263]

Accurate figures on the population of the camps were not available. On February 19, 1943, the French representatives supplied to the Commission the following estimates of persons detained in North Africa on November 8, 1942:

French —   900 on political grounds, 150 on non-political grounds
Spanish—3,200 "   "   "   260 "   "   "
Others —3,000 "   "   "   160 "   "   "

Total   —7,100 "   "   "   570 "   "   "

On that same day the French representatives stated that 1,299 detainees had already been released. This figure comprised 200 Frenchmen, 219 Spaniards and 880 others. The French representatives announced that "there were no persons still detained on account of sympathy shown by them for the Allied Cause before November 8, 1942."

It was never easy to obtain up-to-date, accurate figures of persons interned since many Axis sympathizers, particularly Italians, were being interned each week, at the same time some were released, particularly in Morocco and many other internees were escaping to take jobs in the cities.

The field party left for its first tour on February 25, 1943. After each visit they submitted their reports to the members of the Commission. A number of releases were effected immediately in accordance with their recommendations.

The only internment camps visited were Djelfa and Berrouaghia in Algeria and Missour and Sidi-el-Ayachi in Morocco. All the others were, according to the French representatives, camps of foreign workers (Groupes de Travailleurs Etrangers). The men in these camps were under military discipline, but they worked outside the camps and, according to the French reports, enjoyed a certain amount of freedom within the immediate district. The French also reported that a small number of special disciplinary camps which had existed previously, had already been closed before the field party began its work.

In practically all the camps the majority of the internees were Spaniards, refugees of the Spanish Civil War. Some of them came straight from Spain to North Africa in 1939; others escaped from Spain into France where they were either interned, or joined the French Foreign Legion as volunteers for the duration of the war. These men were transferred to North Africa in 1940, and when their demobilization became necessary under the terms of the Armistice, they were incorporated into groups of foreign workers under military control.

Many nationalities were represented among the other internees, the most numerous being German and Austrian refugees. Many of them had fought with the International Brigade in Spain, while others were living as refugees in France when the war broke out in 1939. Their history from that time was the same as that of the Spaniards.

Generally speaking, the men who were sent to internment camps, rather than to groups of foreign workers were, according to French reports, either men who were not willing to work or men who were considered by the French to be dangerous because of their political views.

The French High Commissariat proposed (1) that nationals of countries represented in North Africa should be placed at the disposition of their representatives; (2) that volunteers should be accepted in the Foreign Legion or Corps Franc; (3) that those who had been working in the groups of foreign workers should be given work contracts with their existing employers at normal wage rates. They would thereupon be free but would be considered as *requis* (i.e. bound to work in the employment allotted to them) in the same way as French civilian workers, under the decrees in force in 1939. The Commission proposed the consideration of the following alternatives: (4) enrollment in the Pioneer Corps of the British Army, (5) and for Spaniards, emigration to Mexico. The American authorities undertook to complete arrangements with the Mexican Government on this question.

Accordingly the field party made the following offers to the men in the camps:

1. Nationals whose country's interests were represented in North Africa were told that they were at the disposition of their representatives. Under this arrangement, many allied nationals had been released to join their national forces before the field party began its work. Others were released later.

2. The Russians, almost all of whom were at Djelfa, were informed that they would have to wait for the arrival of representatives of their government who were expected to visit North Africa and to arrange for the repatriation of those whose Soviet citizenship was accepted. The Soviet Representatives arrived on April 23 and visited Djelfa on April 26 and April 27; 125 Russians were soon transferred to a camp near Algiers where they were cared for by the British and American armies until their departure for Russia on June 15. Only 107 left for Russia, the rest obtained work in Algiers.

3. Recruiting officers for the French Foreign Legion or the Corps Franc had visited the camps with the result that few men were left who were willing to accept this solution.

4. As for enrollment in the British Pioneer Corps, there was an excellent response to this offer on the part of refugees from Central Europe in Algeria. At Colomb-Béchar, Kenadsa and Djelfa recruitment for the British Pioneer Corps almost completely took care of those Central Europeans who were fit for military service.

The Spaniards, however, were much less willing to enlist. Only at Djelfa were there any considerable numbers of Spanish recruits. In Morocco, owing to the expectation of release for civil work, the response was poor among all nationalities. 794 internees from over 15 camps were actually released and enlisted in the British Pioneer Corps and one release of another 106 internees to be enlisted was suggested by the Commission.

The groups of foreign workers were offered civil contracts at normal wage rates with their existing employers. By far the largest employers were the Méditerranée-Niger Cie. at Colomb-Béchar and Bou Arfa and the coal mine at Kenadsa. Smaller employers were the coal mine at Djerada and the electricity company at Im Fout. At Colomb-Béchar, Bou Arfa and Kenadsa few of the men were willing to accept this solution. The great majority of the men had been working for these companies under conditions of forced labor ever since 1940, and were anxious to get away above all from the south into districts where the climate was less severe and where they would be able to lead a more normal life. At Colomb-Béchar out of

442 Spanish employees of the Méditerranée-Niger Cie., only 77 were willing to accept civil contracts and to remain with their existing employer. Elsewhere the proportion of acceptances was no higher.

In addition to the alternatives noted above, the Spaniards were informed that they had an opportunity to go to Mexico. Unfortunately, at the time of the early visits, negotiations between the United States and Mexican governments had not progressed far enough to enable the field party to state with certainty that an unlimited number of Spaniards would be accepted by Mexico. As a result, the men were reluctant to put their trust in a solution that was merely speculative. Generally speaking, those Spaniards who held strong political views were unwilling to go to Mexico, preferring to remain nearer to Spain in the hope that political changes might offer them an opportunity to return.

The field party also offered the possibility of going to Mexico to 76 out of the 158 Spaniards who were serving prison sentences for political reasons for "crimes" committed during the Vichy regime and which were now no longer recognized as punishable, therefore an amnesty was necessary.

At the same time it was clear that the demand for labor on the part of the Allied Forces and of private industry in the north was very great and most urgent. The field party, therefore, upon their return from Morocco, recommended that the internees should be rapidly freed to meet the demand and that the position of those who had already escaped and were working should be regulated.

The same situation, though on a smaller scale, had by this time arisen in Algeria. At the camp of Boghar, for instance, out of a total strength of 491 workers, only 86 were present in camp on April 17, while 244 had been "detached" to civil work, 100 had escaped and 35 were on leave with a view toward finding civil contracts. At Colomb-Béchar and Kenadsa the remaining Spaniards, of whom 254 had still accepted none of the solutions offered them, were in close touch with their comrades in Morocco, and were not prepared to accept any offer except that of release to civilian work in the north. It appeared to the field party that the demand for labor, though smaller than in Morocco, was nonetheless sufficient to absorb the majority of the men. Moreover, it seemed desirable to give the men in Algeria the same opportunities as those in Morocco. The field party therefore expressed the opinion that work contracts should be sought and that those whose services were required should be released.

On April 28, after much negotiation, General Giraud signed an order closing down the camps and workers groups, the text of which reads as follows:

Since November 8, 1943, General Giraud, desirous of returning to the liberal traditions of France, has set his mind on improving the conditions of political refugees of foreign origin, imprisoned or interned in camps in North Africa.

Following thorough investigations with the different French services in North Africa and the Allied Governments, it has appeared possible to liberate all these aliens, except those nationals belonging to Axis powers.

Therefore, the General Commander-in-Chief of French civilians and military has decided:

Art. 1. Alien internees, nationals of countries who have consular representatives in French Africa are put, except those who have any objection, at the disposal of their respective representatives, these latter having the responsibility of ensuring their repatriation or their support.

Art. 2. All alien political internees in North Africa, other than those referred to in Article 1, and excepting nationals of Axis powers, will be liberated on condition they volunteer either for the Foreign Legion, the Corps Franc d'Afrique or the British Pioneer Corps, depart for a foreign country which will accept their immigration, or sign work contracts with public or private enterprises in French Africa, accepted by the Commander in Chief, contracts which, if not accepted freely, will be proposed to the internees by the Service of Algerian Economy or by the management of Public Works, Communications and Labor in Morocco, considering the professional worth and the conduct of the interested persons. A right of priority is granted to ex-soldiers of the Foreign Legion.

Art. 3. In the absence of the conditions referred to in Article 2, and in application of the decree-law of April 12, 1939, alien internees other than the Axis nationals, will be submitted to civilian requisition.

Art. 4. However, alien internees recognized as unfit for any effective work by a Medical Commission to be created for that purpose, will be put into a Rest Camp, the administration of which will be confided to a Committee of the Red Cross.

Art. 5. Alien nationals other than requisitioned civilians and those referred to in articles 2 and 4 of this decision, will be furnished with a worker's identity card valid for one month and renewable. This card, as well as the work contracts referred to in Article 2, will be considered as a temporary residence permit, the lack of which will cause the offenders to be treated according to the laws and regulations fixing the conditions of residence of aliens in North Africa.

Art. 6. The groups of alien workers, other than those employing Axis nationals, are dissolved.

Art. 7. However, a special group of alien workers will be constituted in

Algeria and another one in Morocco, to which will be attached administratively the alien nationals referred to in Article 5.

Art. 8. Allowed to benefit from a departure to a foreign country, under the same conditions as in Article 2, are alien nationals held for political offenses, who will accept the offer made them by the Allied authorities on behalf of the country of immigration.

Art. 9. The Secretary for the Interior is responsible together with the Secretary of Foreign Relations, for the execution of this present decision.

A final meeting of the Commission was held on May 8, 1943 to discuss the recent decisions of the French authorities and to arrange for solutions of problems still pending. It was explained that the United States Army had agreed to sign six-month contracts with all internees left in camps who were able to work. At the same time the Algerian government agreed that all men in camps could choose, if they wished, to take jobs in the Algerian economy and would soon be released on permission to find work and sign contracts. Those Spaniards who wished to go to Mexico did not need to wait in camps until that became possible, but were to sign contracts with the proviso that they would be annulled if opportunity to emigrate arose.

It was further agreed that the Commission would not distinguish between men in camps and work companies and political prisoners. The Commission agreed to consult with the French authorities about an immediate amnesty for these men.

By the end of June, all the internees and foreign workers were freed on labor contracts, except for a few still considered by the French to be dangerous. In these few cases the Commission negotiated with the French so that only those men actually proven to be dangerous would be detained in the camps. There remained at the end of July only about 25 such cases. By now the French authorities had either satisfied the Commission in most cases that those maintained in internment were considered dangerous, or had liberated the last few. In all cases, the men concerned were German or Italian nationals.

Amnesty for the men in Port Lyautey, Lambèse and Berrouaghia and also Maison Carrée prisons was finally granted and the men freed on the 12th and 13th of July. Amnesty for the men in Port Lyautey was authorized by the Committee of National Liberation on July 16 and the men freed 5 days later. This meant that all of the men interned before November 8, except the few exceptional doubtful cases mentioned above were freed.

When the Allied Forces landed in North Africa early in November 1942, there were probably 7,000 men in internment or work camps. At the time of the establishment of the Commission there were, according to French figures, about 6,300. By the end of July, none remained except for the above-mentioned number whose liberation seemed to the French with, in most cases, the Commission concurring, undesirable. Of this group of 6,300, the following disposition was made:[264]

British Pioneer Corps	1,100
Voluntary contract Méd-Niger R.R.	200
Repatriated to U.S.S.R.	107
Inept	40
To Allied Armies	200
On contract with the American or British Armies, or working with a private contract	4,653

XXV. "Anything Which Might Offend French Susceptibilities Has Been Omitted"

On January 3, 1943, the following letter was sent from North Africa to the Free French Forces in London:

I want to advise you of the true situation in Algeria. You have so far been informed only through indirect channels. It is urgent that you should realize its extreme gravity . . .

The landing and installation of the anglo-american forces in North Africa and particularly at Algiers between November 8 and November 10, were made possible through the help given them by sympathetic elements among which ours formed the majority.

In the night of November 7 to November 8, about 400 men occupied the strategic points of Algiers, disarmed the fascists, held in respect the soldiers, made generals prisoners as well as high officials hostile to the Allies including Admiral Darlan, thus allowing the allied commandos to land without trouble and to occupy the town quickly. This was not done without peril. We are still counting the dead among our people.

Be assured that I am telling you all this without the slightest intention of exaggerating, without an excess of bitterness. Such is the truth, believe me.

As soon as the armistice was concluded between Admiral Darlan and General Eisenhower, everything went back to 'normal'. That is to say: All the Vichy officials, without exception, resumed their functions, nearly all the imprisoned fascists were released, the S.O.L., the Legion, yesterday's collaborationists, are keeping the controls, the same orders are in force.

The same men are in charge of the censorship, the radio, the police and the general administration, etc. The control of the telephone and of the vital Algerian posts remains in the hands of the people selected and placed in these posts by the German and Italian armistice commissions. All the military communications are controlled by the friends of the Axis. Most of the Algerian advisors of Mr. Murphy, the representative of President Roosevelt, are ex-supporters of the Axis. The High Commissioner's office and the Prefecture can continue the Vichy policy with impunity, encouraging acts of insubordination and of resistance by military and civilian personnel. The mobilisation of the French army is being sabotaged. In the outlying districts of the country, it is not uncommon to see officers send back to their homes men who have come to answer the official call. The 'Corps Franc' organized by General Monsabert is practically boycotted. The natives are subjected to a public propaganda inciting them to refuse to carry arms for the Allies under the pretext that the Allies are starving them, violating their wives, and will one day be thrown out by the liberating Germans.

At Oran, General Boisseau—the very man who ordered the troops to fire on the Allies on November 8th, is ruling in company with Prefect Boujard, posting in every staff and in all the anglo-american military services men known for their devotion to the Axis under the guise of interpreters, secretaries, phone operators, drivers, etc.

In Algiers . . . the press—which is still in the same hands, praises what it used to condemn. But the communiques of the P.S.F. and the Legion are the only ones to be passed for publication. The communiques from our organizations, reconstituted at great pains and under ground, are consistently refused. The labor unionists who are trying to rebuild their unions are tracked down 'as in the good old days,' and their leaders are kept in prison. A dozen of the young men who took part in the fight during November 7 and 8 have been arrested and are threatened with court martial because they pasted little stickers proclaiming their French and Gaullist faith. Allied authorities refuse to 'intervene in French internal politics.' They refuse to intervene to obtain the release of these young men. They refuse to intervene to stop the internment—decreed after November 8—of democrats and pro-allies guilty of having manifested their wish to see de Gaulle come here and of having publicly affirmed their feelings. The native Jews are mobilized in separate units in labor camps at Cheragam and are sent to build roads. Colonels Rente and Varene, notoriously anti-Jewish officers, are in charge of them.

The group 'Combat' representing the faithful expression of Gaullism remains illegal. Its leaders are being pursued. All the French and foreign political internees remain in concentration camps and the communist deputies are still locked up in the Maison-Carré with other anti-fascists. No official, railwayman, mailman, teacher or employee of the public utilities who had been dismissed for his political activity, his philosophy or his racial origin has been reinstated. Not a single physician, dentist, lawyer, newspaperman or judge who had been dismissed under racial decrees and decrees on secret societies, has been reinstated. Jewish children are still refused access to ordinary schools, and young Jewish students cannot enter the universities. The administrators of the services of economic aryanisation are still in office to control Jewish property. The 'Legion' has not been dissolved, its sections still meet; its propaganda is still officially distributed all around the country, 'resistance to the Allies, fidelity to Marshal Pétain.'

On December 29, on orders from Governor-General Chatel, General Bergeret and General Juin, the mobile guard began a vast police round-up, starting at eight o'clock at night and continuing until the next morning. The official communique indicates that the people arrested will be prosecuted on the three following charges:

1. Complicity in Admiral Darlan's assassination;
2. Organization of an attempt on General Giraud's life;

3. Organization of an attempt on Mr. Murphy's life.
But who were the people who were arrested? Those who were arrested were our own friends, authors of the putsch which helped the Allies take Algiers. Such is the truth that you should know. The police round-up officially organized by the enemies of the Allies against the republicans (the friends of the Allies), made it appear as though those who were denouncing the assassin were his accomplices, and as though Mr. Murphy's actual supporters were his would-be assassins. Who was sent to the concentration camp at Bohar? [Here the letter gives the names of the persons arrested.] [264a]

According to Consul General Willey's report of February 7, 1943, the release of political prisoners and internees in Algiers proceeded "more slowly because of lack of centralization of records and because a large number were sent from France without any record regarding their cases."[265] Moreover, was the report of the Joint Commission reliable?

The official report of the Commission was presented on August 25, 1943, by Eric W. Johnson, Secretary of the Commission. However, Major K. G. Younger Reported that:

The official report on the recent visit to Colomb-Béchar, Kenadsa and Bou Arfa is to be signed by the U.S., British and French members of the party. Anything which might offend French susceptibilities has therefore been omitted from it. The present note is intended to fill in the gaps in the official report, and to indicate something of the atmosphere which prevails among the foreign workers and internees.

Following are some excerpts from a report given by an internee to Younger:

Moreover, a mobilisation appeal was sent to our friends who are still at liberty. What must we think? To whom must we listen? Many of our friends are discouraged. The public dares not understand. The natives are restless. Equivocation triumphs, threatening to engulf us in civil war and anarchy. It is sufficient to state that you are our friend, to lose all credit in the eyes of the representatives of the public power. We have a feeling that we have been disarmed, chained up and abandoned by our own friends, the Allies. We see the valiant men pay for the bad ones. Yesterday's regime continues to exist and is becoming worse. The prisoners are locked up in their gaols; a great number of them die every week. At the very time when the radio announces the liberation of the men detained in concentration camps in Algeria, they see their status getting worse, and machine-guns threatening them.
Must this continue, and can it continue without danger to the Allies?
We had to throw light on these machinations worked up against our cause

... I know what you want, and others with you; the liberation of our territory; I am not acting as a partisan in asking for your help. The months spent in internment—and what an internment!—have made me strong and completely lucid and calm. Personally I am not expecting any other reward for our common action other than to sacrifice still better than I have done up to now. Neither my friends nor myself are afraid for our lives. They have taken everything from us: Nationality, freedom, property, health. I come out of a concentration camp gravely ill. This has absolutely no importance. What we want is to serve the true France.

Maj. Younger further reported:

Colomb-Béchar is the administrative centre of the 'territoire Ain-Sefra', and is the headquarters of the military Chef du territoire Col. Liebray. He is responsible for the administration of the territory in all its aspects. There is no civil government.

The internal administration of the camps, however, comes directly under a central authority in Algiers, the Service des Camps. The head of this service until recently was Col. Lupy, whose representative at Colomb-Béchar is Captain Alexandre.

The economic activity of the territory, and in particular the employment of the foreign labor in the camps, depends almost entirely on two commercial undertakings, the Houillere at Kenadsa and the Méditerranée-Niger which employs labor on the building and maintenance of the railway—the desert roads. The director of the Houillere at Kenadsa is M. Signard; the director of Méditerranée-Niger is M. Laserre, whose headquarters is at Colomb-Béchar.

These three authorities, the Chef du territoire, the Service des camps and the commercial companies, have between them completely controlled the lives of the foreign workers and internees, ever since 1940. Hardly any of the foreign workers or internees owe their detention to any fault of their own. A high proportion, especially of the Central Europeans, were refugees in France in 1939, and joined the French forces as volunteers for the duration of the war. On joining up they appear to have been given a promise of residence in France if not of French citizenship on the termination of their contracts. Those who are not ex-volunteers are mainly men who fought on the Republican side in Spain and became refugees in 1939.

After the Armistice in 1940 the volunteers remained at first in their units, but later had to be demobilised. At the same time the economic situation in North Africa caused the authorities to undertake the development of the coal at Kenadsa and to make a start on the long projected Trans-Saharan Railway. The work was in both cases hard, the district remote and the climate trying. Voluntary labor was not likely to be attracted. The authorities therefore decided to carry out the work by means of the forced labor of the 'travailleurs étrangers' who were deprived of their military status, but were compelled to work under military control for the commercial companies.

No attempt was made to ensure reasonable conditions of work or commercial rates of pay. On the contrary the workers lived in barracks or camps, were fed by the camp authorities, and were paid from 4–10 francs a day. The full weight of the official machine was available to assist the employers to resist demands from the workers. Any obstinacy on the part of a worker was likely to earn him a period in the disciplinary camp at Hadjerat M'Guil.

It is quite clear from the accounts given by numerous internees that the companies took full advantage of the situation, and that they should be regarded for practical purposes merely as one part of the official instrument of repression. This is no matter for surprise, since the companies depended upon a ready supply of cheap labor, which only the camp administration could provide.

Under this system the material condition of the workers was unhappy enough. Their bitterness has been greatly increased by the attitude shown towards them by both military and company officials. Col. Liebray, a dug-out colonel of an antiquated type, undoubtedly thinks that all republicans, socialists and communists are simply 'Reds,' and consequently dangerous beasts. In conversation he made no attempt to conceal this attitude, since he was obviously unaware of its absurdity. His subordinates are mostly men of the Legion, accustomed to deal with native troops. Captain Alexandre has spent long years in the sun and is, at best, careless of everything except his own 'retraite.' His assistant is a German, Schwabe, a refugee from the Kapp putsche, who has since done fifteen years in the Legion. His appearance lends support to the stories of sexual perversion which are currently told of him. Another officer at Kenadsa, Lt. Letor, has a reputation as a fascist with anti-allied sympathies.

M. Signard, director of the Houillere at Kenadsa has the same reputation among the internees. The 'field party' had no opportunity for investigation, but all sensed his hostility and had a bad impression of him.

M. Laserre is more interesting. He is a clever man who has done big engineering work in many countries. He gave an impression of ruthlessness and left no doubt that he would use any method to get the maximum work from his men, with little regard for their welfare as human beings. It is probable that he can do exactly what he likes with Colonel Liebray. During the visit, Laserre asserted that numbers of Spaniards were on strike and he wired to Algiers for authority to get the military to take strong action. Investigation on the spot satisfied the field party that Laserre was staging a strike in the hope of discrediting the commission. A number of men who had refused to go to work on a site some miles away were questioned by Mr. Wiley. Mr. Wiley formed the view that Laserre had hand-picked a number of men and had given them an order which he knew they would refuse on more or less reasonable grounds. There is no doubt that if the field party had not been on the spot, Laserre would have had no difficulty in persuading the military to arrest the 'strikers' and to break up any ensuing demonstrations. This incident illustrates the close alliance between the military and the companies, which has been operating unchallenged for two and a half years.

There can be no doubt that the foreign workers in the territory, apart from any material hardships they may have suffered, have been made by all the officials to feel that they are, in the words of Arthur Koestler 'Scum of the Earth.' This must be borne in mind in considering their attitude to the improvement which was recently made in their conditions.

The Spaniards working for Méditerranée-Niger were all 'liberated' on February 10th to continue work with the company at standard wages. The new conditions are on the whole reasonable. It cannot however be expected that the internees will regard this as freedom. They are still compelled to live in the same place. The company officials are unchanged and have even been supplemented by the transfer to the companies of reserve officers who were formerly on the staffs of the camps. The workers know quite well that the unholy alliance between the military and the employers has not been shaken. How true this is, is shown by the episode of the 'strike' described above. So long as the same authorities remain in the territory, and so long as there is no trade union or other body to watch the interests of the men, the sense of injustice will remain and no improvement in material conditions will remove it.

For this reason alone it is not enough to establish decent working conditions, and to leave the bulk of the men where they are. On the political plane, neither they nor their supporters in the U.S.A. and England are likely to accept it as a satisfactory outcome of the Commission's work. Moreover, it is quite possible that the men themselves, feeling at last that they have some friends, may begin to stand up for themselves. In present conditions in the territory this will cause trouble.

Another cause for anxiety is the steady inflow of axis prisoners-of-war and internees, who work in contact with the anti-fascist workers. If there are disturbances between Italian fascists and Spanish republicans, the Spaniards will probably start the trouble and will get the blame. But the fault will lie with the French authorities for allowing the situation to exist. In all the places visited the number of axis prisoners or internees is rapidly increasing, so that an effort should be made to remove from the area in the near future as many of the anti-fascist workers as can be absorbed elsewhere.

The French authorities are at present strongly opposed to the release of large numbers of the Spaniards for work in towns in North Africa. They point out that there is already an uncomfortably large Spanish population in Oran, and that the Spanish-Moroccan border is not far away. These arguments might be sound enough if a wholesale uncontrolled release of Spaniards were proposed. It is difficult to believe that they would apply to a considered scheme of releases of workmen for work connected with the war effort in approved places.

The trouble is that any such scheme requires collaboration between the French Bureau du Travail and the French Security authorities, in order to release the right men to sensible jobs. It will require strong pressure to make the French administration do a serious job of work of this kind. During the stay at Colomb-Béchar numerous examples of the callous inefficiency of French officials came to the notice of the field party. The so-called 'commission de criblage' which had been to the camps, had signally failed to do any proper sifting, even among the most deserving cases; and even since the 'commission's' visit, further inoffensive legionnaires and other foreigners are being sent to the camps when their contracts expire. There is no evidence whatever of an intention on the part of. the French administration to clear up the mess on their own initiative. If they are to be persuaded to do so, all the drive will have to come from the Anglo-American side, and the commission will have to insist that orders are not merely given in Algiers, but are carried out on the spot.[266]

In another report dated April 21, 1943, Major K.G. Younger added a few more facts about Moroccan camps "not mentioned in the official report." At two of these camps "important work is being done," Younger wrote. These were the camps of Djérada, near Oudjda, where there was a reasonably productive coal mine, and Im Fout, near Settat, where there was a barrage which could assist in irrigating a large stretch of plain and furnish electric power. Unfortunately, these camps were probably "the worst of the camps from the point of view of climate and amenities." The foreign workers at both camps were anxious to get away, owing largely to the legacy of bitterness which had remained from the old regime. Since no important work was being done at Settat and Oued Akreuch, there seemed no reason why they should continue to exist, unless they were to be improved and made into rest camps. By far the worst problem was that of Bou Arfa, a very large camp far to the South. The employer there was the Mediterranean Niger which had a "bad reputation." The work did not seem to be of any great importance; it could either be stopped or carried on by prisoners of war. In the opinion of Maj. Younger one could have closed all the camps completely, ensuring the continuation of the work where necessary by the normal process of treating the workers as "requis" (requisitive workers) and offering them normal conditions of work.

Some of the instances of brutality recorded in Algeria undoubtedly existed in Morocco. There were two particularly bad disciplinary camps there which were closed down some months earlier, Younger reported. In several camps, including Missour, the commandant of the camp was in charge only since November. For this reason the staff of the camps made a better impression than in other areas. In the populated areas in the plain round Casablanca, the officials were rather unpleasant and Maj. Younger sensed a certain hostility. The chief official of the Production Industrielle, Col. Kiesler, claimed to have been a leading Gaullist and "resistant." He had, however, a "most unpleasant bullying personality," and several people told Maj. Younger that Kiesler was a confirmed Fascist who was on excellent terms with the Germans. Younger was also told by an officer in charge of one of the camps that the Controleur Civil at Settat had been a leading collaborator, responsible for many arrests. A humorous incident occurred as Younger was leaving the camp at Settat. He and his party had given a lift to a French air force captain. The *Controleur* asked them in for a drink, and was somewhat embarrassed to discover that the captain had been an inmate of the camp, recently released.

On the whole, there seemed to be more bitterness in Morocco about collaborationists still holding good jobs than there was in Algeria. The gradual process of sifting out which had occurred in Algeria was not noticeable in Morocco.

Maj. Younger found an entirely different situation in the hill country round Missour, Midelt and Azrou. These places still retained the character of military posts and most of the officers above the rank of captain had served under Lyautey in the Moroccan campaigns.[267]

In still another report submitted by Major Younger and sent by Robert D. Murphy to the Department of State the following points were made:

> The French stated that on February 2, 1943, the 903 of the Moroccan internees had been released. On February 8, 1943, they said that a further 357 men had been released in Algeria. I do not feel sure that these figures are complete either as to totals or as to numbers released. The French should make a fresh statement to the Commission at an early date.
>
> The French state that, in pursuance of Article 11 of the "Darlan Agreement" they have already released all persons who were interned for pro-allied activities or sympathies. They propose to produce a list of these persons to the Commission at the next meeting. They state that this is the full extent of their contractual obligations.
>
> In deference to Allied public opinion, however, they propose to release other Frenchmen who are willing to rejoin the French armed forces, provided they are favorably reported on by the camp authorities. "Etrangers" will also be released to work on the same condition.
>
> The impression gained was that the numbers who would pass the required test would amount at most to an odd hundred or two. This applies especially to the French internees classed as "communists." No indication of a general change of attitude to alleged "communists" has percolated as far as Major de la Chenelière, presumably because there is indeed no change in the attitude of the higher authorities.
>
> Those not released unilaterally by the French will be handed over willingly by the French to the Allies for release, provided the Allies remove them from French North Africa. It is not entirely certain that they would release the men en masse for enrollment in British or American units in French Africa, but it is

probable that they would do so if pressed. In a number of individual cases they have proved obstructive when asked by special British services to release men for special work in North Africa not involving incorporation in combatant units.

It is the contention of the French that, under Article 11, they are not bound to give the Commission any facilities whatever, whether by way of statistics, nominal rolls or visits to camps for investigating the situation of any internees other than the "pro-Allied sympathisers" referred to in the article. Any further information will be given, if at all, purely as a matter of grace.

Accordingly, they do not intend to supply the Commission when it next meets with any nominal rolls or other particulars about the vast bulk of the internees who do not come within Article 11. They are prepared to tell the Commission what are the main types of internees involved. If the Commission can agree in principal on the disposal of all or any part of the categories in a manner acceptable to the French authorities, facilities can then be given for suitable allied officers to see the categories in which they are interested.

There can, however, be no question of the Commission presuming to decide in individual cases whether the men classed by the French authorities as dangerous are, in fact, dangerous or not. In other words, this is an internal French matter in which the allies have no locus standi. Their only course is to accept the French decision as binding for French territory, and to take the man, if they wish to free him, out of French jurisdiction.

The French contemplate that the limited visit will take place under the auspices of the Haut Commissariat, and not under the auspices of the Inter-Allied Commission, which, in their view, will be wound up as soon as it receives the French report stating that all pro-Allied sympathisers have been released.

In the meantime there would be no objection to a visit purely for "welfare" purposes by the International Red Cross, or any other humanitarian organization of a similar kind.

It will be seen that the French view, as given by Major de la Chenelière, is *rigid and somewhat ungenerous*. It should, however, be emphasized that Major de la Chenelière showed the utmost goodwill throughout and let me look even at the documents which he does not feel obliged to furnish officially to the Commission. He asked that I should try to settle "off the record" any points which were proving troublesome. My impression is that he, and presumably his superiors, are standing on their rights for *reasons of prestige,* but that they are extremely anxious to reach a friendly settlement of the whole question *without further damaging publicity.*

An immense proportion of the internees are undoubtedly entirely harmless from an Anglo-American point of view—with few exceptions they are solidly in favor of the Allied war effort and those who are fit are anxious to fight.

Their treatment has, however, made them bitterly anti-French, so that the French have good reason to object to large-scale releases unless the men can be removed from the country or at least segregated from the local population.

Large-scale releases depend, therefore, on the ability of the Commission to take complete charge of the men released.

The disposal of those claiming Soviet protection seems unlikely to present serious difficulties. The total of these is, at most, a few hundred. These will all or mostly go to U.S.S.R. via U.K.

The Spaniards may be accepted in Mexico. Alternatively, the Director of Labor, Brig. Innes-Irons, has stated that he urgently requires an almost unlimited amount of European labor to be formed into Pioneer Units of the British Army. He would readily absorb anything up to 10,000 men within a few days. He can provide for them at once and supply British officers and N.C.O.'s. He only requires cabled authorization from W.O. about which he anticipates no difficulty, other than the political one.

Brig. Innes-Irons would also welcome International Brigaders, of whatever nationality, whom he could use in the same way.

Only the political objection to employment of Spaniards stands in the way of the almost immediate release of all supporters of the Spanish Republic who are fit and willing to join the British Pioneer Corps.

Brig. Innes-Irons states that no Spaniards enrolled need be used anywhere near Spanish Morocco. He also points out that enrollment of this labor will save the shipping space which would otherwise be required to bring labor from U.K. In view of this, an effort should surely be made to overcome the political difficulties.

There seems no reason why recruitment of the International Brigade should not begin independently of the Spanish question. The French can provide nominal rolls showing the location of the men, in order that they may be visited and medically tested.

It is obvious that a great deal of labor will be saved if the Spanish question can be promptly solved and all recruiting can be done in a single visit to each camp.

The second and most troublesome category outstanding is the Frenchmen interned for communist activities or offenders against discipline and morale in the French armed forces.

The French undoubtedly expect the Commission to refrain from inquiring into the rights and wrongs of these cases. Moreover, it is doubtful if they would allow the recruitment by the Allied Forces of Frenchmen who are legally liable for French military service.

Nevertheless, this category almost certainly contains many of the hardest cases. It is common knowledge that such phrases as "communist" activity were used by the Vichy régime to cover almost any form of opposition to the Government. The Commission cannot possibly report that it has obtained the liberation of all "pro-Allied sympathisers" until it has inquired into the truth of these cases for itself. This is likely to provoke strong French opposition since an inquiry of such a nature implies disbelief in the information supplied by the French to the Commission.

This issue should be found. Moreover, I do not believe that the French are in a position to hold out if the Commission persists on pursuing the inquiry.

One suggestion would be that the men should be allowed to join the French forces in U.K., or if practicable in the Middle East. The political difficulties of this are obvious, but if the Commission can satisfy itself that many of these men wish to fight for the Allied cause, the interests of the war effort surely demand that they should be allowed to do so. Moreover, the continued imprisonment of these men is a public scandal which is likely to attract the attention of the Anglo-American press as soon as the question of Spanish Republicans has been settled.

The position of naval and military personnel convicted by court martial is even more delicate and might well be left until the other problems have been tackled. There is, however, ample evidence from escapees arriving in U.K. that the "framing" of charges against Allied supporters has been a common feature of the Vichy regime. Though this problem should eventually be tackled I am not, at this stage, prepared to recommend how it should be attempted.

Major Younger reported that the French had supplied information about the following types of camps in Algeria—seven camps (Akbou, Berrouaghia, Bossuet, Djelfa, Djenien-Bou-Rezg, El Aricha, Mercheria), two labor camps (Boghar, Colomb-Béchar) and three prisons (Berrouaghia, Lambèse, Maison-Carrée). And in Morocco—one camp (Sidi-el-Ayachi), one labor camp (Bou Arfa) and three prisons (Casablanca, Meknès, Port-Lyautey). In addition, there existed "Groupes de Travail" which had from time to time been transported from the main camps to temporary camps. However, Major Younger added:

It is probable that the French members of the Commission are acting in entire good faith. They depend, however, for their information on other authorities whose main interest is to conceal the worst cases and the worst places. Appeals reaching the American and British Consulates General have mentioned a number of places of detention which do not appear in the French lists. Some of these may be dissolved or the places may have been inaccurately stated. Nevertheless, it must be one duty of the Commission to insure that no place of detention is overlooked, and in particular that Groupes de Travailleurs working in makeshift camps in remote places are included in the survey. An inquiry of this sort will meet with obstruction. It can only be carried out if the Commission empowers its Field party to insist, even at the cost of unpleasantness, on having access to every place to which its attention has been drawn.[268]

It was difficult to estimate the number of Jewish internees. At one time (March 3, 1943), Consul General Willey reported from Algiers that out of a total of 4,326 internees in Algeria, only 194 were Jews, "but this is believed to be on the low side. Information from other sources believed reliable indicates number of Jewish prisoners is probably close to 400." Of

1,447 in Morocco, only 30 were believed to be Jews. However, on March 10 he again reported:

> It is believed that at least 80% of the Central European refugees at the camps visited are Jews. Existing records list as Jews only those few who declared themselves as such and it was not deemed expedient to make specific inquiries since some former commissions have done so and left an impression that persons declaring themselves Jews would be discriminated against.[269]

In a press release of the Commission given earlier to the press (on June 23, 1943), it was stated that

> during the visits to internment camps the field party of the Joint Commission for Political Prisoners and Refugees also visited prisons in which political prisoners were confined. There are now in prison approximately two hundred foreign refugees who, although they have been duly sentenced by Courts, should be considered as political prisoners since the offenses consist chiefly of infractions of discipline in internment camps or political demonstrations involving violence. The greater part of these prisoners are Spanish Republican refugees. The French authorities agreed to liberate from prisons all Spanish Republican refugees for the purpose of proceeding to Mexico. The Joint Commission suggested, however, that these prisoners should be liberated and allowed to make their own dispositions. Dr. Jules Abadie, former Secretary of the Interior and now Commissioner of National Education, Justice and Public Health, has given an assurance that an amnesty will be granted to these prisoners after their cases have been examined in regard to military security. The granting of these amnesties has been delayed by the temporary confusion resulting from the transition from the High Command to the French Committee of National Liberation, but is expected soon.[270]

However, on March 4, 1944, Eric W. Johnson reported to the AFSC in Philadelphia of the difficulties he encountered by the AFSC in taking an "active role in arranging for the liberation" of the internees, "with a government which was far from enthusiastic about the idea."[271]

It is worthwhile mentioning some problems discussed at the meetings of the Joint Commission. At the meeting of January 8, 1943, General Walter Bedell Smith, Eisenhower's Chief of Staff, remarked that the former members of the "International Brigade was anathema to many people in the United States." The suggestion was made by Murphy that some of the Spaniards might be able to go to Mexico; in fact, some of them might even have Mexican visas. General Smith said that "Mexico was a little too close to the United States" and suggested "Chile as a likelier spot for them to settle."[272]

Warburg asked at the meeting of February 19 if the French were to be included in the Commission visiting the camps and why an advance French Commission had been sent and the visits had not been made simultaneously. Ronin said that it was too late to discuss that since the French Commission had already set out. Fred K. Hoehler of the Office of Foreign Relief and Rehabilitation said he had wired to Secretary of State Hull to have funds made available to Consul General Willey for clothing, medical care, reading matter and other supplies and services needed in the camps, and afterwards to provide means of support for the internees after they were released until they could find suitable jobs. He said he thought the men should be released unconditionally. The interest of Great Britain and the United States in this internment question was very keen and it was suggested that certain individuals should be sent from the United States to assist in this work. He added that he would like to be able to send a telegram to the United States to the effect that a decision had been reached to do a careful, thorough job. Col. H. Richmond of the Judge Advocate's office supported this point of view saying that it was his feeling that political prisoners should be released and become free agents and not be offered work on railroads, in coal mines or the British Pioneer Corps. He said that if there was money for these people, there was no need to adopt that course and that with the funds, they would not become public charges. Dr. Edouard Wyss-Dunant of the International Red Cross said the clothing question was of great importance and that from what he had seen, the men could not possibly begin to look for work in the clothes in which they would be released. The impression must be avoided of these people have been forced into labor camps.[273]

The French authorities complained that as a result of the many interventions of the Joint Commission in favor of the internees and visits to the camps discipline there had become a serious problem. Many internees left the camps without permission.[274]

Only when the complete files of the Joint Commission are found will it be possible to present a complete picture of the struggle between the Allies and the French authorities over the internees in North Africa after November 8, 1942. However, even on the basis of the existing documents, one may conclude that the pressure exerted on France by the non-French members of the Commission saved the lives of many internees. That there was not enough pressure is another question.

For a long time Algerian censorship did not permit any writing about the volunteers in the Foreign Legion and their internment to be reported in the press. In the summer of 1943, after most of the internees had been liberated and censorship unable to impose a policy of silence on the camps, the press started to publish evidences on the assassinations and other cruelties committed at Hadjerat M'Guil, Djenien-bou-Rezg, and other camps. The French authorities could no longer ignore the demands for punishment of those responsible for such acts. This resulted in two military trials which were held in February and October of 1944. In the first trial, Lt. Santucci, Commandant of the Hadjerat M'Guil camp and his assistants Finidori, Dauphin (*Chef Compatable,* Chief Accountant, called by the internees *chef coupable*) and Riepp were sentenced to death. Santucci and Riepp were executed, but the death sentences for Finidori and Riepp were commuted to forced labor for life. Six other torturers were sentenced to forced labor. The second trial took place in October 1944, when the military tribunal could afford to be lenient. Lt. Ticko of the Djenien-bou-Rezg camp was tried and sentenced to six years in solitary confinement.[275]

Nobody demanded reparation from the French government or the semi-official compagnies. The latter could always prove that the internees signed up as volunteers . . .

About 150 Italians, members of the anti-Fascist *Unione Democratica Italiana* were sent to concentration camps in Algeria. Among them were some who had helped in the landing of the American forces. They could have played an important role in North Africa, especially in Tunisia, among the Italians there, who were Fascists. The *Unione* did not belong to any political party but was a large movement of Italians of anti-Fascist leanings. The French, however, had nothing better to do than intern them. In Morocco, Frenchmen of Fez protested against the liberation of Italians from concentration camps. Greeks, who had resisted the Italian invasion were also interned in Morocco because officially they had been Italian protégés. On March 25, 1945, the Delegates for the Study of Foreign Affairs of the Consultative Assembly and representatives of the Italian anti-Fascist parties in Tunisia (Republican Party, Socialist Party, Communist Party, Libertarian Party) had met in closed session. An O.S.S. memorandum reported on this meeting:

> The anti-Fascist delegation presented a report which allegedly described the position of the Italians in Tunisia. They pointed out that many of the dangerous and still active Fascists who are wealthy and influential have either been

liberated from concentration camps or have never been interned. On the other hand, anti-Fascist and honest Italians, who were interned two years ago for security reasons only, are still imprisoned. The delegation asked that these Italians be liberated and allowed to return to their work as fishermen, farmers, etc. and to assist thereby in the reconstruction and rehabilitation of Tunisia. The property of the small farmer and the small businessman is still confiscated; the property of the wealthy is untouched. Italian workers subject to compulsory labor laws are underpaid, they said, and many French employers have been forced to supplement their salaries; however, other employers have taken advantage of the workers' nationality to underpay them. The delegates stated that the Italian workers are not placed in positions for which they are best qualified; that pharmacists are made gardeners, mechanics made gravediggers, students made street-sweepers. In addition, all Italian workers must wear white bands with the initials "TI" to single them out from their co-workers.

The delegation asked that anti-Fascists be allowed to help in the work of destroying Fascism in Tunisia, of suppressing fifth-column activities and of re-educating the masses who had been poisoned by Fascist propaganda. They expressed the hope that the problem of Italians in Tunisia would be solved and that a sincere and permanent harmony would soon prevail between the French and the Italians.[275a]

Mention should be made of the civilian refugees in North Africa after November 8, 1942. On April 23, 1943, the State Department sent the following cable to Murphy:

> Please present the following matter to General Eisenhower with the request that he consult General Giraud also and that we be advised as quickly as may be practical of the decision:
> The American and British Governments are meeting in Bermuda to discuss ways and means for saving refugees, a number of whom have found their way out of German military jurisdiction and some of whom are now in Spain. The delegates at Bermuda are impressed with the thought that Spain is the only effective channel of escape for these unfortunates who remain in Western Europe composed of various nationalities. They feel it is of supreme importance that this channel be kept open as the consequences of closure would be that the admission of additional refugees would be prevented by the Spanish Government; that the Allies would be deprived of persons who are useful to them in North Africa; and that world opinion would come to the conclusion that we were not making any serious effort to deal with that problem if something were not done about the situation in Spain. There are six or seven thousand persons of this category in Spain who are not of French nationality but who are largely Jewish, and of either enemy nationality or are stateless persons. The proposal is that they be transported to North Africa because of the scarcity for

long journeys shipping and the proximity of that region to their present residence. Further that they be assembled there in a camp to be built, if necessary, the site of which would be selected by the military authorities there, and with the consent and approval of the French authorities . . . To keep them in Spain would prevent the advent into Spain of additional persons. Provision for the number mentioned in Africa would be for purposes of a temporary domicile until another place could be found to which to move them and with the assumption that persons later arriving in Spain might fill their places in such a camp in Africa after the persons there had been moved to other jurisdictions.

We are advising the Bermuda conference that the matter involves consultation with the military authorities and approval by the French authorities in North Africa.

The Department will appreciate receiving a reply as promptly as possible considering that the conferees in Bermuda will be entering the second week of what was expected to be a short conference.[276]

In July 1943, President Roosevelt and Prime Minister Churchill agreed to open in North Africa a camp for refugees from Spain. Grace W. Teller of the War Refugee Board wrote on January 12, 1944:

At first the French attached to their approval certain conditions . . . which were unacceptable to the American and British Governments. It was felt that these conditions would place the refugee center in the category of an internment camp rather than a refugee center.[277]

In November, 1943, M. Dugardier, the Chef du Cabinet des Affaires Politiques at Rabat told a representative of the American Quakers (AFSC) that after all, America had a real responsibility in the refugee problem, since, although Americans complained of the treatment refugees received in North Africa, they were unwilling to do anything themselves for them.[278] (Indeed, in a similar American experience with refugees the latter were put in the camp—"shelter"—Oswego).

On February 22, 1944, H. Earle Russel, American Consul General, wrote to Selden Chapin, Counselor of the Embassy at Algiers:

There have been reports that they [the refugees] have sometimes been badly treated notably by certain sections of the [French] Sûreté Militare, which is stated to have forced them into the French Foreign Legion or have kept them in prison for various periods under rather bad conditions.[279]

Chapin also reported on July 25, 1944 that the French tried to recruit the refugees at Fédalhah refugee camp for the Foreign Legion.[280] On

November 4, 1944, Leonard E. Ackerman, representative of the War Refugee Board in North Africa, reported to John W. Pehle, Executive Director of the Board about the "dilatory tactics": "The highly technical, obstructionistic tactics of the low-ranking French officials had already unduly delayed the movement of the refugees."[281]

It should also be noted that Jacques Oettinger of the HICEM was very pessimistic about the realization of the Spanish-North African aspect of the Bermuda conference.[282]

XXVI. Volunteers Forced Not to Fight

The New York *Post* of January 13, 1943, published the following cable sent by the Jewish Telegraphic Agency from Lisbon and reprinted by *Free France:*

> Jewish officers in the French army in North Africa have had all their rights restored since the landing of American forces and are now actively participating in the organization of the French army under Gen. Giraud, it was reliably reported today from Algiers.[283]

Very soon the press began reporting how Jews were really being treated in the armed forces of liberated North Africa.

Prior to the American landing in North Africa, before the alien Jews, former legionnaires in the forced labor camps could hope to be liberated, more Jews arrived into camps. These new arrivals were Algerian Jews, who had lost their citizenship under the Vichy regime. On April 25, 1941 Algerian Jews of military age were sent to Camp Bedeau (a former camp of the Foreign Legion to the South of Sidi-bel-Abbès) to serve in the *Groupement des Travailleurs Israélites*—GTI (Grouping of Jewish Workers) where they were kept under military discipline. By March 1942, the lot of these Algerian Jews became identical to the lot of the alien Jews. The name of the unit was later changed to *Groupement des Travailleurs Algériens*—GTA (Grouping of Algerian Workers). They were called Corbeaux (ravens), because their military uniforms were taken away from them and they were dressed in black civilian clothing. The camp became an actual concentration camp which was under the surveillance of the old-time legionnaires, who constantly called the workers "dirty sheenies" and "dirty ravens."

After the Allied landing, the Algerian Jews were not immediately liberated or drafted into fighting units. They were placed into Special *Batallions des Pioniers Israélites*—BPI (Battalions of Jewish Pioneers). Only the name became liberated, it sounded like the British Pioneer Groups, or like a Jewish army unit. In reality, however, it was neither, and the old regime of a special camp continued. In the Department of Oran alone, over 12,000 Algerian Jews were mobilized into these units, with a few token French Jews of Algeria and Morocco as a decoration. René Pierre Gosset wrote: "Special calling-up measures were taken for Jews, which meant, on closer examination, that they were to be sent to break stones on the road to Chéragas."

The staff still consisted of old-time legionnaires, many of them of German origin. Boitel, the commandant, was a former chief of section SOL (Service d'Ordre Légionnaire) formed by Vichy. A group of workers were severely punished for having shouted to passing American jeeps, "Hello, boys!" The jail at Bedeau was always full; even the chaplain, Zaoui, was incarcerated for a time. New camps were opened for the BPI in each department, Chéragas (Algiers) and El-Guerrah (Constantine). The French authorities openly admitted that this step was necessary in order to avoid future recognition of Jews as *anciens combattants* (war veterans). The new camps for "Jewish Pioneers" were, in reality, penal institutions. The "Pioneers" of Chéragas were transferred to Aumale where the officer Collomb called the Jews "Army of Jerusalem." To a superior officer who was visiting the camp, Collomb protested against permitting Jews to sleep in the same rooms as Frenchmen. On December 3, 1942, the Commandant of Bedeau prohibited "all conversation and manifestation concerning their religion," i.e. about their political and civil status, among Jews.

By an order of December 30, 1942, Algerian Jews were permitted to volunteer for fighting units, but only if allowed to do so individually. Even the ranks of the Foreign Legion were not open to them.

While the Allied soldiers were fighting for their and France's liberty at the borders of Tunisia, the French authorities found nothing better to do with the "Jewish Pioneers," among them many experienced veterans of previous campaigns, than to cut esparto-grass and trees.

The Comité Juif Algérien d'Etudes Sociales reported to the World Jewish Congress in New York:

> The Anglo-American landings, the renewed struggle against the Axis powers were greeted with profound joy and emotion by the Jewish population and have given rise to new rightful hopes.
> The explicit declarations of President Roosevelt, the war aims of the Allied Nations, the examples of their interventions in the freed countries such as Syria, Madagascar, and other French colonies, led to the belief that legislation inspired by racial hatred would be at an end. For over two months now the Jewish population has been experiencing one disappointment after another. In

vain did the Chief Rabbi of Algiers write to the Governor General of Algeria requesting the abrogation of this [anti-Jewish] legislation. In vain did Professor Henri Aboulker, President of the Algerian Jewish Committee of Social Studies, put before Admiral Darlan, High Commissionar of French North Africa, the same request. The only result was that on December 17, 1942, Admiral Darlan, in a statement to General Eisenhower, promised the "suspension" of all laws inspired by the Germans or dealing with persecution because of race or religion.

The vague terms of this declaration, its reticences, the absence of any promise of abrogation of the racial legislation created strong disappointment among the Jewish population and caused the Algerian Jewish Committee of Social Studies to deliver to the Public Authorities a motion asking for the abrogation, pure and simple, and without further delay, of all this legislation of oppression. What happened, however, is rather an intensification of this legislation.

Already, on the strength of the law of June 2, 1941, bearing on the Status of Jews, the Jewish officers and non-commissioned officers had been barred from the regular army. The day after November 6th, Jewish soldiers were somehow barred from the army, being mobilized into separate units, as workers; thus, in spite of the Allied landing, in liberated North Africa, when Frenchmen are called to fight against Germany, those of Jewish origin are, as in the land of Hitler, herded into groups of workers. This time, then, it is not even a question of legislation imposed by Germany, but a new application of the law of Hitlerian mobilization. In each department (Chéragas for the department of Algiers, Bedeau for the department of Oran, El-Guerrah for the department of Constantine) a concentration camp was formed for Jews mobilized as workers. In Bedeau the head of the camp was the old Chief of the L.O.L. of Ekmul. This shows in what spirit this mobilization was put into effect.

Only late in January 1943, Algerian Jews of the camps were permitted to volunteer for active duty. However, this was done in an atmosphere of distrust, of telling the volunteers that they will have to serve as native Algerians instead of French citizens, of forcing even experienced officers to pass through elementary infantry training. Thus, the volunteer movement became suspicious. Even so, Algerian Jews volunteered en masse for active duty. The entire 205th Company left Bedeau singing the *Chant du Départ*. In the end, however, they were used as "Pioneers" near the front lines, for the construction of air fields and other tasks. Many of them were killed by enemy bombs without having regained the status of combatants, resulting in the volunteer movement being regarded as a trap. French public opinion, witnessing no change in the status of Jews since the Allied landing, began believing that the Vichy attitude toward Jews could be continued in Algeria. Lt. Klotz came to the Bedeau camp to recruit volunteers for the armored units. Those who signed up found themselves again sent to "pioneer" units of the Magenta camp which was famous for its concentration camp character. At Chéragas, commandant Suchet continued his brutal practices, including that of sending pioneers to El Méridj where the men spent six months in intensive forced labor. He even formed a *Section Special* (SS) where the Pioneers were punished with 14 hours work every day and 10 hours in the *tombeau*. The higher military authorities did nothing to stop Suchet's practices.

On February 16, 1943 Rabbi Trojman, chaplain of the Jewish Pioneers at Bedeau was advised by Lt. Lemoine of the 209th Company that General Boisseau wanted to see him. Boisseau was the Commanding General of the Oran Division. General of the region Borboissel and officers Boitel and Lemoine were present at the meeting. The following conversation took place:

Gen. Boisseau: Were you a scout?
Trojman: Yes, my General.
Gen. Boisseau: Good, I hope that you will be able to introduce a spirit of scoutism at Camp Bedeau. They [the Jews] serve their fatherland as Pioneers or combattants. I cannot do anything about their French citizenship, this is not within my jurisdiction, this is a matter for higher authorities. My task is to find volunteers. Surely, those who will leave as volunteers will have advantages, more than the others, *but I don't promise anything* . . .
Trojman: Ah, my General, here is the injustice. The Jewish Pioneers of the Bedeau camp are waiting for your promises.
Gen. Boisseau: I cannot do anything now. One must wait that the first volunteers depart and prove themselves.
Trojman: What proofs do you expect from them, my General? Look at these Pioneers, didn't their fathers prove themselves in 1914–1918? They themselves, did they not prove themselves in 1939–1940? Call them directly into the regular units and they will gladly reply to your appeal, but as soon as you talk to them about volunteering . . .
Gen. Boisseau: Yes, yes, I am familiar with the situation, but I cannot do anything; I am in charge of recruiting volunteers . . .
Gen. Borboissel: You were a scout?
Trojman: Yes, my General.
Gen. Borboissel: Then we depend on you to advise your coreligionists.

In fact, the creation of "Jewish Pioneers" did not serve the interests of the fighting forces of the Allies but were the smokescreen for a savage anti-Jewish policy conducted under the very eyes of the American and British armies.

A memorandum entitled "The Use of Jews in the Army" (Utilisation des Israélites dans l'armée), dated January 30, 1943 and signed by Major General René Jacques Prioux and General Louchet contained the following two clauses:

> (1) Jewish commissioned and non-commissioned officers and men in the reserve will generally be assigned to special non-combatant work units; (2) This measure appears necessary in order to avoid having the entire Jewish population gain the title of war veterans, which might prejudice the status given these people after the war.

A copy of the document was obtained by Paul Jacob, a French lawyer and former army officer, then living in the United States where he was secretary of the French Republican Committee. Jacob stated that by a prior order of December 30, 1942, Jewish officers expelled by Vichy in June 1940 could be reinstated only on the condition that they were wounded or cited for bravery during the First or Second World War and their reinstatement application approved by higher authorities. Two of his friends, Jacob disclosed, were discharged from the army in Morocco because they refused to join a non-combatant unit. "In Morocco," said Jacob, "General Lascroux ordered that Jewish physicians and pharmacists in the 22nd Army Medical Corps could not exceed 3% of the total number of men in the corps." These charges were confirmed in April by R. Maillard Stead, the *Christian Science Monitor* correspondent in North Africa. Earlier, on April 1, 1943, the New York *Times* had published the following cable sent from Algiers by C. L. Sulzberger: "Despite some slight improvement in the status of the Jews since General Giraud's liberalizing decrees were issued, they are far from the status they had attained under the French Republic. If a Jew goes into the army, he enters a labor corps, not a line unit."

The French military mission in the United States did not deny the existence of such a memorandum by Giraud. It only said that "the authenticity of the document did not matter, since it was several months old, and that the recent statements and acts of the general showed that he intended to remove discrimination."

When the dissolution of the non-combatant-Jewish units started at the end of April 1943, it, too, was accomplished in a spirit of anti-Jewish discrimination. Stephen S. Wise appealed to Henry C. Stimson, Secretary of War, against this discrimination. (Senator Edwin C. Johnson of Colorado had proposed earlier that all the Jews of military age in North Africa "be organized into a separate unit within the ranks of the American Expeditionary Force"). On June 2, 1943, the French military mission in Washington advised Henry Torrès, president of the Representative Committee of French Jews, that all discrimination against Jews in the army be abolished. However, the *Bulletin de la Fédération des Sociétés Juives d'Algérie* (Bulletin of the Federation of Jewish Societies in Algeria) of July 1943 confirmed the existence of such discrimination, and in September 1943 de Gaulle found the status of Jews in the armed forces of North Africa unsatisfactory.[284]

It is worthwhile to mention that a large number of Jews of Tangier who attempted to volunteer with the French Corps Francs were arrested in May and June 1943 by the Spanish authorities.[285]

In connection with Rabbi Trojman's above-noted recollection of the military record of the Algerian Jews in both world wars, it is important to recall a few facts. During World War I General Gallieni was in command of the 6th Army fighting at the Marne. The 45th Division, formed at Oran under the command of General Maunoury and consisting mainly of reservists, was attached to Gallieni's Army. In some units of the Division, a third or a half were Algerian Jews. Algerian Jewish soldiers of the Marne front fought at Barcy, Vaeeddes, Entrepilly, Chambry, and in four days covered over 100 kilometers to Soissons and beyond. When General Foch defeated the German offensive at the Marne, his small 9th Army was reinforced by a division from Morocco consisting mainly of young soldiers from Algeria, among whom many were Jews. This division fought bravely at the plateau of Mandemont. The Paris firemen who were in charge of burying the dead after the battle of Oureq, noticed a large number of bodies with *arbekanfes* worn by Orthodox Jews. Shortly afterwards Narcisse Leven died. He was secretary to Adolphe Crémieux and helped to prepare the Crémieux Decree that granted French citizenship to the Algerian Jews in 1870. The Chief Rabbi of the Paris Consistory recalled this fact in connection with the bravery of Algerian Jewish soldiers.

Algerian Jews were drafted but there were 87 others who volunteered (including 34 for the Legion), of whom 27 were killed in action. Twenty members of one family named Belahsen volunteered for service.[286]

XXVII. "Incredible" Politics of Compromise

At a meeting of the Joint Commission on Political Prisoners, held on January 8, 1943, Maj. Gen. Walter B. Smith asked "why there was so much interest in the Jews at this time." In the minutes of the meeting it was noted:

> It was brought out in discussion that the repeal of strictly Hitler laws was desirable. Strong pressure groups in the United States were pressing for Jewish freedom in Africa. The removal of restrictions, such as the prohibition of Jews from practicing medicine, might be advisable. On the other hand, it would be undesirable for the Jews to get control of the distribution of supplies. *It was agreed* that a start should be made in Algeria rather than in Morocco. In Morocco the Jewish problem was more acute than in Algeria. Trade in any case would for the time being remain in the hands of the Government agencies. Darlan had in fact, before his assassination, agreed to repeal the anti-Jewish decrees. This had been held up only because of his death.
>
> Mr. [Harold] MacMillan said that he considered it important that the existing anti-Jewish measures should be rescinded, simply on the ground that they were a survival of the Nazi regime. It was not necessary to do more than restore the *status quo* as at the time of the Armistice, and there need in his view be no question of giving the Jewish community any more privileged position than they had enjoyed at that time.[287]

According to one source, MacMillan, British Minister in North Africa, stated "the attitude toward the Jews must be changed because the present attitude will never be acceptable to the British and American peoples."[288]

At a later meeting held on February 19, 1943, Capt. Paul Felix Warburg, an American Jew, said that

> pressure was being brought to bear from the United States as to the question of the Jews and that from the point of view of all Governments concerned it was imperative that an announcement was not made which would cause an outcry from the public.[289]

Indeed, not only Jews protested. On February 3, 1943, Leslie T. Pennington was asked by seventeen parishioners of The First Parish In

Cambridge (Mass.) of The First Church (Unitarian) to send the following letter to Cordell Hull, Secretary of State:

> We are deeply disturbed by word that the anti-Semitic laws in French North Africa are allowed to stand, that these Nazi-dictated policies are only to be "relaxed" and not to give way to the prior laws of the French Republic which we are fighting to free. Nothing in this war has so outraged the conscience of civilized man as Hitler's treatment of the Jews, and it seems incredible that this magnificent American occupation of North Africa should be clouded by compromise with one of the deepest evils of Hitler's influence. The peoples of the world who love freedom and justice are watching America, will be influenced by her example, will be cheered by every evidence of the cleanness of her aims, and disillusioned by evidence of such compromise. Surely our influence with the French leaders in North Africa is sufficient to effect this reform, and if we fail to use this influence, to whom can the conscience of civilized man turn?[290]

Antisemitism was very much part of the general atmosphere after the liberation of North Africa and this had an influence on the situation of the internees in the camps. On December 15, 1942, Radio Morocco broadcasted an article by Pierre Bouton, Professor at Rabat and an active member of the antisemitic Action Française. He said,

> Before this spring will be born for us, we shall have to fight and France will have a hard winter, a winter that may last more than three months. You will not believe the fight for which we are preparing here is that of Jews and Liberals. We who fought the Red flag because it did not belong to our race and our history shall not be taken in by the threat of Freemasonry. We know how to deal with it, and that disorder when it is not supported by the Government is easily swept away by a few squads of bold young men. And, besides, what disgrace if we expected from the Germans protection against our Jews and our revolutionaries! We have fought in civil struggles against the conception which finally surrenders man to gold. We are not going to change our opinion, but it is clear enough that Paris and Marseilles are being occupied by Jews and Freemasons who have dismissed our last source of strength and independence in the mother country—the Army.[291]

Prof. Bouton was not arrested. However, seventeen persons, including the Algerian Jewish leader Dr. Henri Aboulker and his son José, who played an important role in the preparation of the American landing of November 8, 1942, were arrested on December 29. All interventions on their behalf failed. Robert D. Murphy told a delegation of the Jewish community that this was an internal French affair and refused to intervene. (Jews engineered the uprising at Algiers which neutralized that city and forced its surrender to the Americans.) The Moroccan Jew Jacob Cohen was condemned, on December 2, 1942, to six months of hard labor for having expressed his enthusiasm for the Allies.[292]

The Comité Juif Algérien d'Etudes Sociales reported to the World Jewish Congress in New York that on November 21, 1942, Pierre Bouton was summoned to the High Commission at Algiers where the post of Chief of Services of the Interior was entrusted to him. The same report, made public in New York, stated:

> Prior to the arrival of American troops an anti-Semitic campaign, bordering on a veritable call to pillage and murder, had been staged by such official or semi-official organizations as La Legion Française de Combattants. The spokesmen and organizers of this anti-Semitic campaign, hampered in the execution of their plans by the arrival of the American troops, were not reconciled to the collapse of their criminal schemes and even while the Americans marched through the main streets, skirmishes were being fomented, the Jewish quarter was overrun; children, women and old people were assaulted and stripped of their belongings and several synagogues were stoned and desecrated. Immediately, the anti-Semitic leaders formulated a series of slogans, designed to arouse the population against the Jews and here are the most prevalent ones:
> The Americans have come to avenge the Jews.
> The American President is a Jew. (An accusation of German origin, used by Hitler agitators, to the effect that Roosevelt, in fact, is Rosenfeld.)
> The American trucks and vehicles are marked with the yellow star which, in France, the Jews are forced to wear on their chest.
> The Jews are lifting their heads and they are going to give orders from now on.
> Protected by the Americans, the Jews no longer recognize the authority of the pachas or of the Sultan.
> Posters appeared again: "This is still a Jewish war."
> Because the Jews had wildly manifested their joy upon the arrival of the American troops, the anti-Semitic agitators, toward the middle of November, took their revenge upon them through beatings, slashings, pillage, destruction of property. In some cities, the agitators were helped by the Administration which made sporadic arrests and inflicted severe penalties upon the Jewish population. Certain functionaries, in spite of the arrival of the American troops, continued to give free reign to their anti-Semitic feelings and succeeded, even during American occupation, singularly enough, in mistreating certain parts of the population, namely Jews, for the officially expressed reason that they had acclaimed the Americans. Here are the proofs substantiating the above:

(1) At Rabat, an American asked Ben Guira for a match. He was arrested by the police and taken to prison; he was released three days later, his father being a Brazilian.

(2) A waiter in a cafe had made friends with American soldiers and they asked him to go for a walk with them to show them the city. When he returned, he was arrested by a policeman, just as he stepped out of a car, and was taken to the police station. The next day, the tribunal of the pacha sentenced him to three months imprisonment.

(3) At Ben Ahmed, a small locality, a few American soldiers were passing through. Some Jewish schoolboys stopped to look at them and Jewish women, too, greeted the American soldiers. The civil controller, chief of the district of Ben Ahmed, Mr. Costaud, whose anti-Semitism is notorious and who has always discriminated against the Jews, even to the extent of depriving them of the rations they were entitled to, summoned the director of the Jewish school there, to appear before him and told him that the Jewish women had indulged in reprehensible demonstrations, going as far as to kiss the feet of the American soldiers. He immediately summoned all the Jewish notables, in the presence of the Caid, and notified them that he would not tolerate any demonstrations toward the Americans by the Jewish population. As a result, when American soldiers visit Ben Ahmed from time to time, the Jews, being frightened, flee the Americans, and even shut themselves up in their homes, to the great astonishment of the American soldiers.

(4) The Community of Beni Mellal is an example of a community handed over to a civil controller, Mr. E. and his assistant, Capt. T., who even in the presence of the American troops, mistreat their Jewish subjects. The hostile regulations against the Jews subject them to a regime of oppression and terror. Needless to say, that in the distribution of food brought by the Americans, the Jewish population is being defrauded by these officials.

What was the attitude of the French refugees in North Africa? The same report noted:

The French refugees came principally from the departments of the North and from Alsace-Lorraine. They were a democratic element who only submitted to the New Order by necessity and were not at all anti-Semitic. The same holds true today [after November 8, 1942]. They rarely mix with the hybrid French element in Morocco. By a special irony they replaced the Jews in the administrative positions. A great many became employees in the organizations.[292a]

On January 30, 1943 the State Department was informed that, in the opinion of a Gaullist publicist, Algerian colonists, especially Neo-French, were "slave traders who lack both humanity and national sense." Disagreement among Frenchmen in Africa was aggravated by the Jewish question. "Hated by Mussulmans and suspected even by moderate

French, Jews were ostracized by the Algerian administration on orders from Vichy and to please Berlin. Moderates nevertheless preferred this solution to that of Third Republic." The joy of the Jews with the arrival of the Americans strengthened the rightists. American authorities advised by Murphy, made possible, it seemed, the acceptance of the Darlan-Giraud solution of the Jewish problem.[293]

Many Frenchmen of Algeria were just not ready to give up the Jewish properties which had been confiscated and sold to them.[294] On January 19, 1943, the anti-British, antisemitic Marcel Peyrouton, former Vichy Minister of the Interior, was appointed Governor General of Algiers. This provoked great apprehension and resentment. Within a fortnight, on January 30, Gen. Henri Honoré Giraud insisted that the Jewish question was an internal affair of the French administration, and that he would not tolerate outside pressure to remove anti-Jewish restrictions. He promised that confiscated property would be restored to Jews and that Jewish children would be readmitted to the schools, but added, however, that even "these moves must be made gradually."[295]

It took a long time before the most restrictive anti-Jewish laws introduced during the Vichy regime in North Africa were abolished. On *April 27, 1943*, Robert D. Murphy reported on the opening session of the Conseil Général of Algeria:

> An item of possible interest at the opening session at Algiers was a brief speech by a Jewish member who pointed out that while at the moment he could not exercise his full powers as a member of the Conseil Général (because of the loss of citizenship when the Crémieux decree was abolished), he expected to attend the meetings but would refrain from taking part in the debates or voting until such time as the situation was corrected.[296]

On March 14, 1973, Gen. Giraud declared all Vichy legislation against Jews null and void. On the very next day, however, the British and American public learned that they had been misled; Giraud did not annul the abrogation of the Crémieux Decree. Hannah Arendt wrote then:

> Since Jews had no personal status but were entirely subject to French law, they were French citizens not by privilege but by right. General Giraud's abrogation of the Crémieux decree introduces into Algeria a new criterion for French citizenship and creates a distinction between natives and citizens that is in flagrant contradiction to all French laws, to all French institutions and to the whole of French colonial policy. This distinction, abandoning as it does the

basis of French law, language, and civilization, cannot be based upon anything else than racial origin.

If General Giraud, instead of abolishing the Crémieux decree, had extended French citizenship to all natives prepared to accept French civil law and to renounce personal status (as was proposed by Cuttoli in 1935), it might have been dubious whether under the present circumstances he had any legal right to make such a constitutional change. But, at least, he would have acted according to the standards of traditional French colonial policies, and he would have put into effect a law which had been discussed time and again before the Parliament. The possibility of repealing the Crémieux decree, however, had not been mentioned in Parliament for more than forty years.

General Giraud pretends to have nullified the Crémieux decree because it caused inequality among the natives and gave a privileged position to the Jews. Actually, he has acted as an agent of those French colonials who always wanted to bring under their "dictatorship" the only part of the Algerian population that so far had escaped their arbitrary and selfish rule. The French colonials, in other words, took advantage of France's defeat and of their freedom from the control of the mother country in order to introduce into Algeria a measure which they would never have been able to obtain through legal channels.[297]

Admiral William D. Leahy wrote that there were reports that pressure was being brought to bear on Roosevelt to receive de Gaulle and that this "was being instigated by a group of Jews and Communists in this country who feared Darlan's 'Fascist' attitude." The Joint Chiefs of Staff advised Roosevelt that if he should confer with de Gaulle at this time, this might seriously affect the North African campaign. On December 8, 1942, Gen. Eisenhower wrote to Gen. George L. Marshall that Darlan was grateful to Roosevelt for realizing that "there is a local Jew-Moslem problem that is full of explosive possibilities unless carefully handled."[298]

The Joint Chiefs of Staff acted on the advice of Robert D. Murphy who was the chief architect of Allied policies in North Africa. According to him

> It was essential to move very cautiously in revoking Nazi decrees while the outcome of military operations in Africa was still indecisive. German propagandists were agitating the Arabs by broadcasting that the United States was controlled by Jews, and if Americans won the war they would elevate Jews to supreme power in North Africa. Great care was necessary if we were to prevent racial uprisings which would be detrimental to the Allied military campaign.[299]

There is no doubt that Murphy was biased against Jews in general and that he accepted the Jew-Bolshevik bogey. Thus he wrote in his memoirs that anti-semitism was already widespread in France during the period of the "phony war," "aggravated by the fact that some prominent Communists were Jews." However, there were almost no "prominent Jews" among the French Communists at that time. Murphy also wrote that Marcel Peyrouton, who, as the Vichy Minister of the Interior promulgated the first decrees against Jews and was later nominated Governor General of Algeria after the Allied landing, was a victim of his "alleged" antisemitism.[300]

Murphy recalled in his memoirs that a group of American-Jewish soldiers in Algeria called upon him and told him, "We are informed that you have been in Algiers for more than a year, yet you have done nothing about the Jews here! Don't you think you have outlived your usefulness in Africa and should get out fast?"[301]

Major Paul Felix Warburg, a member of a well-known Jewish banking family, was on Murphy's staff for many months. He would constantly advise the American authorities to avoid playing into the hands of the Nazi propagandist by insisting the French give the Jews back their rights too soon. When Secretary of the Treasury Henry Morgenthau, Jr., visited Algiers, Warburg "prudently" recommended that he avoid public meetings with the Jewish community, "lest such association appear to confirm Nazi propaganda."[302]

Later, on May 5, 1944, a certain Hoffman who was on the staff of the War Refugee Board (WRB) reported the following in connection with the activities of Leonard E. Ackermann, representative of the WRB for North Africa:

> As far as I know, Warburg has never contributed anything to the alleviation of the condition of the Jews in North Africa, and at the moment, because of his position and close relations with the State Department in the area, he is likely to be a hindrance to Ackermann's operations.[303]

Kenneth G. Crawford wrote in his *Report on North Africa* that incipient pogroms occurred in Casablanca when the Americans attacked the harbor on November 8. Jews had celebrated the event, proclaiming the imminent arrival of their deliverers. When Americans arrived with stars painted on their vehicles, the Arabs were convinced that these soldiers were, indeed, warriors fighting under the star of David. American officers "submitted reports which later prompted, or helped prompt, the abrogation of the Crémieux Decree and stirred up an international storm." The decision regarding the Crémieux Decree was finally made, along with many other decisions affecting North African policy, at the so-called Anfa conference in January, 1943 where President Roosevelt met with Prime Minister Churchill. They were advised by American and British agents that at any moment Arab unrest might erupt into revolt behind Allied lines, requiring the diversion of troops to put down the uprising. This was a chance they did not want to take. "Yet, if Roosevelt and Churchill placated the Arabs by some positive gesture, they would run a risk of alienating the French colonials, whose cooperation they also needed. Thus the decision to placate the Arabs by depriving the Jews of suffrage." Washington authorities pointed out that the Jews had lost nothing, that their citizenship would remain academic for some time because there had been no election in France since the beginning of the war, etc. The North African Jews and the French Jews living in exile did not see it that way. Crawford wrote: "Why Americans thought it necessary to play up to the Arabs at the expense of the Jews is something of a mystery. Except for minor incidents at Casablanca, I heard of no evidence of violent Moslem unrest."[304]

Giraud's decree returned sequestered Jewish property and removed lesser discriminating practices but failed to restore the Crémieux Decree.

French officials further distorted the real problem by stating that "most Jews prefer to get citizenship independently. Most Algerian Jews are townspeople, well educated and able to pass the educational tests necessary for qualification. They are keenly aware of the dangers of a Moslem uprising in this period."[305]

Baron Edouard de Rothschild, representative of the Franco-Jewish community in exile, protested against the French administration's complicity with the Allies in depriving the French Jews of their citizenship. Later he characterized as "erroneous and inaccurate" the opinion given by "an unbiased specialist familiar with the various legal points involved," who was quoted by Under-Secretary of State Sumner Welles in defending General Giraud's action.[306]

French official Jean Monnet tried to obtain an opinion which could be used against Rothschild from Justice Felix Frankfurter. He sent a message to Frankfurter through Consul General Willey explaining the Darlan-Murphy-Warburg position ("accurate statement made after consultation with an unbiased and best qualified legal specialist"). Justice Frankfurter sent the following message to Monnet on March 27, 1943:

Greatly appreciate your message. Have neither knowledge nor concern for de

Rothschild. For my own understanding should like to be clear about scope and implications of abrogation of Crémieux decree. Does it deprive of French citizenship anyone who possessed it prior to Vichy decrees. If so how many and what is the justification for such deprivation. Warmest regards.[307]

On April 17, Consul General Willey advised the State Department that

The formula adopted by the French contemplates in effect the reversion to the pre-war status without causing, it is hoped, a violent reaction from the Moslem population which the authorities believed the direct revival of the Crémieux Decree might inspire.[308]

On the same day Villey acknowledged in a cable to the State Department, which was seeking further reason for rejecting the criticism of Allied policy toward Jews in North Africa by Rothschild and others, that it was indeed "correct" that General Giraud, by abrogating the Crémieux Decree had deprived French Jews, born and bred as Frenchmen for the second, third or even fourth generation of their citizenship. This "temporary suspension of citizenship will be removed by the further ordinances previously reported as in preparation which it is stated will shortly be promulgated. They will enable the native Jews in this category to acquire citizenship by a simple form of procedure." He further reported that French laws in general are not retroactive (article two of the civil code). "For this reason Algerian Jews did not cease to be French nationals or lose their rights as such when the Crémieux decree was abrogated." The French Conseil d'Etat had, however, frequently held that certain laws with respect to citizenship and specially the right to vote may be retroactive since the electoral statute is a part of the political system. On the same day Murphy reported that Rothschild's attack was based on a "misconception." While it was true that most of the native Jews of Algeria had lost their citizenship as a result of General Giraud's abrogation of the Crémieux Decree, in no instance did they lose their status as French subjects. As French subjects, they retained all the rights of French citizens, including the right to vote for local assemblies, etc. The only two exceptions were the right to vote for Deputies and Senators and the right to hold public executive office such as governor general, prefect, or judge. Jews could fill minor administrative positions, however.[309]

The New York *Times* of October 25, 1943, published a protest by Jacques Maritain, President of the Executive Committee of the Ecole Libre des Hautes Etudes against the abrogation of the Crémieux Decree.

Maritain wrote:

1. It is a profoundly regrettable contradiction that a law of the French Republic should have been "abrogated" at the very same moment when Algeria solemnly proclaimed its return to the laws of the republic.

2. This abrogation is unjust in itself and is contrary to all the traditions of French law, because

   a. It penalizes retroactively persons who are in no way guilty of any offense, and thus infringes upon the principle of non-retroaction of laws, which in all civilized countries is the very safeguard of acquired rights.

   b. It deprives of their citizenship men who are French by birth. . . .

   c. In modern legislative practice the withdrawal of citizenship rights is a very serious penalty meted out to nationals who have committed the crime of espionage or treason. As a result of the abrogation of the Crémieux law a whole category of citizens find themselves thus penalized for the sole reason of being Jewish—a sanction which is without precedent except under racist law.

3. The normal way to remedy the unequal treatment of which Algerian Arabs may be complaining is progressively to lead to French citizenship those of them who will have proved their sincere desire to become a part of the French community. . . .

4. The exceptional circumstances created by the state of war and by the troubled situation in North Africa forbid the turning of any protest, even legitimate, into an occasion for agitation in Algeria. If the Jews of Algeria therefore abstain from such agitation this does not mean that they recognize the invalidation of their rights. . . .

5. It should also be stated that if patriotic duty and concern about victory sometimes demand the temporary acceptance of factual situations in which certain rights are sacrificed, nevertheless the abrogation of a law of the republic without the consent of the French people is and remains by nature an act without juridical value.

6. Finally, if those who today declare themselves in favor of a measure contrary to law, in the name of expediency, give as their reason the unequal treatment of the Arabs—an argument whose validity we deny, because unequal treatment is not remedied by an even greater injustice—still we feel that such an argument deserves to be discussed and refuted.

But if an attempt were made to justify the abrogation of the Crémieux law merely as a measure of appeasing the anti-Semitic feelings developed by German propaganda and by the servility of the Vichy regime toward Nazi Germany, such an argument would deserve only to be branded as unworthy of the cause for which the free peoples are fighting. A precedent of this kind would involve the greatest dangers for the future reconstruction of Europe and cannot be accepted by the human conscience. Anti-semitism is the vehicle of all Nazi poisons, and in no event must any concession be made to it.[310]

On July 14, 1943, during a visit to the United States, Capt. Warburg drafted the following reply by the State Department to Congressman Emanuel Celler's intervention in connection with the Crémieux Decree:

On March 14th 1943 General Giraud abrogated the Vichy Laws and the Crémieux Decree. I feel it my duty to fully inform those interested in this subject as to the political and military situation at that time. It is important for you to know that when our troops landed in North Africa the German propaganda machine started a campaign in Arabic by radio and by word of mouth. This propaganda was to the effect that the American Army was really a Jewish Army, that it had come to liberate the Jews of North Africa and to enslave the Arabs. Laughable as it may seem, they even went so far as to point out that our military equipment stamped with the American Star was not an American Star at all, but the Jewish "Star of David." Since the very beginning this type of propaganda has never ceased and unfortunately has met with a certain amount of success among the Arabs.

The Germans' plan in Tunisia was, wherever they occupied French territory to take the French Colonial farms away from their rightful owners and give them to the Arabs. They also paid the Arabs high prices for their produce and curried their favor in many other ways. This as you can well understand met with great success in the Arab world as unfortunately they have never been satisfied with the treatment they have received from their French conquerors. This catering to the Arabs and at the same time continuing their propaganda that the American Jewish Army was in their land to enslave the Arabs, created a ticklish situation between these two groups which had to be reckoned with.

Your representatives in North Africa were instructed to use every influence on the French Authorities to abrogate the Vichy laws. General Giraud and his advisors took the position that while heartily in agreement with this plan, but because of the United Nations' weak military position in Tunisia, an Arab uprising might be promulgated by the Germans and therefore preferred to wait until such time as our military situation improved before abrogating this law. It should be recalled that these negotiations were started way back in January and at that time the German Armies in Tunisia were pushing back the United Nations' troops.

This is the background of the situation which actually existed during the negotiations with the French authorities but because of our constant pressure, notwithstanding the bad military situation, General Giraud on March 14th issued a proclamation abrogating these Vichy Laws. This meant that all European and Metropolitan Jews were once again reinstated to their full economic and political rights. This he could justify on the basis that it did not disturb the native Jewish-Arab problem. Whereas, the Crémieux Decree which makes all native Jews citizens of France and does not automatically make the Arabs citizens of France, could not be abrogated at this time because of the tense situation which I mentioned above.

It is probably true that the Arabs do not wish French citizenship but there are economic advantages which they have been trying to obtain. These demands have fallen upon deaf ears. It is my considered opinion that now that the military danger is over, the Crémieux Decree should and must be reinstated, but it is my hope that at the same time certain economic advantages be given the Arabs. The Arab leaders feel that they have been unjustly treated by the various French administrations, as they feel that they have always been treated as guests in their own land.

I believe that the reason the Crémieux Decree has not been reinstated nor a machinery set up to enable the native Jews to reestablish their French citizenship is because of the unwillingness of the French administration in North Africa to give any concessions to the Arabs at this time. This whole problem is no longer in the hands of General Giraud but a matter to be decided on by the French Committee of National Liberation and I hope that pressure will be brought to bear on this Committee for a prompt solution.

The same points were made by Warburg in a memorandum stating his personal opinion on the subject.[311]

Murphy wrote in his memoirs (published in 1964) that Warburg had acted as liaison between Giraud and the Chief Rabbi of Algiers, Maurice Eisenbeth, who "endorsed every phase of Giraud's program." He further stated:

What the Jewish people in the United States did not understand, and Major Warburg and the Grand Rabbi understood very well indeed, was that to restore the Crémieux law required extremely delicate handling, in view of the passions which had smoldered for generations among Algerian Christians as well as Moslems. . . .

In 1943, like the Grand Rabbi of Algiers and High Commissioner Giraud and Governor General Peyrouton, I realized that the conditions in Africa were very different from conditions in America.[312]

It so happened, that in 1945 Chief Rabbi Maurice Eisenbeth of Algeria published his memoirs of the 1940-1943 period in which he described in great detail his strongly worded protest against the Darlan-Peyrouton's action without mentioning the fact of his ever having accepted Giraud's, Murphy's, or Warburg's advice. Whom should he believe? Surely, Rabbi Eisenbeth's memoirs as well as the numerous documents he cites are more reliable. He did not specifically deny the allegations by Murphy and Warburg simply because they were then, in 1945, unknown to him. Even earlier, in November 1942-1943, Rabbi Eisenbeth's protests were known in the United States and later, in 1950, were again published by Michel Ansky.[313]

On October 21, 1943, the Crémieux Decree was again in force. Actually, this came about not by any positive act of justice on the part of the French Committee of National Liberation, but by technical default. When General Giraud withdrew French citizenship from the Algerian Jews by not restoring the laws Vichy had abrogated, he stipulated that within three months, further regulations would be laid down that would serve to implement his decision. The three months had passed without the enactment of such ordinances. As a result, according to the Committee of National Liberation, the abrogation of the Crémieux Decree had never become effective. Thus the decree was again in force. The *Jewish Frontier* commented, "We admit we should have preferred a less involved and franker method of bringing it about, a method more in the spirit of President Roosevelt's recent statement, with respect to our own Chinese exclusion laws, that a nation can sometimes make a mistake." On the other hand, at the meeting which accepted the decision, M. de Menthon, an outstanding French resistance leader, pointed out that the resistance movement had always regretted and resented the abrogation. In addition General Georges Cartoux, who, as Governor General of Algeria and Commissioner for Moslem Affairs knew the trend of Moslem opinion, was willing just the same to take the step even though some of the strongest opposition came from members of his own staff. (J. Rives Childs of the American Legation in Tangier reported on September 10, 1942, that the Sultan of Morocco had ordered to apply the anti-Jewish laws with the utmost vigor to French, German and other Jews living in Morocco but to use restraint in regard to Moroccan Jews.)[314]

POSTSCRIPT

In September 1941, I came to the United States as a refugee. A short time later, I was drafted into the United States Army where I served as a paratrooper with the 82nd Airborne Division. In the course of my basic training, I became an American citizen. I cannot remember even one instance of having been insulted, mistreated or even reminded of the fact that I was not a native American.

The world has changed greatly since the two World Wars, for Jewry as well as for France. It seems unlikely that the tragic events described here will be repeated yet a third time. Unlikely? Unless a strict French law is enacted making it illegal to enlist aliens in the Foreign Legion in the case of war the tragic story of Carency may be repeated. Just the same, this story no doubt has lessons for us and thus is surely worth telling.

I may be criticized for having written a biased book, for not being objective, for always looking at the worst aspects of the Legion, etc. To these critics I can only say this. Look at the photograph of the prison in the sand of a camp in North Africa and try to write an objective book! What happened to the Jewish legionnaires in the camps of France and of North Africa before and after the liberation is part of the history of the Holocaust, and one cannot write an objective book about any aspect of the Holocaust.

On the other hand, I do not believe that I am biased because the facts are undeniable. Others have described them in articles, books and official reports. I may be further criticized for not having limited myself merely to the two World Wars. Why involve the French Foreign Legion at all? But, if there had not been a Foreign Legion the tragic facts of Carency in World War I and the camps of North Africa in World War II would not have existed. Alien Jews of France, Loyalist Spaniards and many other aliens were ready to fight for France without their being forced to serve in the Legion. But having no choice, they fought and died in spite of the Legion.

There might be yet another argument against my position. All these terrible acts were not perpetrated by the France of 1789, 1830 and 1848. It was by the Vichy government alone, acting on its own initiative and on orders from Germany which was responsible. In an earlier book published in 1966 *(Analytical Franco-Jewish Gazeteer 1939-1945. With an Introduction to Some Problems in Writing the History of the Jews in France during World War II)* I describe in detail the conditions in Argelès, Aubagne, Barcarès, Brens, Catus, Gurs, Lambesc, Les Milles, Montguyon, Rieurcos, Saint-Cyprien, Saintes, Septfonds, Le Vernet and all the other camps which had been in existence long before the Franco-German armistice of June 1940. These camps were maintained by a government that pretended to represent the spirit of 1789, 1830 and 1848.

Many of the camps were first used for the internment of Spanish Loyalist soldiers and their families who sought refuge in France after Franco's victory. In fact, it was for these people that the French concentration camps were first established. Later, the Spaniards shared the camps with the Jewish refugees. Thus, the fate of these two groups became intertwined.

A law of November 2, 1938 authorized the internment of "undesirable aliens" in camps ("étrangers indesirables dans les centres spéciaux"). By then, however, the number of internees was already quite large. Ironically, a Franco-Jewish Minister of the Interior, Georges Mandel, who himself fell victim to the anti-Jewish policy, was in charge of the camps for a time. Of course, these refugees were not interned because they were Jews, but most refugees were Jewish. As early as the summer of 1939, more German, Austrian and even Polish Jews were interned. A law of December 31, 1939, extended the scope of such internment. Many refugees, taken off ships, both enemy ships and neutral ships, were interned. According to HICEM reports at the end of 1939, about 6,000 Jews were interned in approximately 70 camps. However, the number of camps was underestimated. Many refugees were also imprisoned and were rarely freed. When the law of October 4, 1940 gave the Prefects of the free zone the right to intern Jews, there was no shortage of camps.

Officially, the concentration camps of 1939-1940 were rarely designated as such by this horrible name. They were imaginatively called, "centers," "supervised lodging centers," "reception centers," etc. Thanks to this "hypocrisy," to use the expression of one historian, the system of camps became recognized as a legal institution in a civilized society. This "hypocrisy" was continued after June 1941 until the very end of the War.[315]

There is something to say in the "defense" of those who continued to intern the legionnaires—volunteers for the defense of France—in concentration camps after the liberation of North Africa and that is, the United States and Great Britain have a share in the responsibility.

There is yet another reason for my writing this book. Bruno Weil expressed it when he cried out in his memoirs about a French camp, "Ich liebe Frankreich. Darum habe ich dieses Buch uber das lager Le Vernet geschriben'' (I love France. It is because of this that I wrote this book about the camp Le Vernet).[316]

APPENDIX
Military Service of Russian Jews in England

During World War I, there was more freedom of expression and less official censorship in England. Thus, even immigrant Russian Jews were able to explain in the press and through leaflets their reasons for refusing to return to Russia and serve there or in the Allied armies abroad. As the situation had many similarities to that in France, it may be worthwhile to give a few excerpts from printed documents.

1. Memorandum by Lucien Wolf, secretary of the Conjoint Foreign Committee of the Board of Deputies and the Anglo-Jewish Association. [317]

Russian Jews who have sought and found an asylum from persecution in this country ought to be in favour of compulsory military service for two reasons:

(1) Because they should wish to share fully in the burdens and sacrifices of the native Englishmen who have treated them so generously; and,

(2) Because they should wish to be saved from their shirkers.

Unfortunately, compulsion is required for other and less heroic reasons. The only question is whether it should be direct or indirect.

Compulsion is really indispensable if the Jewish community are to be spared an explosion of anti-Semitism, and if their good name in this country is to be maintained.

Without compulsion, the response to the invitation of the War Office is likely to be very small, and, even if it is large, the Russian Jews will still be victimised by their shirkers, and the dangers of anti-Semitic calumny and agitation will remain.

In a word, compulsion is needed to save the Russian Jews from being compromised by the less worthy elements among them, and in this way to tranquillize public opinion.

It would, however, be exceedingly imprudent to apply compulsion crudely and directly.

To compel aliens to serve in the army would be against all principles of constitutional and international law. It would afford a disastrous example to anti-Semitic countries, like Rumania, and it would supply the Jewish shirkers themselves with a grievance which they may be trusted to exploit very effectively.

The Russian Jews declare they are attached to this country, but they urge that, if they are to serve in the army, they should only do so in the capacity of full citizens.

In my opinion, the proper course to pursue is to take them at their word.

Let the Government offer naturalisation to all Russian Jews, and their immediate dependents, eligible by reason of good character and conduct, and the permanence of their residence in this country. Permanent residence should be tested, not by the length of residence, but by the intention of the resider, as shown by his willingness or not to go back to Russia.

If this were done, all else would follow automatically.

Russian Jews naturalised in this way would be liable to the Army Service Act like other Englishmen.

Those who refused naturalisation would *ipso facto* affirm their Russian nationality and their attachment to, and preference for, Russia. They should consequently be compelled to discharge the military obligations they owe to that country. If they have no military obligations in Russia, they should have none here.

Russian Jews who, by reason of bad character, are ineligible for naturalisation, should be deported to Russia as undesirables. Where, however, the circumstances justify an exception, they should be offered the alternative of enlisting in the British Army without naturalisation.

Some such scheme as this would leave no loop-hole for opposition in the Russo-Jewish community, and all danger of overt agitation against military service would be overcome. It would present itself, not as an act of compulsion, but as the gracious bestowal of a valuable privilege. It would also meet all the necessities and equities of the case.

There need be no fear, in my opinion, of any public disapproval of such apparently wholesale naturalisations. The anti-alien agitators cannot have it both ways. If they want the Russian Jews to serve, they must make them Englishmen. If they do not want to make them Englishmen, then they must cease from reproaching them with not serving. Moreover, as none would be naturalised who were not legally eligible, except perhaps in the strict term of residence, there would be no reasonable ground for objection.

One or two subsidiary questions remain to be mentioned.

There is, in the first place, the question of exemptions in Russia. It is difficult to get proof of exemption, as the Russian authorities refuse to supply the necessary documents. In cases, however, where Jews have come to this country with clean passports since the outbreak of the war, exemption in Russia may be safely presumed, and, as pointed out above, such exemption should be valid in England.

Another question which will have to be decided is how far service in the British Army will atone for non-service in the Russian Army. If the Jew serves in the British Army, steps should be taken to relieve him, and his relations in Russia, of the penalties he has incurred by failing to report himself to the conscription in Russia.

Russian Jews have further asked whether they will be eligible for promotion, even if they are not naturalised, and whether their rank will be recognised in Russia.

The question of Kosher food, and other ritual observances, is very largely a question of numbers. If the Jews are conscripted in full measure, this question will be solved as easily as it is solved in the case of Indians, etc.

2. *What Awaits Those Who Will Be Deported to Russia?*[318]

The reason given by the Government in the House of Lords and in the House of Commons for deporting to Russia those Russian subjects of military age who refused to enlist "voluntarily" in the British army, is to afford the Russian Government the opportunity of "making the most effective use of their reserves in men"; or, in other words, the object of the measure is to augment the fighting forces of Russia by as many as would be deported from England.

A glance at the Russian Military Service Regulations will show us that far from increasing the strength of the Russian army, the only effect of the measure of deportation will be to fill the prisons and the disciplinary battalions of Russia, already taxed to their utmost capacity, with the fresh arrivals from England.

According to Article 145 of the law promulgated on the 23rd June, 1912, amending the Military Service Regulations, and Article 514 (2) of the Penal Code, vol. xv., part I:—

"All Russian subjects abroad who have not, at the proper time, presented themselves for military service, are liable, upon their return to Russia, whether they have appeared voluntarily or not, after the 15th February of the year following that in which they were called, and provided they are below the age of 34, to imprisonment for a period of from eight months to one year and four months; and all those who have attained the age of 34, to the forfeiture of all special rights and privileges, either personally acquired or belonging to their status, and to imprisonment in a correctional prison for a period of from one year and a half to two years and a half."

The same applies to all young men below the age of 21, who were called up in 1915. If discovered with the precincts of Russia after 1st November, 1915, they will be liable to the same punishment. This is in accordance with Article 514 (2), note 2 of the Penal Code, and Article 392 (2), note 2 of the Military Service Regulations (Code of Laws, vol. iv., continuation 1912).

In August, 1914, a decree was published to the effect that Russian subjects residing abroad and liable to military service need not return to Russia but may join the armies of the Allies. On the 22nd February, 1915, a decree was published revoking that issued in August, 1914, and calling upon all Russian subjects abroad, who are liable for military service and who have not already joined the armies of the Allies, to return to Russia to fulfil their military obligations there. The decree was to come in force on 1st March, 1915.

All Russian subjects liable to military service under the Russian law, who are at the present moment in this country, will consequently, upon their return to Russia, be tried under the one or other of the laws and regulations cited above and sentences passed accordingly upon them.

Needless to say the great bulk of the Russian and Polish Jews in this country, as well as the Letts, Poles, Lithuanians and members of other nationalities, who had fled from pogroms, massacres, and the general persecution and oppression of the Russian Government, were not at all anxious to return to Russia to fulfil their military duties. A considerable number of them have actually deserted the Russian army. One who has had a glimpse of the conditions under which a Jewish soldier is placed in the Russian barracks will understand why such a large number of them run away, at great peril and risk, from the army. The Jewish soldier, who, however educated, cannot hold any commission, is at the mercy of the whims and caprices of the roughest N.C.O. He is the butt-end of all obscene jokes, continually made sport of, sneered at, beaten, spat upon, physically and morally tortured and treated like a dog. Military service for a Jewish soldier in Russia is veritable hell.

There is also a number of deserters in this country who have participated in the various military and naval risings during the revolution, and there are others who were serving in the various punitive columns which were sent to the Baltic and other provinces during the revolution and who had run away in order to avoid participating in the orgies of murder and rapine with which the punitive expeditions have distinguished themselves.

It is obvious that not military service but prison, torture and execution awaits those whom the Home Secretary will deport to Russia.

3. *The Proposed Deportation and Compulsion for Russian Subjects.* [319]

.... As Russian Jews, who in their country of origin were deprived of elementary citizen-rights, and subjected to all kinds of restrictions in movement, trade, education, etc., to constant insults, to persecutions, massacres, unspeakable horrors—we consider that deportation to Russia would be for us the most terrible of fates, and for Britain a most inconceivable act of inhumanity. It was owing to these political conditions that we came here, fleeing from brutal laws and criminal violence. We have been victims of the political régime in Russia, and therefore are all political refugees. We cannot believe that the Government of Great Britain, where the Right of Asylum has been sacred for centuries, will overthrow that noble tradition. We must especially emphasize that the Right of Asylum has always been known in History to extend to all those who left their native countries owing to persecutions, and to whom can it apply with more cogency than to ourselves? What political refugees have had grievances

The alleged object for deporting us to Russia is that we should fight for the Russian Government. On that we can in full conscience declare, that although we are at one with the Russian peoples, have the same aspirations as our fellow-workers of all the other nationalities of Russia, and although many of us have actually fought the battles of freedom for the well-being of the popular masses of Russia, yet we, as well as all other people who have fled from the persecutions of the Russian Government, have no obligations towards that Government, who have nothing for us but oppression and persecution and treat us as outlaws.

The position of our Jewish brethren in Russia is certainly not better, but even worse than that of the Armenians in Turkey. Have not Rabbis been hanged, without guilt or trial, in the market places of our native towns and townlets, in the enforced presence of the horror-stricken Jewish population? Have not the most prominent members of our communities been taken as hostages by the Russian Authorities and shot against the wall for crimes never committed? Have not our sisters and daughters been dragged into barracks and subjected to unspeakable horrors? Have not hundreds of thousands of our Jewish brethren in Russia been ruthlessly driven from the homes of their ancestors—neither the infants, the aged, the sick nor the afflicted being spared—their lives and homes ruined for ever? And all this at a time when the flower of the Jewish male population is shedding its blood on the battlefields of Poland and Galicia for the Russian Government and its Allies!

Would not there be an outcry of horror if an ally of Turkey would propose to deport Armenians to that country? In view of the horrors experienced by our people in Russia can it then be denied that the need for the preservation of the Right of Asylum in its full integrity has ever been greater than in our case?

We further submit that the invitation to join the British Army under the threat of deportation to Russia, being in effect compulsion, and compulsion of the most drastic character, has a much wider aspect involving the whole position of foreigners, who never, until now, have anywhere been pressed forcibly into the Army of a State which is not their own, and that such a precedent would gravely jeopardise the status of our Jewish brethren who, owing to their intolerable position in Russia, are scattered all over the world. We have not enjoyed all the rights and privileges of the British citizen, neither have we been able to take part in shaping the policy of Great Britain, and compulsory service cannot be extended to us directly or indirectly. We therefore hope that the British Government will not do an injustice to us by going beyond the limits of absolute voluntary enlistment.

In conclusion we beg to say that as Jewish Workers and Trade-Unionists we consider it below our dignity to deal with the false and malicious alarm-cry of the anti-Semites that we are "Job-snatchers" and could only be rendered harmless by being forcibly pressed into the Army. These unscrupulous mongers of race-hatred, these heroes of the "no Jews, no-dogs" advertisements know quite well that 95 per cent of us always have been and still are engaged in trades which were introduced, developed and built up by ourselves. They consider, however, these distressing times opportune for their vile agitations against us, but we have sufficient confidence in British public opinion to be convinced that the fair-minded British people will treat this agitation with the contempt it deserves and will recognise the terrible difficulties of our position and see the justice of our contentions . . .

4. *To the Emigrants from Russia.*[320]
Comrades and Fellow Citizens!

Never yet have the emigrants from Russia, resident in London, gone through so difficult a time as the present. Under the glamour of War an attack is being made upon the existence of the right of asylum in Great Britain, that seemed until now unassailable. It is the right of asylum that attracted into remote London tens of thousands of emigrants—in their own lands victims of oppression; it attracted the Jews who fled from the unparalleled persecutions and horrors of the barbarous Russian régime, Poles, Lithuanians, Letts, and numbers of other oppressed nationalities of immense Russia. The right of asylum attracted also fighters for a better future for Russia's unhappy people, revolutionary champions who were compelled to save themselves from the revenge of Tsarism. We came here, counting upon safety—and now it is proposed to carry us forcibly back to Russia from which we escaped, unless we submit to the act of brutality demanding from us that we should enter the British Army.

We, the emigrants from Russia, a mere handful, are without political influence, and without the power that is given by wealth. But in acting unitedly, in joining our forces, even we can obtain a desired end, and can bring the present conflict to a successful issue. Our strength is in unity. We can influence the difficult situation only by concerted action.

A strong source of such concerted action can be found in our organisations, in the London groups of the Socialist Parties of Russia. We are small groups, but in those groups the Russian Socialist Parties step forth and act; they, the representatives of the labouring and exploited masses of Russia in their struggle for a better future for themselves and for the whole human race; they, the defenders of the oppressed nationalities, untiringly struggling against the persecutions and oppressions to which these nationalities are being subjected. The organised vanguard of Russia's workers stands behind us. It gives moral and political weight to our voice and to our actions. And as in Russia our activity consists in fighting for the interests and the better future of the labouring and exploited masses and against the persecutions of oppressed nationalities, so also here, in this remote foreign country, our groups have done all they could, and are now straining all their forces, in order to save the emigrants from Russia from the great misfortune that threatens them.

The Committee of Delegates of the Russian Socialist groups in London has already worked for some time past, in preparation for this present struggle. For even when there was no compulsion of foreigners, it foresaw the coming of this danger and prepared to repel it. And now that the threat has drawn near, the Committee had developed that broad activity of which no doubt you have heard. At the present moment, it addresses itself to you, comrades and fellow citizens, in order to carry on its work in close association with you. We ask for your support, we ask for your confidence, we hope that you will listen to our voice.

And our chief lesson to you is—BE MANFUL. There is an obvious intention to act upon you by terror, and by threats to compel you to submit to brutal force. DO NOT YIELD TO FEAR, not under its influence take any course opposed to your convictions. As Socialists, as representatives of the militant vanguard of the workers of the world, we say to you: By resisting the brutal attack that is being prepared against us, we are not only struggling for our rights, we are struggling against the world-wide reaction embodied in its advocates here. In resisting this new crime of capitalism and militarism, we participate in the struggle against both that is being carried on by those workers of all countries who remain faithful to their ideals. We struggle against the violation of the right of asylum, whose conservation is a necessity for the first rank fighters of the oppressed, to whatsoever country those fighters belong.

Remember, we do not stand alone. The eyes of the Socialist International are now turned upon us. What we say here, what we do here, finds a sympathetic echo in the conscious vanguard of the working masses of all countries, and will find still stronger echo tomorrow. Let their sympathy be for you a source of fortitude, inspiring you to continue the struggle. Give no ear to those who would fill you with despondency, telling you that all is lost. It is a fraud and a lie, it is a perfidious attempt to deprive you of the whole-hearted energy and strength necessary in effectually defending yourselves against danger. We are not vanquished; there is still possibility of a successful issue. United, we will repel the attack. Steadfastness will ensure success. And may those, who after us will carry on the struggle against brutality and oppression, remember you as manly fighters, who at a critical moment were able to stand for yourselves.

5. *Statement by the London Groups of Socialist Parties of Russia.* [321]

We, the London Groups of the Socialist Parties of Russia, representing all its various nationalities, most emphatically protest against the alternative, which, according to Mr. Herbert Samuel's statement in the House of Commons on June 29th, it is proposed to be put to Russian subjects in this country, of either joining the British army or being deported to Russia. And in protesting we speak as those, who have escaped from death sentences, penal servitude, prisons, Siberia—fighters for labour's emancipation and for freedom, and also as those, who have fled from pogroms, savage persecutions and all kinds of oppression. We know that we are speaking in accordance with the views and feelings of the whole political emigration from Russia in foreign countries, and that these views correspond to the attitude of the organised labour movement in Russia.

We especially protest against the violation of the principle of the right of asylum, sacred for genuine democracy, the abandonment of which is one more significant proof of the Russianising and Prussianising of Great Britain. We must emphasize the fact, that the principle of the right of asylum has been for many centuries considered as extending to all those whom political, religious, or national persecutions would await in their native countries—to the victims of the Spanish Government who fled from the Netherlands, and to the Huguenots who left France under Louis XIV, and must necessarily extend to the victims of all the various kinds of persecutions, perpetrated by the Torquemadas and the Alvas of modern Tsarism.

We protest against the proposed compulsion of Russian subjects into the British army, a compulsion which is all the more repugnant as it is carried out not openly, but treacherously, under cover of the threat of deportation to Russia. We protest against this infringement of the elementary rights of foreigners, who, without having all the rights of British Citizens, and being subject to constant restrictions, are nevertheless pressed into cannon-food. We point out the monstrous iniquity of compelling those victims of Tsarist tyranny who sought here safety and severed every connection with their persecutor the Russian Government, to shed their blood for that same Government that caused them so much suffering. We emphasise the treachery of the trap in which the whole Russian emigration in England has been caught, seeing that it came to England with the certitude of freedom and safety, and is now not even allowed to depart to a land of its own choice.

We consider that it would be the greatest of crimes to hand over to the most barbarous of Governments not only us, its political adversaries and victims, whose fate in Russia would be physical and moral torture, but also all those, who fled from its national, religious and other persecutions and oppression, and who would be faced after their enforced return with renewed brutalities. Deportation to Russia would be the only alternative to Russian Socialists who are true to the Flag of International Labour Solidarity, and are irreconcilably opposed to all capitalist Governments and to participation in this Imperialist war.

We place our protest before the British workers and before all those, for whom freedom and democracy are not empty words.

We place our protest before our comrades in Russia, who will not forget, that the British Government, with its lip-service to freedom, has allowed itself to become the accomplice of Russian reaction and of the terrible nightmare that is oppressing all the peoples of Russia.

We place our protest before the International proletariat who have remained true to their ideals —before the reviving International Labour Movement.

6. [*Statement by the Committee of Delegates of the Russian Socialist Groups in London.*][322]

In view of the fact that there is abroad an erroneous impression that the Government have modified their attitude with regard to the question of Deportation to Russia of Russian refugees who will not enlist in the British Army, we find it necessary, in order to combat that wrong impression, to make the following statement.

(1) As seen from Mr. Herbert Samuel's declarations in the House of Commons on July 24th and on August 1st and from Lord Sandhurst's statement in the House of Lords on July 27th, to all intents and purposes Mr. Herbert Samuel's scheme remains the same. Whilst perhaps there may possibly be a few exceptions, the alternative for the Russian refugees still remains: either the British Army, or deportation to Russia.

(2) The problematical exceptions are those, who will be exempted by tribunals on grounds of "Work of necessity to the country" or on grounds of "Domestic hardships." As for those who in the eyes of the British Government will be "Genuine political refugees," their future fate, as referred to in various utterances of Mr. Herbert Samuel, is not clear at all, and quite unsettled.

(3) We must point out that every attempt of definition of Political Refugeeism by representatives of the British Government or, even more so, of the Russian Consulate, will of necessity be absolutely arbitrary. The circumstances of the position render it impossible to draw a hard and fast line as to what is or is not political refugeeism. Numerous individuals who have during their past lives in Russia been only for a time, sometimes indeed very remotely, connected with the movement for freedom, are not

even known to the Russian Socialist Organisations, while their names are still retained on the records of the Russian police. Even such who took a prominent part in the Revolutionary movement and underwent heavy sentences of penal servitude, are very often not able to produce documentary proofs of this fact, and for obvious reasons cannot make known their past activities and the happenings of their lives. Further, members of oppressed nationalities, especially Jews, even though in the past they have taken no actual part in the movement for freedom, would nevertheless in case of their enforced return to Russia incur the revenge of the Russian authorities, only too often in the most drastic form.

(4) Even the exceptions referred to above are not definitely guaranteed and are very vaguely outlined.

(5) These vague promises obviously tend to bring confusion into the minds of Russian emigrants, to divide their forces and to lead some categories of emigrants to relax their efforts in the fight and by concentration on their own personal safety to weaken the fight as a whole. Such vague promises too, may and in some cases certainly do, mislead even those Britishers who regard the Right of Asylum as precious, and who may now be labouring under the delusion that it is preserved by Mr. Herbert Samuel, of whom Lord Sheffield said in the House of Lords on July 27th: "His words and his acts do not correspond."

The Committee of Delegates of the Russian Socialist Groups in London hereby declare that they are on the alert, and they call upon the Russian emigrants and upon their British friends not to let themselves be misled by such illusory perspectives that are not an adequate solution of the present problem in its totality.

7. *The Yellow Press, the Danger of Pogroms and the Home Secretary.* [323]

... In the troublous times of brewing discontent, when the semi-conscious masses of the people gropingly endeavour to find out the cause of their miseries and misfortunes, and the ruling classes are in fear and tremble—it is the Yellow Press that rushes to the rescue. It swoops down amongst the surging, raging waves of humanity and rides the storm. In a thunderous voice it champions the cause of the people, shedding bitter tears over their miserable lot, fulminating against their oppressors, and when the crowd, their confidence won, their ire and wrath brought to boiling pitch, turns in eager expectancy for advice and for an indication of the oppressor—it flings its venomous, treacherous cry. When the miners went out on strike a few years ago, asking for a paltry increase of their miserable pittance, and the coal-owners, taking time by the forelock, had raised the price of coal, bringing misery and desolation to thousands of homes, the Yellow Press started a furious campaign against the strikers—the miner was the enemy!

The most potent cry, however, is always the foreigner! He is the enemy!

The Yellow Press knows that the prejudices of the masses is their trump card, and it plays skilfully upon these prejudices; it foments and fans feelings of race hatred, sets the workers by the ears, one section against the other, those of one nationality against those of another. Its fiendish work done, the blind victims of misery venge their wrath on others. fellow-sufferers like themselves. ...

Now, what are the facts of the situation? Since the war began, there has been no immigration into this country from Russia. The number of Russian subjects here has even diminished; a good many had left in the early months of the war, and others have joined the army. Those who remained are pursuing the very same trades and occupations in which they were engaged before the war. The greatest bulk of the Russian Jews are engaged principally in the tailoring and mantle making trades. The latter was introduced by the Jews in this country, which previously imported mantles from Germany; the tailoring trade was developed by the Jews on lines hitherto unknown in England. During the war, only an insignificant number went on war work outside of their own trades, but in that case had naturally to give up their former jobs. It is, therefore, inconceivable how the Jews or anybody else could snatch up the jobs of the English who went to the war, unless every Jew or foreigner was endowed with a number of doubles, and whilst the original was busy with his needle in a tailoring shop in the East of London, his double No. 1 was working away in a munition factory somewhere in the Midlands, and his double No. 2 was officiating at a shop captured from a poor fellow who went to the front. It is ridiculous to talk of job-snatching and job-stealing at a time when the whole nation is practically put on war work, and there are more jobs going than there are hands to take them up. As a matter of fact, Danish labour is at the present moment being imported into this country, and there is talk of importing Chinese.

The absurdity and mendacity of the job-snatching cry is obvious, and is on a par with the other cry which the Yellow Press had raised before, that there was a quarter of a million "friendly aliens" of military age walking the streets of London; whereas from every reference book the fact was staring one in the face that the total foreign population of all ages and both sexes did not exceed that number in the whole country. According to the Home Secretary's statement, the number of Russian subjects of military age was about 20 to 25 thousand all told, from which a considerable number would have to be deducted, who, for one reason or another, are not fit or are ineligible for the army.

It was the stirring up of race-hatred and trouble in the East End of London and elsewhere that the Yellow Press was after.

Perhaps we should point out that the presence of a large colony of Russian subjects in this country is due to the political régime in Russia, which probably would have fallen long ago under the blows of the revolutionary forces there if not for the millions of money advanced to the Russian Government by the "Western Democracies"—France and England, together with Germany. If not for this foreign gold Russia might have been a free country, and there would not have been here such a large number of Russian subjects who now give so much trouble and heart-burning to the Home Secretary.

One would have expected Anglo-Jewry and its Press, "The Jewish Chronicle" and the "Jewish World," who know, or, at least, ought to know the facts, to clear up the situation and take up the cudgels on behalf of the Russian Jews against their attackers. And it must have come as a surprise to many an Englishman that the financial magnates who lead Anglo-Jewry and their Press should themselves have joined the chorus of the Yellow Press, and taken an active part in the hunt organised against the Russian Jews. In fact some of the leaderettes of these worthy organs were fit to grace the columns of the anti-Semitic "Novœ Vremia." The explanation, however, is very simple, English Jewry represents a very small community belonging almost exclusively to the moneyed parasitical classes. The foreign Jews, on the other hand, belong almost entirely to the working classes. The contempt and hatred of the English Jew for his Russian and Polish "brethren" is deep-seated, and is in the nature of things; it is the contempt of the parasitic rich for the hard-working poor. There was not much love lost between these two sections, even in pre-war time. Only now the opportunity was afforded to the rich English Jew to drag out his animosity towards the Russian and Polish Jew on the wider arena of British politics. The result is that the financial magnates who lead Anglo-Jewry stand disclosed before the whole world in their abject ignominy, fully meriting the contempt of all those in England who have remained true to the traditions of the past.

The Anglo-Jewish Press has thus joined hands with the scurrilous Black Hundred Press of this country, and has imperilled the position of the Russian Jews here.

A clear statement on the part of the Government of the actual facts of the situation would have been sufficient to take the wind out of the sails of the vile anti-Semitic fomenters of strife, and would stultify their whole agitation.

It was, however, idle to expect such a statement from the Government, who, up till now, knuckled down to every cry the Yellow Press was pleased to raise. And now, when the Home Secretary, Mr. Herbert Samuel, deems it fit to take up the cue, in the matter of compulsion and deportation for Russian subjects, from the Yellow Press, and repeats their callous and gross allegations and misrepresentations, we are in duty bound to enter our most emphatic protest.

In attempting to justify the unjustifiable measure of compulsory military service under the threat of deportation for the victims of Russian Despotism, Mr. Herbert Samuel had advanced in the House a sort of poser-argument—what would people say of him in the "very possible eventuality, perhaps stimulated by a violent press agitation, of riots and disturbances breaking out in the East End," and "those families who had seen their young men taken away adopted violent measures in protest when they saw their trade being captured by others living in their midst, etc. . . ."

And hence his monstrous proposal.

We have already pointed out the absurdity of the charge of job-stealing and trade capturing. We may, however, assure the Home Secretary from the experience of Russia, that however great the power for mischief of the Black Hundred Press, whether in England or Russia, there is no danger of riots or pogroms breaking out unless the Government desires such outbreaks.

When a deputation of the Progressive Bloc, in the Duma, urged the Russian Government, on the 9th September, 1915, to open villages to the Jews, the Government replied that such a measure would bring about pogroms. The answer of the deputation was that pogroms occur only when the authorities aid, abet, and foster them. That is true, not only for Russia, but for every other country.

So far, the British Government have not given any indication that they are determined not to have any pogroms in this country. On the contrary, Mr. Herbert Samuel, in his speech on 1st August, is discounting this "very possible eventuality," before which he capitulates in advance, proposing either to deport Russian subjects to Russia or to slave-drive them into the British Army.

It is speeches and utterances like those made by the Home Secretary that create a real element of danger, because they serve as an official sanction of the false statements spread by the Yellow Press, and as a sort of indication to the latter to continue their nefarious work and bring about those very events, i.e., riots and pogroms, which might provide the postulated justification for the Home Secretary's policy, affording him at the same time some cover from the attacks directed against him by the British public opinion for his violent destruction of the Right of Asylum.

Let all Russian subjects here, and the friends of freedom in this country and abroad, ponder over the utterances of the Home Secretary, fraught as they are with the danger of pogroms, so that should anything untoward happen they may put the blame where the blame is due.

8. Brief Summary of the Activities of the Committee of Delegates of the Russian Socialist Groups in London.[324]

... The Committee was formed on March 13th, 1916, and consisted of the Delegates of the:

... At that time rumours were only beginning to circulate about the impending plan of compulsion of Russian Subjects to enlist in the British Army, under the threat of deportation to Russia. The Committee utilized the connections that had been created by the previous activity of the Russian Socialist Groups in London, in order to prepare the ground for the struggle against the danger that threatened the Right of Asylum. Realising the necessity of making the question widely known through Parliamentary discussion, the Committee entered into communication with Members of Parliament, in the first place with Comrade Snowden. Amongst the Radical Members of Parliament, an energetic part in the fight for the Right of Asylum has been taken by Mr. Joseph King (although he differs fundamentally from us in principles and tactics), with whom comrades from the Russian Socialist Groups had previously been in touch in connection with the acts of repression against Refugees (the affair Anitchkine, the affair Petroff and others). Great interest in the maintenance of the Right of Asylum has been shown by a Liberal Peer, Lord Sheffield, who, in the House of Lords on July 27th, made the most weighty speech for the defence of the Right of Asylum. Other public men have also been interested in this cause. The work and aims of the Committee have been made widely known in Socialist, Trade Union and Radical circles by Comrade Mrs. Bridges Adams, who has worked with the Committee throughout.

In March and April many Russian Subjects were forcibly taken into the Army in Scotland; in consequence of the action of Messrs. King and Snowden in Parliament, to whom the Committee addressed itself, the Military Authorities withdrew these measures.

In the middle of May, the Yellow Press began a violent campaign against the friendly Aliens not serving in the British Army. The Committee officially communicated with the British Socialist Party and the Independent Labour Party, began to get into touch with the local British Socialist and Trade Union Organisations, and did its best to organise a campaign in the Press, especially in the Socialist and Trade Union organs. Letters dealing with the impending threat were sent to numerous Parliamentarians, to other public men, and also to literary men. In view of the especially great importance of the activity in the East End, the Committee entered into close touch with the Jewish Social Democratic Organisation in Great Britain, and since then works hand in hand with it.

In the beginning of June, the situation having been discussed by the Russian Socialist Groups, the general meeting of these groups definitely fixed the line of action which the Committee has followed unswervingly, that is the line of struggle without compromise against the violation of the Right of Asylum—this impending new crime of Imperialism. The same meeting also adopted a resolution saying that the Right of Asylum must extend to all those who fled from the political regime in Russia.

. . . Looking back upon the work done until now, the Committee of Delegates of the Russian Socialist Groups in London has the right to state that it has done a very great work in rousing advanced British public opinion in the struggle for the Right of Asylum. Numerous resolutions adopted by Socialist and Labour organisations, many utterances of the adversaries of Mr. Samuel's policy in Parliament, in the press, at meetings—have been in a large measure influenced by the activity of the Committee. Being the unifying organ and the expression of the will of the London Organisations of the Russian Socialist Parties, the Committee has introduced into the action of the emigration from Russia at this critical time a consequent line of principle, based upon the system of views of the international socialist working class faithful to its banner. In the sense of these views the Committee illuminates the problems facing now in England the emigrants from Russia. It has decisively and categorically made clear to the Government and to the whole British society that the idea of compelling by threats the whole Russian emigration to submission to the intended act of brutality is a baseless illusion. The Committee has not asked for the reception of deputations from it by a Cabinet Minister and would have refused to take part in such deputations, but it has opposed to the Government the only force that cannot be crushed, the force of the consequent action based upon principle of the conscious working class, indissolubly connecting the struggle carried on here with the international struggle of the proletariat of all Countries against world wide reaction, and seeing in the problems that face the Russian emigration in England only a partial expression of the general, fundamental problems of the present historical moment.

9. *To the Workers—Refugees from Russia.*[325]

. . . A fight for principle is a source of great moral force. Our uncompromising line of action and our faithfulness to principles have brought about some important results. We have succeeded in arousing public opinion on this question. Numerous British working class organisations have supported our cause. Our influence lies not in rifles nor guns, but in the determined firm stand against all the attempts of reaction to intimidate or to demoralise us. Threats of deportation, of compulsion, of economic pressure must not affect us. Better to be the victims than the accomplices in the crime planned by the forces of reaction. And those threats can only be carried out on a large scale, if we are weak, disunited and lacking in steadfastness. Every concession of principles in face of those threats would only make our position worse. For only in a fight for a principle are we justified in appealing to British democracy and to international Labour for support and help.

Our opponents too understand this. And the Home Secretary, Mr. Herbert Samuel, has declared his readiness to give special consideration to the position of those, whom he called "genuine political refugees" as distinct from the remaining bulk of the refugees. But the members of the Russian Socialist Groups have rejected any privilege, proving thereby, that the preservation of principles is more important to them than their personal safety. Thereby they greatly strengthened our solidarity and increased our moral force.

And with the same faithfulness to our principles our whole tactics should be inspired. We must still further close our ranks and continue our fight with still greater determination. We must let reaction know, that no acts of repression will alter our firm resolution to stand by our principles.

We must especially warn you against every attempt to demoralise us by so-called "compromises." Some individuals propose that we should abandon our principles, and on their own responsibility they suggest, that then the Government will perhaps agree to give us better conditions, less dangerous service, "work of national importance" (fine phrase for slave labour) and so on. The class conscious worker understands that to accept such a proposal would mean to betray his own class. But even to those outside our movement it is clear, whither all those plans are leading. To propose such a compromise is to recognise the right of the Government to compel the foreigners to military service, that is to say to put us entirely at the mercy of the British Government. In practice all these proposals can have only one effect: To undermine the unity of the Russian refugees and to weaken or even totally to destroy their moral force, by making them appear as cowards, concerned only for their own safety. This cannot be allowed. Remember, our steadfastness is our strength.

In the stormy days of the great world-crisis a serious situation has arisen for the refugees from Russia, involving great responsibility. Their voice must now be heard. Upon their attitude, upon their faithfulness to principle, upon the strength with which they fight will the verdict of the future depend. Two ways are open to them. One, that leads through personal aims, through undignified compromises to deplorable results today, and which will cover their name with shame in the future. The other way is the way of a courageous stand for our principles, for our class ideal. It gives the certitude that the future will recognise that they fulfilled their class duties and took their place amongst the fighters against oppression and for the liberation of humanity.

The class conscious worker knows, which way to choose. And with the sympathy and the help of International Labour he will continue the struggle.

10. Data on Russian Refugees. [326]

... The situation of the Jews in Russia since the outbreak of the war is such, that no words could express its horrors. Even the Armenian atrocities could hardly be compared to the unheard treatment meted out to the Jews by the official authorities in Russia. ...

From the above it is obvious, that the overwhelming majority of Russian subjects in England have full right to the claim of "genuine" refugeeism on political or religious grounds. When they came to this country, they were told as it were by the British authorities: We have no part in your quarrel with your oppressors. As a democratic country we have our door open for you, offering you only foreigners' rights and requiring from you only foreigners' duties.

It appears now, according to the utterances of Mr. Herbert Samuel, that a mental reservation was made which implied that as the price of hospitality the refugee was to pay "the Shylock's pound of flesh."

11. To the Jews of London. [327]

England wants her sons to fight for her today in this Great Struggle against the Enemy, and we Jews should be among the first to come forward in this sacred cause.

In this land of Liberty, the Jew is proud to stand shoulder to shoulder with his neighbour in defence of all that Englishmen hold dear, and fight the battle of Justice and Freedom.

Read what the Very Rev. Dr. Hertz, our Chief Rabbi, has said upon the duty of the Jews at the present hour:—

"In this solemn crisis of our Nation's life, when our beloved country is calling upon her children to fight her righteous cause, all my Jewish brethren will, I am sure, fully realise the supreme duty of the hour.

"Once more we will prove that the old Maccabean spirit is still alive amongst us. We will offer our lives to defend Great Britain's ideals of Justice and Humanity: in ever larger numbers will we continue to join the army of our King.

"Be strong and of good courage. The God of righteousness is with us, He will guard our going out and our coming in."

Already, thousands of Jews living beneath the shelter of the glorious Union Jack have joined H. M. Navy and Army. On the sea, in battleships and torpedoboats and submarines, in France and in Belgium, in the trenches, and on the battlefield in large numbers, they stand side by side, fighting to uphold the honour of the Empire. Truly, the Jews of England have proved by their courage and enthusiasm that the spirit of their Maccabean ancestors is not dead within their hearts.

All who are able must follow this splendid sample. We have not yet done enough. "Send us more men," our soldiers call to us from the battlefield. We have a strong enemy against us, the war is far from ended. We must all do our best to help to win a great victory that shall lead to a permanent peace for the world.

More young men are wanted. Every Jewish man, who is a British subject and is between the ages of 19 and 38, should offer himself for King and Country. The Government gladly welcome Jews into His Majesty's Forces.

You can enter any Regiment you like, whether you know anything of drill or not. A number of relatives and friends may join together wherever they please, and can remain together for the whole time of the war.

Now is the time to join and strike a blow for your King and Country. Join as Jews and bring honour upon your Faith.

Public Recruiting Meetings will shortly be held at which prominent members of the Community will speak. Notice of the dates will be given on placards and in Yiddish papers.

Why recruits are wanted.

Because their country is engaged in a War

To protect the Civilization of Europe.

To protect the Freedom and Honour of England.

To crush the cruel and despotic power of an unscrupulous enemy.

Those who are eligible for enlistment.

All strong and healthy men between the ages of 19 and 38 who are British subjects.

Why Jews should serve.

Because this Country has always been the refuge of the oppressed.

Because England has always given absolute freedom for all religions and all sects.

Because it is voluntary in this country to serve, and it is an honour to do so.

Because it is one of the finest Jewish ideals to crush militarism and strive for an honourable peace.

Why parents should send their sons.

Because so many of the Jewish parents have found safety in England from oppression abroad.

Because they would lose their right and freedom if England were conquered.

Because their sons are cleanliving, healthy young men and would make the best soldiers.

All regiments are open.

All friends can serve together in the same Company of the same battalion of the same regiment.

Enlistment is for the War only—the more men offer the quicker the war is over.

Men will be discharged after the War and can return to their homes and their ordinary occupations. . . .

12. [Appeal by Lord Leopold de Rothschild and Baron Louis Samuel

Montagu Swaythling.]³²⁸

We urge you to read carefully the accompanying documents, in which you will find particulars of the scheme adopted by His Majesty's Government for the voluntary enlistment in the British Army of Russian subjects residing in this country.

All Jews, and more especially Russian Jews, owe a deep debt of gratitude to England, the historic champion of freedom throughout the world. They have found in England a generous welcome, security for their persons, schools for their children, and the same opportunities as are enjoyed by Englishmen themselves. Now, when she is once more waging a great war for the liberties of Europe and asks your help, you cannot in honour or in gratitude hold back.

In all the countries of the Grand Alliance our co-religionists have responded to the call with the utmost enthusiasm and self-denial. In your own land 400,000 Jews are now fighting, not only for their Fatherland, but for the honour of Jewry and for the liberties the War will assuredly bring them and all their fellow countrymen.

England offers you the most generous conditions of enlistment. No difference will be made between you and the British soldier by whose side you will take your place, except that every concession it is possible to give will be given to enable you to observe Jewish laws and customs. In the proportion of the numbers enlisting Jews will be grouped in batches. So far as military exigencies permit, you will be afforded opportunities of celebrating the Jewish festivals at home. In your equipment you will find the Hebrew Prayer Book, and in the camps and on the battlefield you will meet Jewish Ministers ready to minister to your spiritual wants. In the matter of pay, pensions and promotion you will be treated precisely in the same way as the native Englishman, and those of you who desire it will be naturalised as soon as possible after you join the colours, without paying any of the customary fees.

You may either enlist at once or show your good will by attesting. If you attest, you will be able later on to apply for exemption should your circumstances not permit you to serve, and in that case your appeal will be heard by a specially constituted Tribunal on which Jews and other trusted friends will sit, so that you may rely upon a sympathetic hearing.

Until October 25th the scheme is voluntary, but after that date you may be treated in the same way as the ordinary Englishman in England or Russian in Russia.

Your adopted country is calling upon you to defend her. Let your answer be worthy of your traditions and of the cause you are invited to assist.

13. Military Service (Conventions with Allied States) Act, 1917.³²⁹

A Convention has been made between the British Government and the Provisional Government of Russia providing that British subjects of military age in Russia and Russian subjects of military age in this country shall either return to their own country or serve in the Army of the country in which they reside. The Convention has this day been laid before Parliament.

Notice is hereby given that any male Russian subject of military age who desires to return to Russia rather than to stay in this country may within 21 days after 19th July 1917 make application accordingly at the police station where he is registered under the Aliens Restriction (Consolidation) Order 1916.* No such application can be made after the 9th August and no application made before the 9th August can be withdrawn after that date.

Arrangements have been made for conveying direct to Russia those who wish to go and any man who applies to return to Russia must be ready on receiving notice to start at any time after the 13th August. The notice which will be sent or delivered to the applicant will contain full information as to the date on which he must be ready to embark for Russia and other necessary details.

If an applicant fails to sail after receiving such notice he will at once become liable to service in the British Army, and will have no right of application to a Tribunal for exemption.

The Government cannot undertake the responsibility of conveying women or children by sea to

Russia from this country under present conditions. Men desirous of returning to Russia should make arrangements for the maintenance of their dependents during their absence.

Russian subjects who prefer to remain in this country will come within the operation of the Military Service Acts as if they were British subjects ordinarily resident in Great Britain on the making of the necessary Order in Council. It is the intention to make this Order in Council on or about the 20th August and before the thirtieth day after that date, any Russian who has not applied to return to Russia may apply to a Tribunal for exemption from military service on any of the grounds open to British subjects for claiming exemption. On the thirtieth day after the making of the Order in Council, i.e. on or about the 19th September every male Russian subject between the ages of 18 and 41 who has not satisfied the conditions as to return to Russia will be deemed, subject to the statutory provisions as to exemption, to have been enlisted in the British Army for the duration of the war and to have been transferred to the Reserve. Russian subjects who hold a certificate of exemption issued by or on behalf of the Russian Embassy in London will not be liable to military service in this country.

Those who serve in the British Army will have the same rights and privileges in regard to pay, pension, separation allowances, etc. as British subjects. They will also be granted certificates of naturalization without fee after three months' satisfactory service in the Army if they apply to the Home Office and satisfy the statutory conditions.

Any Russian subject who has attested for service in the British Army and has not actually joined for service, may, if he chooses, apply to return to Russia in the manner explained above; if he does so, his attestation will be cancelled. On making application to return he must inform the local military authority.

This notice does not apply to Russian subjects now serving in the British Army.

14. *Conscripting the Alien. The New Military Service Act,* by Lucien Wolf.[330]

The Military Service (Conventions with Allied States) Act, which has just received the Royal Assent, deals with the problem of the able-bodied alien of Allied nationality, very much on the lines I ventured to suggest in "The Daily Chronicle" last September. Unfortunately, the lapse of time and certain concessions made in the Act render it doubtful whether it will afford a really effective solution of the problem, even when the conventions it contemplates have been successfully negotiated. Neither the War Office nor the Home Office seems to have grasped the fact that this Act is a logical and necessary corollary of the Military Service Acts of last year. In the old days, the stranger within our gates, even when of Allied nationality, enjoyed a perfect immunity from military service, not because of any right of asylum or other doubtful "maxims of international law," but because we did not practise conscription ourselves and we strongly disapproved of it in others. With our adoption of military alliances and compulsory service, this state of things should have automatically come to an end, but it did not. We had made our revolution of military policy, in order to exert the man-power of the Alliance to its utmost, on a uniform plan of conscription, and yet we continued to give immunity from service to some 30,000 subjects of our Allies domiciled among us, because in our muddle-headed way we could only think of them as foreigners of the ante-conscriptionist era.

AN ABSURD ANOMALY

It is difficult to imagine a more absurd anomaly. It has cost us sixteen months of valuable time, besides social embitterments and complications, which in certain districts have given the police and others cause for some anxiety. The work has now to be done under much greater difficulties than would have presented themselves in March 1916. It is not only that the Conventions with our Allies may prove less easy to negotiate, but the machinery of the new Act, especially in regard to the transport of the conscripts to Russia, is likely to be seriously impeded by the new conditions of the war. What with these difficulties and the appeals to the Tribunals and the Ambassadors, no very appreciable additions will be made to any section of the armies of the Alliance from this source, for a very long time, if at all.

Even during the debates in the House of Commons—there were virtually none in the House of Lords—the real scope and significance of the problem found little appreciation. Only one member, Mr. Caradoc Rees, discussed it in terms of Allied manpower. The others appear for the most part to have been haunted by obsolete conceptions of the status of the alien, or to have envisaged the question as chiefly one of local import, arising out of certain popular discontents in the East-end and elsewhere, and limited in its possible solution to service in the British Army or deportation. The result is, among other defects, the fatal concession by which the aliens affected are to be afforded an opportunity of returning to their own countries before they are held liable to military service here.

This concession is likely to defeat the whole purpose of the Act. There can be no doubt that the overwhelming majority of the aliens will avail themselves of it, and the result will be that, as we cannot transport more than a small proportion of them beyond the seas, we shall add nothing to the armies of the Alliance, either at home or abroad, and we shall not appreciably diminish the social irritation caused by their presence in our midst. The matters will remain pretty much as they are. But even if we can manage to send some thousands to Russia, the hardships of the voyage to Archangel and the ruin of families left behind will only make fresh complications for us in other directions.

A CONCESSION THAT COULD HAVE BEEN AVOIDED

All this could have been avoided had the unity of the Allies in the matter of manpower been realised in the conception and drafting of the Act. Had that been done it would have been seen that the alien liable to military service in an Allied country has no inherent right to be sent to that country. All he has to do is to render his military service whenever and wherever he is duly called upon under the authority of his Government. Questions of place or time are for his military superiors—in this case the Allied staffs—and they should determine them in accordance with the needs or convenience of the Allied armies. Thus Russians in this country could quite fairly have been called up, trained and embodied here, under the authority of a convention with the Russian Government, and the only option allowed them should have been whether they would serve in existing British regiments or in separate and special units.

Following out the wrong-headed idea that, in conscripting aliens under the new Act, the military benefit would accrue, not to their own country, as a part of the Alliance, but exclusively to the British Army, it was frequently urged during the debates that naturalisation should accompany enlistment. The argument was that it was unreasonable to ask people to fight for any particular country without giving them the full rights of nationals of such countries. This argument, however, has no cogency if the larger significance of the Act is properly understood. There is no necessity to naturalise, seeing that the recruited aliens, even if called up for service in this country, will be serving their own country just as much as Great Britain.

The plea might, however, have been urged on other grounds. Under the Army Act, aliens enlisted in the British Army are incapable of holding commissioned rank. This might operate very unjustly if enlistment were to prove successful under the new Act. Besides, the whole conception of the alien recruit as a soldier of the Alliance, liable to all his normal obligations, and enjoying all his normal rights, wherever he may be serving, would be defeated. It is true that there is some difficulty in dealing with the question, as it involves negotiations with the Dominions, who are partners with us in the naturalisation laws; but it certainly ought to be dealt with if a humiliating disability is not to be created. The best plan would be to repeal the alinea of section 95 (1) of the Army Act, under which the disability now exists. On the whole perhaps the only real merit of the new Act is that it settles in principle the vexed question of the military obligations of aliens of Allied nationality under the present military and political conditions in Europe.

15. The Right Way (Foreign Jews and Military Service). [331]

The Anglo-Russian Convention on Military Service is now a fact. It cannot be abrogated.
For the Russians in this country two ways only are open:
   To serve in Russia or
   To serve here.
Everyone ought therefore to consider what he intends to do.

THERE ARE ADEQUATE NUMBERS OF SHIPS

First of all do not let yourselves be led astray by those who tell you that the Government has not sufficient shipping for sending you all away and that it will be forced to let you stay in this country through the winter.

All this is a tale for naïve children, but not for grown up people.

Let us not deceive ourselves and let us see in short how the things stand.

For carrying one person with all his belongings two tons of tonnage are wanted, thus for 1000 persons only one ship of 2000 tons is sufficient. Even if we assume that 30,000 men will register for returning to Russia, the Government will be able to send them all on 10 vessels at 6,000 tons each.

Generally speaking a ship of 6,000 tons is not an extraordinary thing, as this is the average displacement of a ship. There are immense numbers of ships of this tonnage on the shores of England, as according to the official naval reports, England has more than 15,000,000 tons of tonnage.

Thus you will plainly see that the shipping question is no question at all, and not for nothing has therefore Lord Derby announced that the men concerned should not deceive themselves with the belief that there would be no ships. The issue is clear.

In a few weeks' time *ALL* of you, whatever the numbers, will be packed in the ships and despatched.

THE JOURNEY OVER THE SEA

It is not very safe to travel for a fortnight over the seas. Even neutral ships risk great dangers, the more a ship packed with able bodied young men going to serve in the Russian Army. Such a ship will be considered as a military transport, which will be chased by the sea monsters—the submarines.

The transport of soldiers from one port to another has always been fraught with dangers, though the transports have always been protected by war ships.

Even from the shortest sea routes, news about disasters is arriving.

Let us take, as an illustration, the transport of troops over the Mediterranean, which lasts only from 3-4 days: attacks by submarines and mine explosions are quite frequent, and it is very advisable to think before one undertakes a journey of 14 days over a sea which is so close to Germany's shores.

We have pointed out all this, not in order to frighten the people, but to make them consider the matter before they take their decision.

THE SITUATION IN RUSSIA

Let no one be deceived with regard to the happy prospects of serving in the Russian Army into which you would be incorporated immediately after your arrival at a Russian port.

"An iron discipline is to be introduced" is the order of the new Prime Minister Kerensky—and this discipline is being introduced.

It has to be introduced because Anarchy raised its head, chaos began to engulf the Army; therefore, the most severe military order had to be established and the most cruel measures had to be taken.

You can easily understand how the Officers and N.C. Officers, who were so roughly handled at the outbreak of the revolution, will treat the soldiers now when they have to establish the necessary military discipline.

Neither can we refrain from dwelling upon the general conditions of life in Russia itself.

The railway traffic is disorganised and consequently food is not easily transported from the remote districts. Hence the dearth of everything and the fact that there is almost no bread in the country.

The Army also suffers from shortage. During the last few months it has many times happened that soldiers were receiving half of their rations.

Besides, do not forget the severe Russian winter which is moving on. It was with extreme difficulties that Russia passed through the last winter, when considerably better conditions prevailed. In the coming winter the ten million strong Russian Army will suffer badly from lack of food and coal.

ANTI-SEMITISM

And after all we are Jews and you have only to remember what that means.

Whatever happens, the blame is always thrown upon us.

Now in Russia the old despotic pogrom-mongering régime is trying to re-occupy its lost positions, conducts an anti-semitic propaganda in the Army, in the towns, in the villages.

Whatever happens in such a chaotic state of affairs, the Jews, and especially the Jewish soldiers will be the first to suffer.

THE POSITION OF YOUR FAMILIES

And if we even admit that out of your great love for Russia, you make up your minds to go and to serve there, have you thought of what would become of your families? In whose charge will you leave them?

You know what the pay of a Russian soldier is. The separation allowances are paid by the local authorities and these allowances never exceed 7 Roubles a month for a woman with one child.

Do you think that on this money your families will be able to exist here? Or do you rely upon the support of Charitable Institutions? Why should you make your children beggars?

THE BEST CHOICE

For all the above reasons, it is clear that for those who must serve, it is better to serve here than there, and if the choice for serving here is made, it is more practical to join the Jewish Legion which the Government has decided to form.

We know that the idea of a legion has opponents, but this opposition is in no way justified.

If every Jew, whose fate it has become to serve, earnestly reflects on the sort of service he has to select, he will come to the conclusion that the Jewish Legion is the best choice for him.

WHY A JEWISH LEGION

In a Jewish Legion, the Jewish soldier will not be suddenly turned away from the Jewish World and Jewish surroundings. A religious Jew will be able to live there according to his religious convictions. The food and all the ways of its preparation will be the same as those to which Jews are accustomed and the Jewish soldier will have his rest day on Saturdays instead of Sundays.

In a Jewish Legion, the Soldiers during the period of their training will be given facilities for keeping their cultural life. A Library will be established, lectures and concerts will be arranged. All this is a thing which a Jewish Soldier could have in no other legion but a Jewish one.

THE MISTAKE

Many of you think that dangers connected with service in the Jewish Legion are considerably greater than those connected with service in other units.

This is a mistake. We do not believe that any difference is being made between English and Non-English soldiers, but if we even admit this, we see no special dangers for us.

The Legion itself is the best guarantee against any sort of misuse. The Jewish public opinion of the whole world will be keenly interested in the fate of the Legion, and under the watch of this public opinion the attitude towards the Legion will be exactly the same as that towards any other unit.

But the main thing is that the Jewish Legion is destined to serve in Palestine. Those who serve in other regiments must take into consideration that they will have to go to France, and everyone having an idea of what the battles in France are, will see that the dangers at the Palestine front are not half so great as those in France.

FOR PALESTINE (ERETZ ISRAEL)

Now we come to the most important point of all—to the idea of the Jewish Legion—and we think that we need not dwell at length on this idea.

In the hearts of the Jewish masses, the old love for Palestine is now stronger than ever, and manifests itself plainly in all countries. Never before have the old hopes of Jewry to become a nation and to return to their own country, burned as brightly as now, and if we have to fight, why should we fight under foreign flags and among foreign peoples as an insignificant minority which is lost in the large numbers of others; why should our sacrifices be credited to somebody else and not to our own account.

FOR THE JEWISH FLAG

Hundreds of thousands of Jews are in the Armies of all the peoples which are involved in the war, but there can be no doubt that from the point of view of the Jewish future, a few thousands of Jews of the Legion will have more importance than all these masses. On the Day of Judgment of Nations, the Jewish flag in the hands of the Jewish heroes will demand its acknowledgment as a right, which nobody would be able to deny.

JEWISH MEN TAKE YOUR WHITE-BLUE FLAG IN YOUR HANDS

Cowards try to impress upon you that it will be obnoxious for Jewish interests to have a Legion. Do not believe them. Every free nation and even the enemy will have the greatest respect for us, if we come forward and openly defend our old right to Palestine. No one despises an open enemy, on the contrary, one counts with him and acknowledges him as a living nation.

JEWISH MEN STRENGTHEN YOUR HEARTS

IT IS YOUR LOT TO CARRY ON THE WORK OF YOUR ANCESTORS THE MACCABEES WHO FOUGHT THOUSANDS OF YEARS AGO FOR PALESTINE IN CONDITIONS MORE DIFFICULT THAN THOSE AT PRESENT AND STILL HAVE WON. LET THEIR SPIRIT FOLLOW YOU. COME IN CLOSED RANKS. FIGHT AND WIN. FOR THE NATION AND FOR THE LAND.

16. *An Interview with Dr. David Jochelman on the United Russian Committee for Matters of Military Service.*[332]

"The Committee came into being," said Dr. Jochelman, "at the request of the representative of the preliminary Russian Government (the Kerensky Government), Mr. Nabokoff, and the then First Secretary and now Chargé d'Affaires, Mr. Sablin, in order to assist in the carrying out of the military convention between this country and Russia. The cardinal point of this convention was that British subjects of military age living in Russia might, if they so desired, enter the Russian Army, and conversely Russian subjects living in England, if they wished, might enter the British Army, but both parties had the right of going to their own country for the purpose of military service. The result was that a certain percentage—I do not know off-hand how many—joined the Army here, and another lot of Russians went to Russia to serve in Kerensky's Army. I do not feel myself competent to enter into the psychology of either group for the purpose of arriving at the motives which prompted the choice of either alternative, but the fact remains that those who decided to go to Russia went at a time when the Russian Army was still in existence, and we know as a fact that many were actually received as soldiers. The British authorities here treated the scheme as seriously as the Russian authorities did. A special tribunal was set up by the British Government to investigate the cases of Russians of military age, and my Committee was invited through the Embassy to advise as to the appointment of the Russian members, and the Vice-Chairman of the Committee, Mr. A. Krougliakoff, was appointed member of the tribunal. The Russian Chargé d'Affaires regarded the arrangement as so natural that he started at once paying the families and dependents of those Russians who went back; allowances in the absence of the breadwinners. Several thousand pounds were dispensed by our Committee, on his behalf, in this way. There is not the slightest doubt that had the Kerensky Government kept in power these families would have continued to receive these allowances. It is equally certain that the Russian Government would have insisted on the right of the men concerned to return to England at the expiration of their term of service."

A BRITISH "SCRAP OF PAPER"

You imply that they were not allowed to return?

"Unfortunately, the British authorities have treated the convention as a scrap of paper, and totally disregarded the spirit of the whole treaty. Let me state the facts. The Russian front suddenly collapsed.

Some of the men who went out did, as I have said, actually serve before this *débâcle*. Some arrived when there was no army in existence. Some were captured by the Germans, others died. But a very large proportion are now desirous of rejoining their families here, but unfortunately the attitude of the British authorities is very unsympathetic. I understand that only in exceptional cases has permission been given to these men to re-enter this country."

A QUESTION OF RIGHT

Dr. Jochelman went on to say: "Though personally I am as convinced now as I was when these young men left for Russia, that it would have been better for them to have served in the British army. I am equally convinced that from the point of view of justice these men have an absolute right to come back. But there are still stronger humanitarian considerations, for the men's families are in the most miserable plight which it is possible to conceive, and I am not without hope that the humane characteristics for which the British people are distinguished will ultimately induce the Government to take the right course. But my criticisms apply equally to the Jewish Community, and I say quite frankly that I am very grateful to the Jewish Chronicle for affording me this opportunity of making the facts known. I may say that I have been connected with charitable work for the greater part of my life, and I have in most cases found people humane, and the more so when the distress has been greatest. Especially have I found this feature among our race. But in regard to these unfortunate families I have met with an attitude which amazes me, and I am really surprised and perplexed to see the position which English Jews have taken up towards these unfortunate fellow Jews. On several occasions I have endeavoured to explain the position, the the Jewish Chronicle has helped me, and I have, as you know, tried more than once to raise this question at the Deputies, but, with few exceptions, I have met with a hostile attitude everywhere. The explanation I give is very simple. The Jews note the unfriendly attitude of the Government and the non-Jews in general, and they adopt the same attitude. But I must say that this explanation does not satisfy me. The Jewish Community, as such, should have nothing to do with politics. Suppose for one moment that these young men by going to Russia had committed the greatest crime of which human beings are capable, why should their wives be punished? Let us go a step further, and assume that they acted on the advice of their wives, then why should their little children and aged parents be punished? Have we not, in all civilised countries, societies for helping the families of prisoners? I really cannot understand how Jews can become so callous towards the suffering of fellow Jews. But there can be no question in this case of crime or even of disloyalty."

THE SPECTRE OF POGROMS

Why did these men go to Russia and not serve with the British army? our representative asked.

"I put this question to a group of these people before they left for Russia, and they replied that the reason was because they were absolutely sure that the Revolution was bound to bring in its train massacres of Jews, and they wished to be on the spot to help in defending the lives of their coreligionists. This fact was reported by me at a meeting at Brighton some two years ago, and, if my memory does not deceive me, was recorded in the Jewish Chronicle. Recent events have unfortunately shown how justified this prognostication was. But the main point is that these men have done nothing wrong, even if some of them did leave this country to evade military service, though I have no evidence of this. I would point out that you have a percentage of this class among all the belligerent nations, and Switzerland, as we have recently read, is full of deserters. I repeat that I cannot understand the heartlessness of the community here. The facts which I shall presently give you will acquaint you with the position as it stands at the present moment, when the majority of these unfortunate families are still receiving a meagre allowance from the Government. Imagine what is going to happen when the Government stops this allowance on the 1st of January."

A PROTEST

Dr. Jochelman intimated that the sympathisers with the victims of the situation he had described were casting about for a means of arresting the attention of the Community in dramatic fashion.

"At a conference held last Sunday of the branches of the Jewish Workers' Fund, which lasted almost the whole day, several propositions were made for bringing home to the Community the urgency of this matter. One of these suggestions was that the women should be told that the working classes were no longer in a position to support them, and that they should demonstrate before the houses of the leaders of the Community. I persuaded the conference not to adopt this course, first of all because I did not expect any help in this way, and secondly because I was afraid this procedure might give cause to some heartless people to call the starving demonstrators Bolsheviks, and thus their position would become still worse. But among the resolutions adopted was one which I confess I suggested, that a group of young Englishmen should go one Saturday to the synagogues and should stop the reading of the Law in order to draw attention to this injustice. It is an old Jewish tradition that when people cannot get justice they should adopt this course, and address the community before the reading of the Law. Believe me I am not in favour of this step, but let those who resent it advise me of a better."

A TERRIBLE PICTURE

Dr. Jochelman drew a terrible picture of the condition of the women and children assisted by his Committee.

"There are about 800 families supported by the local Guardians, but of these we support only 545 women and 1,250 children. Of these, 200 women and 700 children suffer from lung, heart, and internal diseases, and the number increases daily. Twenty women suffer from tuberculosis and consumption, and in most cases the children also show symptoms of the same disease. Fifteen women suffer from heart disease, and one child has at present a serious attack of pleurisy. Twenty per cent of the women are subject to nervous complaints, some of them being so severe that we fear that their minds may become deranged very shortly. Every one is troubled by some internal disease. One woman is in the Lunatic Asylum and her children are in the Workhouse; another is in such a bad mental condition that she may be taken to the Asylum in a few days. One woman was about to sell her children to the missionaries, but owing to our timely intervention they were saved. Another, who was unable to pay her rent, was put into the street with her four children and her few pieces of furniture, and has not yet found a home. The doctors report that they can do nothing with all our cases, as the patients lack even the bare necessities of life. Owing to this fact, their bad accommodation, and the strenuous work to which they are forced, not one of them is in a position to stand alone, independent of support. 80 per cent of the women have never heard from their husbands, and four know definitely that they have died in Russia; 90 per cent of the children require permanent medical treatment; not one family whom we support occupies more than two rooms; 5 of the women are dead, and 9 orphans are left, whom we are supporting. The local Guardians pay 12s. 6d. per woman, and 2s. 6d. per child. Therefore the average income of a mother and four children is 1 per week. Only 10 per cent of the women who have no more than two children can do work, and in no case do their earnings average more than 10s. per week.

"As I stated," said Dr. Jochelman, in conclusion, "I am not very optimistic as to the results of this interview, but perhaps the main reason why the case is as bad as I have painted it is because the Community has not had the facts brought home sufficiently forcibly. I am despondent, but never in my life did I wish more that my judgment may turn out wrong than I do in this case and at this moment."

NOTES

[1] Marcel Pennette and Jean Castaingt, "La Legion extrangera en la intervención francesa," *Historia Mexicana*, vol. XII (1962), pp. 229-73; George Blond, *La Légion Etrangère* (Paris 1964), pp. 53-93.
[2] *Souvenirs du Colonel Fernand V.M. Maire de la Légion Etrangère*, recuillis par Jean-Pierre Dorian (Paris 1936), pp. 184-85.
[3] Charles E. Mercier, *Legion of Strangers* (New York 1964), p. 6.
[4] Geoffrey Bocca, *La Legion!* . . . (New York 1964), p. 115.
[5] New York *Times*, Aug. 5, 1934, p. 5; Feb. 15, 1935, p. 20; Feb. 17, p. 29; Feb. 28, p. 11; March 14, p. 21.
[6] Ouida [Louise De la Ramée], *Under Two Flags*. A novel (Philadelphia 1862); also dramatized as *Cigarette*.
[7] Roland Pertwee, *Gentlemen March* (Boston-New York 1927).
[8] Percival Christopher Wren, *Beau Geste* (New York 1925); Mordaunt Hall, in the New York *Times*, August 26, 1926; Howard Thompson, *ibid.*, Sept. 8, 1966.
[9] Francis A. Waterhouse, *Journey Without End. An Autobiography*. (London 1940), pp. 218-19; New York *Times*, Oct. 27, 1951, p. 10.
[10] George Manington, *A Soldier of the Legion* (London 1907), p. 50.
[11] Isábelle Eberhardt, *Notes de Route* (Paris 1921), pp. 135-36.
[12] Charles Favrel, *Ci-devant Légionnaire* (Paris 1962, p. 9.)
[13] Adrian Liddell Hart, *Strange Company* (h.p. 1953), p. 11.
[14] M. M. [Maurice Magnus], *Memoirs of the Foreign Legion* (London 1924), p. 172.
[15] Major P. C. Wren, "With the Legion," *Living Age*, vol. cccxliii (1932), p. 158.
[16] Ian Scott-Kilvert, "The Mercenary," *The New Statesman and Nation*, n.s., vol. xxiv (Sept. 5, 1942), pp. 155-56.
[17] Capt. R. E. Dupuy, "The Men Who March From Yesterday," New York *Times*, Sept. 28, 1930, v, pp. 12-13.
[18] Franco Arthur Waterhouse, *Five Sous a Day* (London 1933), pp. 6-7.
[19] William Penderel, *Parade of Violence* (London 1937), pp. 18, 25.
[20] NA, RG 59, 851.2225 S.
[21] Brian Stuart, *Far to Go* (London 1947), p. 5.
[22] "The Foreign Legion," *Blackwood's Magazine*, vol. clxxxix (1911), pp. 589-99.
[23] New York *Times*, April 2, 1974, p. 16.
[24] NA, RG 165, MID 2450-C39.
[25] Reginald R. Forbes, *Red Horizon* (London 1932), p. 8.
[26] *Dead March in the Desert*. The Story of Mervyn Pellew, as told to W. B. Bannerman (London 1937), pp. 1-2.
[27] J. M. Sothern, "An Outpost of the Foreign Legion," *Cornhill Magazine*, n.s., vol. lxxiv (1933) pp. 604-05; Erwin Rosen (Carlé), *In the Foreign Legion* (London 1910), pp. 228-29; Michael Alexander, *The Reluctant Legionnaire. An Escapade* (London 1956), p. 156.
[28] *Legion of Hell*, by James Mackinley Armstrong, as told to William James Eliot (London 1936), pp. 200-01, 208.
[29] *From the Abyss to the Foreign Legion*. As told to Edward Clarence Trealawney-Ansel by T. Victor (London 1939), 118-19.
[30] Waterhouse, *op. cit.* p. 51.
[31] Angus McLean, *Vive la Légion* (London 1937), pp. 220.
[32] Waterhouse, op. cit., p. 51; G. Ward Price, "The Lords of the Atlas Submit," *Saturday Evening Post*, vol. ccvii (Nov. 10, 1939), p. 90; René Viliers, "Heat that Kills," *Living Age*, vol. cccxxxiii

(1927), pp. 622-24.
[33]Sothern, *op.cit.*, pp. 600-01.
[34]Roy Baker, *Penal Battalion* (London 1934); Albert Londres, *Dante n'avait rien vu* (Paris 1924).
[35]Sholem Szwartzbard, *In krig mit zikh aleyn* [*In the War With Oneself*] (Chicago 1933), pp. 107-11; NA, RG 59, 851s.22/1.
[36]Irwing Werstein, *Sound No Trumpet. The Life and Death of Alan Seeger* (New York 1967), p. 36.
[37]*War Letters of Edmond Genet* (New York 1918), p. 44.
[38]Bal Hahalomes [Sholem Szwartzbard], *Troymen un virklikhkayt, lider* [*Dreams and Reality. Poems*] (Paris 1920), p. 10.
[39]Maurice Vanikoff, *La Commémoration des Engagements Volontaires des Juifs d'Origine Etrangère 1914-1918* (Paris 1932), p. 16.
[40]*Bal Hahalomes, op.cit.*, p. 10.
[41]Capt. G. F. Eliot, "The French Foreign Legion," *Infantry Journal*, vol. xxxii (1928), pp. 407-12; NA, RG 145, MID 2450-C39.
[42]F.K.B., "The Foreign Legion," *The Spectator*, vol. cxlvi (1931), p. 497.
[43]*From the Abyss* . . . p. 63.
[44]Walter Kanitz, *The White Kepi* (Chicago 1956), p. 188.
[45]*Ibid.*, p. 175.
[46]"The Foreign Legion," *Blackwood's Magazine*, vol. clxxxix (1911), p. 593.
[47]Ernst F. Loehndorf, *Hell in the Foreign Legion* (London 1931), p. 119.
[48]Bocca, op.cit. pp. 45-114; Erwin Rosen (Carlé), *Cafard. Ein Drama aus der Fremdenlegion in 4 Akten* (Munich 1914); "A Deserter Who Was Not Shot," *Literary Digest*, vol. xc (Aug. 14, 1926), pp. 44-48.
[49]Ensio Tiira, *Raft of Despair* (London 1954), p. 48.
[50]NA, RG 165, MID, 2450-C39
[51]*From the Abyss* . . . p. 41.
[52]"What Price Humanity," by Legionnaire "Torato," *Living Age*, vol. cccxxxii (1927), p. 807.
[53]Rosen, *op.cit.* pp. 104-16.
[54]NA, RG 165, MID, 2450-C39.
[55]*From the Abyss* . . . pp. 196-97, 232-33.
[56]*The Souless Legion*. By Ex-Legionnaire 1384, in collaboration with W. J. Blackledge (London 1934), pp. 15-16.
[57]*The Legion of the Damned. The Adventures of Bennet J. Doty in the French Foreign Legion, as told by himself* (New York-London 1928), pp. 77-78, 117, 122.
[58]F. A. Waterhouse, *Five Sous a Day* (London 1933), p. 153.
[59]Reginald R. Forbes, *Red Horizon* (London 1932), pp. 66-67.
[60]Capt. R. E. Dupuy, *op.cit.*
[61]Kanitz, *op.cit.* p. 129.
[62]Cat. Lambert, "The Foreign Legion," *The Fighting Forces*, vol. i (1924), p. 296.
[63]Arthur L. Martin, "An International Force of Tomorrow," *The Spectator*, (London), vol. cxlii (1934), pp. 40-41.
[64]Hans Walter Lehman, *Die franzoesische Fremdenlegion. Eine voelkerrechtliche Untersuchung* (Munich-Leipzig 1915). For a pro-Legion French attitude see Gaston Moch, *La Question de la Légion Etrangère* (Paris 1914).
[65]G2 report from Switzerland, Jan. 11, 1922 (NA, RG 165, MID 2657-R29).
[66]NA, RG 59, 851, 2221 Lensch.
[67]Fritz Klose, *The Legion Marches* (London 1932), p. 284.
[68]Reginald R. Forbes, *op.cit.*, p. 67.
[69]Heintz Pol, *Suicide of a Democracy* (New York 1940), p. 240.
[70]*Death Squads in Morocco*. As told to W. J. Blackledge by Ex-Legionnaire Tercy Brennan

(London 1937); Capt. R. E. Dupuy, *op.cit.*; José Millan-Astray, *La Legión* (Madrid 1939); *idem, Franco El Caudillo* (Salamanca 1939); Carlos Prieto, "Legion of the Lost Ones' Fights in Spain," New York *Times,* Oct. 18, 1936, p. 7; Richard Sablotny, *Legionnaire in Morocco* (Los Angeles 1940); Gen. Carlos de Silva, *General Millán Astray. El Legionario* (Barcelona 1956); George Elmer Ulmer, "Franco Perfected Foreign Legion as Weapon to Seize Rule of Spain," New York *Times,* July 26, 1936, p. 23.

[71] YIVO.

[72] Rosen, *op.cit.* pp. 180-82.

[73] *Victor [Emmanuel] Chapman's Letters from France* (New York 1917), p. 45.

[73a] *Sefer Virushuv* (Tel Aviv 1970), p. 770.

[74] Adrian Liddel Hart, *op.cit.,* pp. 159-64.

[75] G. Bocca, *op.cit.,* pp. 210-13.

[76] Mercier, *op.cit.,* pp. 283-85.

[77] Schwartzbard, *op. cit.,* pp. 19-20; J. Bielinky, "Les Engagements Volontaires des Juifs dans les Armées de la République," *Le Volontaire Juif,* June 1, 1931, pp. 3-4; Juda Tehernoff, *Dans le Creuset des Civilisations,* vol. iv (Paris 1938), p. 309; Mathieu Wolf, "Les Corps des Volontaires Israélites," *L'Univers Israélite,* vol. 70-2, 1915, 529-31; "Les Volontaires Juifs de 1914," *ibid.,* Feb. 18, 1916, pp. 600-02.

[78] Doty, *op.cit.;* Maurice A. Hamonneau, *The Foreign Legion* (n.p. n.d.), p. 7; Kanitz, *op.cit.,* p. 94; Magnus, *op.cit.* p. 172; Patrick Turnbull, *The Foreign Legion* (London 1964), p. 129; Mercier, *op.cit.* p. 228.

[79] Fr. A[lbert], "Un appel entendu," *L'Homme Enchaîné,* according to *L'Univers Israélite,* vol. lxxii-2, 1916, p. 49; "Les Israélites Tunisiens et la Guerre," *Archives Israélites,* Sept. 14, 1916, p. 147; *Le Peuple Juif,* Jan. 1-15, 1917, p. 15, March 4, 1921, p. 5; *Le Volontaire Juif,* Nov. 1, 1931, pp. 1-5, 11.

[80] Schwartzbard, *op. cit.,* p. 36.

[81] *Ibid.,* p. 44.

[82] *L'Univers Israélite,* vol. lxx-2, 1915, p. 46.

[83] *Ibid.,* vol. lxx-1, 1917, p. 447.

[84] A. Saphir, "Les Engagements Volontaires en Août 1914," *Le Volontaire Juif,* April 1932, p. 3.

[85] *Pages de Gloire de la Division Morrocaine,* reprinted in *Le Volontaire Juif,* no. 1, May 9, 1919, pp. 4-6; *Le Volontaire Juif,* May 9, 1931, p. 4.

[86] See p. 126.

[87] Schwartzbard, *op. cit.,* pp. 87-93.

[88] *La Guerre Sociale,* June 26 and 27, and July 1 and 3, 1915.

[89] *A l'Opinion Publique. Au sujet de la situation des réfugiés russes en France.* Publié par le Comité Executif des Organisations Politiques et Professionnels Originaires de Russie (Paris 1916), 11 pp.

[90] *Journal Officiel,* Oct. 27, 1916, p. 3202.

[91] Z. Szajkowski, *Jews, Wars, and Communism,* vol. i (New York 1972), pp. 52-53, 591-93.

[91a] YIVO.

[92] Gustave Hervé, "Le Parlement et les camps d'évacuation," *La Guerre Sociale,* Jan. 13, 1915; Emile Cahen, "Les Suspects," *Les Archives Israélites,* Dec. 13, 1917, p. 199.

[93] New York *Times,* Feb. 20, 1916, i, p. 10.

[94] *L'Univers Israélite,* vol. lxx-2, 1915, p. 364.

[95] A. Lozovsky, in *Nashe Slovo,* Feb. 12, 1915.

[96] Gustave Thiéry, "La France aux Français," *Revue Catholique des institutions et du droit,* Sept. 1915.

[97] *L'Action Française,* July 1 and 2, 1915.

[98] Emile Cahen, "Les Régiments Etrangers," *Les Archives Israélites,* May 20, 1915, p. 87; Mathieu Wolf, *op.cit.* pp. 529-31.

JEWS AND THE FRENCH FOREIGN LEGION 253

[99]"Trois articles d'Hervé. Pour l'honneur de la France," *L'Univers Israélite*, vol. lxx-2, 1915, p. 360.

[100]*La Guerre Sociale*, June 20, 1915; *Les Archives Israélites*, June 24, 1915; *L'Univers Israélite*, vol. lxx-2, 1915, pp. 338-40. See also *Les Archives Israélites*, Oct. 2, 1914, p. 27.

[101]New York *American*, Nov. 28, 1915; *The Day*, Aug. 26 and Nov. 29, 1915; M. Anoutin [Jarblum], "French Stones for Jewish Bread," *Varhayt*, July 16, 1915; *item*, "What Gentiles May Do and Jews May Not," *ibid.*, July 5, 1915; "Days of Fear for Russian Jews in France," *ibid.*, July 5, 1915; J. Schapiro, "With the Russian Jews in Paris," *ibid.*, July 17, 1915; "Arrival of Escapees from France," *ibid.*, July 14, 1915.

[102]Szajkowski, *op.cit.* p. 353; *see* the Appendix.

[103]*Letters and Diary of Alan Seeger* (New York 1917), p. 130.

[104]Schwartzbard, *op. cit.*, p. 155.

[105]Magnus, *op.cit.* p. 172.

[106]*War Letters of Edmond Genet* (New York 1918), pp. 53-54.

[107]Paul Ayres Rockwell, *American Fighters in the Foreign Legion 1914-1918* (Boston 1930), p. 102; Mercier, *op.cit.*, p. 228.

[108]"A Propos des Israélites Russes a Paris," *Les Archives Israélites*, Aug. 29, 1918, p. 138.

[109]*Rusishe Nakhrichten (Russian News)*, published by the *Kolonial Komitet*. For a partial list of evacuees see J. Bielinky, *op.cit.*

[110]*La Renaissance du Peuple Juif*, Aug. 15-Sept. 15, 1917, pp. 15-16.

[111]*La Vérité*, Jan. 26 and 28, 1919.

[112]Edgar O'Ballance, *The Story of the French Foreign Legion* (London 1961), p. 158.

[113]*La Victoire*, July 31, 1918.

On the revolts of Russian soldiers in France see John Reed, *Ten Days That Shook the World* (New York 1919), contains an appendix on the mutinies; Joseph R. Scheftel, "The Russian Soldiers in France," *Soviet Russia*, Oct. 25, 1919, pp. 12-15; Joseph Jolinon, "La Mutinerie de Coeuvres," *Mercure de France*, Aug. 15, 1920; André Obey, "Camarades Rouski," *Revue de Paris*, Dec. 1920 (a fictionalized account of the La Courtine mutiny); Pierre Poitevin, *Une Bataille au Centre de la France en 1917. La révolte des Armées Russes au camp de La Courtine* (Limoges 1937); idem, *La Mutinerie de La Courtine* (Paris 1938). On the mutinies of the army see Szajkowski, *Analytical . . .*, pp. 591-92.

[114]*The Jewish Chronicle*, March 7, 1919, p. 10.

[115]G. Bocca, *op.cit.*, pp. 44-45.

[116]Charles Hora, *Mon tour du monde en 80 barrods*, recuilli par Paul Vincent (Paris 1961), p. 201.

[117]Alan Seeger, *Poems* (New York 1916), p. 114.

[118]Mercier, *op.cit.* pp. 210-11; P.A. Rockwell, *op.cit.* p. 350; I. Werstein, *op.cit.* pp. 41, 49, 51, 68, 108-09, 121.

[119]John Bowe and Charles L. MacGregor, *Soldiers in the Legion* (Chicago 1918), pp. 50-51, 77,103. See also the *Varhayt*, June 16, 1915.

[120]Irving Werstein, *op.cit.* pp. 108-109.

[121]*Letters and Diary of Alan Seeger* (New York 1917), pp. 152-54, 172-73.

[122]*The Lafayette Flying Corps.* Edited by James Norman Hall and Charles Bernard Nordhoff (New York 1920), 2 Vols; Rockwell, *op.cit.*, p. 188.

[123]Carlos Prieto, *op.cit.*

[124]Edward Morlae, "A Soldier of 'The Legion,'" *Atlantic Monthly*, vol. cxvii (1966), pp. 383-96, 813-25; *ibid.*, *A Soldier of the Legion* (Boston 1916); New York *Times*, March 14, 1916, p. 4, March 15, p. 10; "The Charge of the Foreign Legion," *Literary Digest*, vol. lii (March 18, 1916), pp. 770-79.

[125]A. L. Hart, *op.cit.* p. 202.

[126]New York *Times*, Feb. 10, 1931, p. 15, Feb. 21, p. 12.

[127] *Ibid.*, Nov. 6, 1938, p. 12.
[128] *Ibid.*, May 7, 1933, iv. p. 7.
[129] *The World,* July 28, 1925; NA, RG 59, 851.2221/6.
[130] New York *Times,* Aug. 7, 1932, ii, p. 3.
[131] NA, RG 59, 851.222,2221, and 225.
[132] *Detroit Free Press,* Oct. 6, 1915.
[133] NA, RG 59, 851.2225/D.
[134] *Ibid.*, /K.
[135] *Ibid.*, 2222/-
[136] *Ibid.*, 222/M.J.
[137] *Ibid.*, 2226/5.
[138] New York *Times,* Oct. 6, 1932, p. 8.
[139] "Doty's Wild Adventures in the Legion," *Literary Digest,* vol. xcvi (Jan. 21, 1928), pp. 48-52; "Americans Not Wanted in the Foreign Legion," *Literary Digest,* vol. cxiv (Sept. 10, 1932), p. 33.
[139a] NA, RG 84, Casablanca, 711.5. 1942.
[140] Brig. Gen. Lytle Brown to the Chief of Staff, Aug. 6, 1918 (NA, RG 165, WCD 10050-200).
[141] *Ibid.*, 10050-201.
[142] *Ibid.*, 202, 206 and 209.
[143] *Return of Polish Citizens* . . .
[144] Alfred Vagts, "The Foreigner as Soldier in the Second World War. The Military Use of the Foreigner By France," *The Journal of Politics,* vol. ix (Aug. 1947), p. 393.
[145] New York *Times,* Jan. 25, 1935, p. 7.
[146] *Ibid.*, April 15, 1939, p. 6.
[147] N. Sztern, "Le Tribut du Sang (Les Etrangers et la Guerre)," *Bulletin de l' Union des Engagés Volontaires, Anciens Combattants Juifs 1939,* no number [1946], pp. 2-3.
[148] Vanikoff, *La Commemoration* . . . p. 22.
[149] *Revue Juive de Genève,* vol. vii, no. 7, July 1939, p. 467.
[150] Z. Szajkowski, *Analytical Franco-Jewish Gazetteer 1939-1945* . . . (New York 1966), pp. 18-23.
[151] Joseph Ratz, *La France que je cherchais. Les impressions d'un Russe engagé volontaire en France* (Limoges 1945), pp. 63-65.
[152] Benjamin Shlevin, *The Jews of Belleville* (Paris 1948), pp. 237-38 (in Yiddish).
[153] Léon Aréga, *Comme si c'était fini* (Paris 1946), p. 5; Szajkowski, *op.cit.*, p. 25; Franz Verfel, *Jacobowsky und der Oberst* (Stockholm and New York 1944).
[154] Kalman Stein, "Jewish Soldiers in the Polish Army," *Jewish Frontier,* May 1944, p. 18.
[155] HH2, France I/48.
[156] Alfred Vayts, *op.cit.* p. 394.
[157] Mercier, *op.cit.* p. 258.
[158] *Ibid.* p. 260.
[159] Kanitz, *op. cit.* p. 20.
[160] Ratz, *op.cit.* pp. 84-99.
[161] Kanitz, *op.cit.*
[161a] Szaja Appel, "Notre Action au Camp de Pithiviers," *Le Combattant Volontaire Juif 1939-1945* (Paris 1941), pp. 75-77; Joseph Ratz, *La France que je cherchais* (Limoges 1945), pp. 96, 155; Jacob Kaplan, "French Jewry under the Occupation," *The American Jewish Year Book 5706* (Philadelphia 1945), p. 80; Szajkowski, *Franco-Jewish Gazetteer,* p. 24.
[162] Ratz, *op.cit.* p. 109.
[163] Aréga, *op.cit.* p. 353.
[164] Ratz, *op.cit.* pp. 110-11; M. Vanino [Vanikoff], *Le temps de la honte* . . . (Paris 1952), pp.

315-18.

[165] Michel del Castillo, *Child of Our Time* (New York 1958), p. 27.

[166] Szajkowski, *op.cit.* pp. 26-27.

[167] Vanino, *op.cit.* pp. 298-318.

[168] *Ibid.*, p. 306.

[169] HH2, France I, 194.

[170] Ted Harris, *Escape from the Legion* (Condor 1945), p. 9.

[171] Heintz Pol, "Vichy's Slave Battalions," *Nation,* vol. clii (1941), p. 529; New York *Times,* March 30, 1941, p. 25; "Il y a un projet d'envoyer à Djelfa les éléments les plus dangereux du camp de Vernet" (LB p. 55). "La défaite de la République espagnole le ramena en France où il devait être interné d'abord au camp de Saint-Cyprien puis à Gurs puis enfin au camp special pour politiques du Vernet où il reste jusqu'en juin 1941. Lorsqu'ils apprirent qu'il était sur le point d'être envoyé en Algérie, a Djelfa, sa femme et ses amis réussirent à organiser son évasion." "Interné en France au camp d'Argelès, il réussit, alors qu'il allait être déporté en Afrique du Nord, a s'évader" (David Diamont, *Héros juifs de la résistance française* (Paris 1962), pp. 203, 211). "Réfugié belge, interné plus que deux ans dans différents camps en France, actuellement au camp de Djelfa," March 6, 1942 (AIP, 59, p. 15). Golski, *Un Buchenwald français sous le règne du Máréchal* (Périgueux 1945); Eberhard Jaeckel, *Marokko im zweiten Weltkrieg. Unter besonderer Berucksichtgung der Behandlung und Internierung von Juden in der Franzosischen Zone.* Gutachten (n.p. July 1960), mimeographed; *Le martyre des antifascistes dans les camps de concentration de l'Afrique du Nord.* Préface de Virgile Barel (Alger n.d.); Jacques Sabille, *Les Juifs de Tunisie sous Vichy et l'occupation* (Paris 1954), pp. 81-115; "In die Sahara verschickt," and "Der Sahara entlofhen," *Aufbau,* April 25 and Sept. 26, 1941; NA, RG 226, no. 21060.

[172] HHI, XII France A, 15; Michel Ansky, *Les Juifs d'Algérie. Du Décret Crémieux à la Libération* (Paris 1950), p. 281.

[173] A. D. Printer, "Spanish Soldiers in France," *Nation,* vol. clv (1943), p. 489.

[174] AIP, 62, p. 202.

[175] New York *Times,* May 25, 1941, p. 31.

[176] Charles Seville, "Barcarès-Beyrouth-Roanne-Turn," *Le Combattant Volontaire Juif . . .* (Paris 1971), pp. 18-19.

[177] According to Mercier, *op.cit.*, p. 267.

[178] AFSC.

[179] HHI, XVI, All; NA, RG 59, 740.00115Eur.War1939/375.

[180] "Sahara Railway. Hitler pushes Rail Route across Desert toward Dakar Plane Base," *Life,* Nov. 17, 1941, p. 132-34; Lois A. C. Raphael, "Dakar and the Desert Road," *Political Science Quarterly,* vol. lix (1944), pp. 15-29; Kenneth G. Crawford, *Report on North Africa* (New York-Toronto n.d.), p. 31.

[181] Pol, *op.cit.*, pp. 527-29; New York *Times,* July 25, 1941, p. 6 and Aug. 6, p. 16.

[182] NA, RG 59, 851T. 77 Transah./27.

[183] *Ibid.*/21 and 22.

[184] *Ibid.*, /21.

[184a] *Ibid.*, /30.

[185] *Ibid.*, /27.

[185a] World Jewish Congress.

[186] HHi, XVIA, 26-28; World Jewish Congress.

[187] Printer, *op.cit.* pp. 4880-90.

[188] AFSC; HH-i, XVL A 21-22, 25-26; NA, RG 84, Casablanca, 814.2. 1942.

[189] HH-i, XVL A-26; Ansky, *op.cit.*, pp. 264-67.

[190] Rudolf Selke, "Trans-Saharan Inferno," *Free World,* vol. ii (1943), pp. 57-62; NA, RG 226, no. 2160.

190ᵃNA, RG 226, no. 2160.
190ᵇ*Ibid.*
190ᶜMaurice Vanino-Vanikoff, "Le Régime des Camps en Afrique du Nord," *Le Combattant Volontaire Juif 1939-1945* (Paris 1941), pp. 80-82.
191HH-i, XVI A-23.
192AFSC; World Jewish Congress.
192ᵃVanino-Vanikoff, *op.cit.*
193*Ibid.*
194*Ibid.*
195NA, RG 226, no. 2160, Heath's report of Nov. 7, 1942 *(ibid).*
196*Ibid.*
197*Presse Marocaine,* Aug. 28, 1940; *Echo d'Alger,* Sept. 29, 1940.
198Jacques Sabille, *op.cit.,* pp. 94-99.
199"Freedom in Africa," *Jewish Frontier,* Dec. 1942, p. 5.
200AFSC.
201*Ibid.*
202Ansky, *op.cit.,* pp. 265-66.
203AFSC; HH-i, XVI A 26.
204*New Republic,* Nov. 23, 1942, p. 657.
206René Pierre-Gosset, *Algiers 1941-1943. A Temporary Expedient* (London 1945), pp. 206-07.
207Giutonne Zannutelli, "The Disenchanted," *New Republic,* March 1, 1943, pp. 284-85.
208Ansky, *op.cit.,* p. 268.
209Kenneth G. Crawford, *Report on North Africa* (New York-Toronto n.d.) p. 104-111.
210AFSC.
211NA, RG 59, 851R.00/545.
212AFSC.
213*Parliamentary Debates, House of Commons,* 24 March 1943 (London 1943), col. 1728.
214NA, RG 59, 851R.00/545.
215Crawford, *op.cit.*
216*Ibid.,* pp. 108-18.
217AFSC.
218*Ibid.*
219*Ibid.*; LBI.
220*Ibid.*
221AFSC.
222*Ibid.*
223Crawford, *op.cit.,* p. 124.
224*Ibid.*
225AFSC.
226"Note de Service" No. 598/GT,i, signed by Kiesele of the Direction des Communications de la Production Industrielle et du Travail (AFSC).
227AFSC.
228*Ibid.*
229*Ibid.*
230*Ibid.*
231Kendal Kimberland of the Joint Commission for Political Prisoners and Refugees to Pierre Bloch, Commissioner of the Interior of National French Liberation Committee, Feb. 8, 1944 (AFSC).
232AFSC.
233HHI, XVI, A 21.

JEWS AND THE FRENCH FOREIGN LEGION 257

[234] AFSC.
[235] Report of Dec. 29, 1942 (HH-i, XVI A 21); AFSC.
[236] *Ibid.*
[237] Reports by Consul General Willey, March 10, 1943 (NA, RG 59,851R.00/358.)
[238] Drew Pearson in *Daily News,* April 30, 1943; NA, RG 59, 851R.00/481.
[239] AFSC.
[240] *Ibid.*
[241] *Ibid.*
[242] *Ibid.*
[243] Johnson to E. R. Fryer, Chief of Mission February 11, 1944 *(ibid.)*
[244] *American Jewish Year Book 5704,* vol. xliv (Philadelphia 1943), pp. 257-58.
[245] Report by Philip A. Conard of the AFSC, Sept.-Oct. 1944 (HHI, XVI, A 14).
[246] "Il semblerait que les Forces Françaises Libres ne peuvent, pour des raisons purement administratives [!] incorporer les étrangers volontaires dans les Forces Armées régulières de Londres. Ceux-ci ne peuvent servir qu'à nouveau dans la Légion Etrangère et doivent être acheminés en Syrie via l'Afrique Equatoriale Française" (Lisbon, 825. "Situation des Français ou étrangers ayant quitté la France clandestinement pour s'enrôler dans les Forces Françaises Libres").
[247] Paul W. Gordon, Acting Chief of Mission, OFRO, to Michael E. Furcolow, Oct. 4, 1943 (AFSC).
[248] Ansky, *op.cit.,* p. 266.
[249] Cable from Algiers to the State Dept., Jan. 15, 1943 (NA, RG 59, 851R.00/188); AFSC.
[250] E. W. Johnson to the AFSC, Jan. 6, 1944 (AFSC).
[251] *Crawford,* op.cit., p. 118.
[252] Printer, *op.cit.,* p. 488.
[253] "Humiliated, Starved and Tortured," *New Statesman and Nation,* Feb. 20, 1943, p. 118.
[254] "Save the Spanish Loyalists!" *New Republic,* Nov. 30, 1942, p. 700.
[255] NA, RG 59,851R.00/151-254.
[256] AFSC.
[257] Eric W. Johnson to the AFSC, March 4 and 15, 1944 (AFSC).
[258] AFSC.
[259] *Ibid.*
[260] *Ibid.*
[261] David Hartley's reports of March 24 and April 5, 1943 (AFSC).
[262] The records of the Joint Commission "are not known to exist." *Analytical Guide to the Combined British-American Records of the Mediterranean Theater of Operation in World War II,* by Kenneth W. Munden (Rome 1948), p. 100. Some minutes of meetings and other documents used by this author are to be found at AFSC; NA, RG 59,740.0015 European War (1939)/5913 and 815R.00/232, 242, 247, 378, etc.; RG 218 (Records of the U.S. Joint Chiefs of Staff), CC 5-383. 7 (9-6-43).
[263] NA, RG 59, 740.00115EuropeanWar(1939)/5913; 851R.00/242; RG 218, CC 5-383.7(9-6-43).
[264] See Note 262.
[264a] Press release of the Free French Delegation in New York, February 3, 1943. According to a copy sent by G. S. Pettee, Chief of the Sources Division of the Office of War Information, Bureau of Intelligence at the Executive Office of the President, to William Langer, Director of the Branch of Research and Analysis, Office of Strategic Services (NA, RG 226, no. 28564). The New York *Times* of Feb. 3, 1942, had published a summarized account of the letter.
[265] NA, 815R.00/232.
[266] "Confidential report of Major Younger, British member of the Field Party of the Commission" (AFSC).

[267]AFSC.
[268]NA, RG 59,815R.00/378.
[269]*Ibid.*, 342, 358.
[270]NA, RG 218, CC5-383.7(9-6-43).
[271]AFSC.
[272]NA, RG 59, 851R.00/242.
[273]*Ibid.*, /378.
[274]Chadenson of the Trans-Sahara project to the Permanent Military Tribunal of Algiers, Oct. 14, 1943 (AFSC).
[275]Maurice Eisenbeth, *Pages Vecués 1940-1943* (Alger 1945), p. 88; Ansky, *op.cit.*, p. 271.
[275a]NA, RG 84,711.5 Casablanca, 1945; 226, nos. 38928, 80817, 124574.
[276]NA, RG 59, 851R.00/463A.
[277]WRB, 38.
[278]Clarence E. Pickett of the AFSC to Adolf A. Berle, Assistant Secretary of State, May 16, 1944 (WRB, 1).
[279]*Ibid.*, 1.
[280]*Ibid.*, 38.
[281]*Ibid.*, 1.
[282]"Nous revenons à la question de l'évacuation des réfugiés sur l'Afrique du Nord. *Autant que nos informations sont exactes, ces déplacements n'ont aucun rapport avec les décisions prises à la Conférence des Bermudes.* Il s'agit en principe, dans les mouvements actuels uniquement de réfugiés français et de quelques alliés, acheminés en vertu d'accords particuliers, conclus par les gouvernements respectifs avec le Comité National de Libération, ainsi que de personnes arrivant avec la nationalité française présumée, rectifiée à leur arrivée en Afrique du Nord. Nous avons parlé avec des représentants de l'organisation Lehmann de ce projet de la Conférence des Bermudes, que vous mentionnez, et, comme eux, nous avons été fort satisfaits que ce projet n'ait pas encore été réalisé et ne paraisse pas sur le point de l'être, car nous sommes convaincus que sa réalisation ne présente nullement une amélioration pour nos protégés. D'autre part, nous vous avouons que nos informations n'ont peut-être pas été tout à fait complètes, mais le *peux que nous avons appris nous a suffi pour nons rendre adversaire de sa réalisation.*" Oettinger to New York, Nov. 8, 1943. (HHI, XVI, A 10).
[283]*Free France*, vol. iii, no. 2 (Jan. 15, 1943), p. 37.
[284]Eisenbeth, *op.cit.*, pp. 26-28, 113-16. Michel Ansky, *Les Juifs d'Algérie. Du Décret Crémieux à la Libération* (Paris 1950), pp. 272-81, 312-14, 368-69; René Pierre Gosset, *Algiers 1941-1943, A Temporary Expedient* (London 1945), p. 125; Varian Fry, "Giraud and the Jews," *New Republic*, May 10, 1943, p. 626-29; New York *Times*, April 27, 1943, p. 3 and April 28, p. 10; YIVO (documents on North Africa); "The New Zionism," *New Republic*, March 8, 1943, p. 304; World Jewish Congress.
[285]NA, RG 59, 851.222/126.
[286]*Reveil Juif*, March 27, 1931; J. Bielinky, "Les Juifs Algériens," *Le Volontaire Juif*, March 1, 1931, p. 3; "Hommage aux soldats juifs d'Algérie," *L'Univers Israélite*, Sept. 15, 1916, pp. 669-71; "Jewish Heroes of the French Army," *Varhayt*, July 9, 1915.
[287]NA, RG 59, 851R.00/242.
[288]*Jewish Chronicle*, Jan. 22, 1943.
[289]See note 287.
[290]*Ibid.*, /269.
[291]*Free France*, vol. iii, no. 1 (Jan. 1, 1943), pp. 5-6.
[292]Eisenbeth, *op.cit.*, p. 70; Marcel Aboulker, *Alger et ses complots* (Paris 1945); Lucien Steinberg, *La Révolte des Justes. Les Juifs contre Hitler* (Paris 1970), pp. 219-33 ("Le débarquement d'Alger"); NA, RG 84, Casablanca, 800. 1942.
[292a]World Jewish Congress.

[293] NA, RG 59, 851R.00/208.
[294] Albert Krammerer, *Du débarquement African au meurtre du Darlan* (Paris 1949), p. 74.
[295] *Contemporary Jewish Record,* April 1943, p. 178.
[296] NA, RG 59, 815R.00/498.
[297] Hannah Arendt, "Why the Crémieux Decree was abrogated," *Contemporary Jewish Record,* April 1943, p. 123.
[298] William D. Leahy, *I Was There* (New York 1950), p. 136; Alfred D. Chandler, ed., *The Papers of Dwight David Eisenhower. The War Years* (Baltimore n.d.), vol. ii, p. 817.
[299] Robert D. Murphy, *Diplomat Among Warriors* (Garden City 1964), p. 147.
[300] *Ibid.*, p. 159-160.
[301] *Ibid.*, p. 147.
[302] *Ibid.*
[303] Hoffman to J. W. Pehle, Executive Director of the WRB (WRB, box 1).
[304] Crawford, *op.cit.*, pp. 45-46, 86-89.
[305] New York *Times,* March 22, 1943; April 4, p. 7; March 28, p. 4; April 4, p. 7.
[306] *Ibid.*, March 19, 1943, p. 15.
[307] NA, RG 59, 815R.01/42; 815R.4016/32-34.
[308] *Ibid.*
[309] NA, RG 59, 851R.4016/35.
[310] New York *Times,* April 25, 1943.
[311] NA, RG 59, 851R.4016/57 and 61.
[312] Murphy, *op.cit.*, pp. 100-61.
[313] Eisenbeth, *op.cit.*, pp. 72-82; World Jewish Congress . . . ; Ansky, *op cit.*
[314] New York *Times,* Oct. 22, 1943; "The Crémieux Decree 'Restored'," *Jewish Frontier,* Nov. 1943, p. 5; NA, RG 84, Casablanca.
[315] Szajkowski, *Analytical Franco-Jewish Gazetteer* . . ., pp. 19-21.
[316] Bruno Weil, *Baracke 37-Stillgestanden! Ich sah Frankreichs Fall hinter Stacheldraht* (Buenos Aires 1941), p. 11.
[317] June 20, 1916 (YIVO).
[318] One-page leaflet published by the Committee of Delegates of the Russian Socialist Group in London, n.d. (Harvard).
[319] Copy of a letter sent to the Home Secretary Herbert Louis Samuel on behalf of the Conference of all the Jewish Trade Union Committees in London, signed by S. Joseph and I. Lush, Published as a two-page leaflet, n.d. [August 1916] (Harvard).
[320] One-page leaflet published by the Committee of Delegates of the Russian Socialist Groups in London, July 1916 (Harvard and YIVO).
[321] Mimeographed leaflet, 2 pp., [July 1916]. Signed by the London Section of the Social-Democratic Labour Party of Russia; the London Group of the Social-Democratic Labour Party of Russia; the London Group of the Social-Revolutionary Party; the London Group of the Bund (Jewish Labour Alliance in Lithuania, Poland and Russia); the London Group of the Social-Democracy of Latvia; the London Group of the Lithuanian Socialist Federation in Great Britain; and the London Polish Social-Democratic Club (Harvard).
[322] Aug. 3, 1916, mimeographed, 2 pp. (YIVO).
[323] Four-page pamphlet published by the Committee of Delegates of the Russian Socialist Groups in London, reprint of a leaflet published by the Russian Socialist Committee, London, September 1916 (Harvard).
[324] Four-page pamphlet, Sept. 16, 1916 (Harvard).
[325] Two-page pamphlet signed by the Committee of Delegates of the Russian Socialist Groups in London and the Jewish Social Democratic Organisation in Great Britain (London, October 1916). Harvard.

[326] Four-page pamphlet published by the same organizations. Sept. 1916 (YIVO).

The Committee of Russian refugees also published: 1) *An Appeal to Public Opinion. Should the Russian Refugees be Deported?* (London 1916), 4 pp. 2) *Za pravo ubiezestsha!*]London 1916], 7 pp. 3) *The Right of Asylum*. Two thousand copies of the leaflet were seized by the police in a raid on the room of Mrs. Bridges Adams who undertook the distribution. 4) A pamphlet *The National Question in the Russian Duma*, containing the speeches of members of the Duma, translated by E. L. Minsky. Five hundred copies of the pamphlet were distributed during the Trade Union Congress in Birmingham. 5-6) Two statements proving the "impossibility of separating the political emigrants in the narrow sense of the word from the other emigrants. 7) Draft of a resolution about the Right of Asylum, addressed to all Socialist organizations and Trade Councils. 8) A Yiddish leaflet *To the Jewish Workers—Our Situation*, signed by the Committee of Delegates of the Russian Socialist Groups in London and the Jewish Social Democratic Organisation in Great Britain (London Oct. 1916), 1 p. 9) A leaflet published by the Russian Socialist Committee, reprinted in *The Yellow Press* . . . 10) A Yiddish leaflet published by the Foreign Jews Protection Committee Against Deportation to Russia and Compulsion, representing 120 organisations. Signed by Abraham Bezalel, honorary secretary (London, Sept. 12, 1916), 1 p. 11) A leaflet *Report of the Defense Committee*, contains a report of activities and of the conference held on March 4, 1917, by the same organization. 12) A leaflet published by the same Foreign Jews Protection Committee, calling a public meeting "to protect the right of asylum and cheer the Right of Asylum," March 25, 1917. 13) A Yiddish leaflet *Jews, do not be deluded!* published by the same Committee in reply to the Committee for the Jewish Future, which called for the formation of a Jewish Legion for Palestine. 14) In addition the Foreign Jews Protection Committee published a leaflet containing an appeal by the Russian-Jewish (French Refugees) Protection Committee (Harvard and YIVO). On the same subject see also *Di Yidishe Shtime*, London, 12 issues, 1916; Farteydigungs Komitet fun di Oyslendishe Yidn Gegen Tsurikshikung Keyn Rusland . . . *Biuletin*, no. 1, July 18, 1916; I Wassilevsky, *Jewish Refugees and Military Service* . . . (Manchester n.d.), 8 pp. See also Szajkowski, *Jews, Wars, and Communism*, vol. i, pp. 297, 490-91.

[327] English and Yiddish, 4 pp. (Harvard).

[328] Mimeographed, Oct. 4, 1916 (Harvard and YIVO).

[329] One-page official leaflet, July 19, 1917, mimeographed (Harvard).

See also the official printed documents: A Yiddish leaflet of Oct. 1914 (see *News of the YIVO*, Dec. 1946, p. 4); *Russian Subjects and Voluntary Service in the British Army*, published by the Home Office, Aug. 1916, also in Yiddish; *An Agreement Concluded between His Majesty's Government and the Provisional Government of Russia relative to the Reciprocal Liability to Military Service of British Subjects resident in Russia and Russian Subjects resident in Great Britain* . . . (London, July 16, 1917), 3 pp.

[330] Published in the *Daily Chronicle* of July 13, 1917.

[331] A Yiddish pamphlet published by the Committee "For Jewish Future," 8 pp. (Harvard); the translation was made by the Conjoint Foreign Commiteee (YIVO). The same Committee published a Yiddish leaflet calling to enlist in the Jewish Legion, signed by W. Jabotinsky, 1 p. (Mowschowitch).

[332] *Jewish Chronicle*, Dec. 5, 1919. Dr. Jochelman was connected with many Anglo-Russian insurance and transportation companies, member of the Executive Committee of the Anglo-Russian Chamber of Commerce, Vice-President of the Jewish Territorial Organisation, Chairman of the Association of Ukrainian Jews in England, member of the Joint Foreign Committee of the Board of Deputies, etc.

SOURCES

ARCHIVAL SOURCES USED IN THE NOTES

AFSC—Archives of the American Friend's Service Committee, at Haverford College (Haverford, Pa.).
AIP—Archives of the Association des Israélites Pratiquants, at the YIVO Institute for Jewish Research (New York City).
Harvard—Hebrew Division, Harvard College Library (Cambridge, Mass.).
HH—Archives of HIAS-HICEM, at YIVO.
LBI—Archives of the Leo Baeck Institute (New York City).
Lisbon—Archives of the American Joint Distribution Committee and HICEM at Lisbon, at YIVO.
Mowschowitch—The David Mowschowitch Collection, at YIVO.
NA—National Archives (Washington, D.C.).
WRB—Archives of the War Refugee Board, at F. D. Roosevelt Library (Hyde Park, N.Y.).

PRINTED SOURCES

Aboulker, Marcel, *Alger et ses complots* (Paris 1945).
About Military Service, signed W. Jabotinsky (London 1917), in Yiddish, 1 p.; see note 328.
Action (L') Française.
A[lbert], Fr., "Un appel entendu," *L'Homme Enchaîné,* according to *L'Univers Israélite,* vol. lxxii-2, 1916, p. 49.
Alexander, Michael, *The Reluctant Legionnaire. An Escapade* (London 1956).
A l'Opinion Publique. Au sujet de la situation des réfugiés russes en France . . . (Paris 1916).
American, New York.
American Jewish Year Book.
"Americans Not Wanted in the Foreign Legion," *Literary Digest,* vol. cxiv (Sept. 10, 1932), p. 33.
Anoutin [Jarblum], M., "French Stones for Jewish Bread," *Varhayt,* July 16, 1915.
———, "What Gentiles May Do and Jews May Not," *ibid.,* July 5, 1915.
Ansky, Michel, *Les Juifs d'Algérie. Du Décret Crémieux à la Libération* (Paris 1950).
[Appeal by Lord Leopold de Rothschild and Baron Louis Samuel Montagu Swaythling] (London Oct. 4, 1916), mimeographed, 1 p.
Appeal (An) to Public Opinion. Should the Russian Refugees be Deported? (London 1916), 4 pp.
Appel, Szaja, "Notre Action au Camp de Pithiviers," *Le Combattant Volontaire Juif 1939-1945* (Paris 1941), pp. 75-77.
"A Propos des Israélites Russes à Paris," *Les Archives Israélites,* Aug. 29, 1918.
Archives (Les) Israélites.
Aréga, Léon, *Comme si c'était fini* (Paris 1946).
Arendt, Hannah, "Why the Crémieux Decree was abrogated," *Contemporary Jewish Record,* April 1943.
Armstrong, *see Legion of Hell.*
"Arrival of Escapees from France," *Varhayt,* July 14, 1915.
Au Service de la France. Edité a l'occasion du 10e anniversaire de l'Union des Engagés Volontaires

et Anciens Combattants Juifs 1939-1945 (Paris 1955).
Bal Hahalomes [Sholem Szwartzbard], *Troymen un virklikhkayt. Lider [Dreams and Reality. Poems]* (Paris 1920).
Bailby, Léon, "D'autrés embusqués," *L'Intransigeant,* Nov. 30, 1915.
Baker, Roy, *Penal Battalion* (London 1934).
Bannerman, see Dead March . . .
Barel, Virgile, see Le Martyre . . .
Bielinky, J., "Les Engagements Volontaires des Juifs dans les Armées de la République," *Le Volontaire Juif,* June 1, 1931.
———, "Les Juifs Algériens," *ibid.,* March 1, 1931.
———, "Les Juifs Tunisiens," *ibid.,* Nov. 1, 1931, pp. 3-5.
Blackledge, see Death . . . Souless . . .
Bocca, Geoffrey, *La Legion!* . . . (New York 1964).
Bowe, John, and Charles L. MacGregor, *Soldiers in the Legion* (Chicago 1918).
Brian, Stuart, *Far to Go* (London 1947).
Brief Summary of the activities of the Committee of Delegates of the Russian Socialist Groups in London (London, Sept. 16, 1916), 4 pp.
Cahen, Emile, "Les Régiménts Etrangers," *Les Archives Israélites,* May 20, 1915.
———, "Les Suspects," *ibid.,* Dec. 13, 1917.
Castaingt, Jean, see M. Pennette.
Castillo, Michel del, *Child of Our Time* (New York 1958).
Chandler, Alfred D., ed., *The Papers of Dwight David Eisenhower. The War Years* (Baltimore n.d.).
Chapman, see Victor . . .
"Charge (The) of the Foreign Legion," *Literary Digest,* vol. lii (March 18, 1916), pp. 770-79.
Cigarette, see Ouida.
Combattant (Le) Volontaire Juif 1939-1945. Edité à l'occasion du 25e anniversaire de l'Union des Engagés Volontaires et Anciens Combattants Juifs 1939-1945 (Paris 1971).
Contemporary Jewish Record.
Crawford, Kenneth G., *Report on North Africa* (New York-Toronto n.d.).
"Crémieux (The) Decree 'Restored,' " *Jewish Frontier,* Nov. 1943, p. 5.
Daily News.
Data on Russian Refugees (London Sept. 1916), 4 pp.; see note 326.
Daudet, Léon, "La sécurité de Paris," *L'Action Française,* June 28 and 29, 1915.
"Days of Fear for Russian Jews in France," *Varhayt,* July 5, 1915.
Dead March in the Desert. The Story of Mervyn Pellew, as told to W. B. Bannerman (London 1937).
Death Squads in Morocco. As told to W. J. Blackledge by Ex-Légionnaire Tercy Brennan (London 1937).
Delafosse, Jules, "L'Espionage," *L'Echo de Paris,* Jan. 10, 1916.
Dépêche Algérienne, La.
"Déposition de Gustave Hervé," *La Victoire,* July 31, 1918.
"Der Sahara entlofhen," *Aufbau,* Sept. 26, 1941.
"Deserter (A) Who Was Not Shot," *Liberary Digest,* vol. xc (Aug. 14, 1926), pp. 44-48.
Diamont, David, *Héros juifs de la résistance française* (Paris 1962).
Dorian, see Souvenirs du Colonel . . .
Doty, see The Legion of the Damned.
"Doty's Wild Adventures in the Legion," *Literary Digest,* vol. xcvi (Jan. 21, 1928), pp. 48-52.
Dupuy, Capt. R. E., "The Men Who March From Yesterday," *New York Times,* Sept. 28, 1930, pp. 12-13.

Eberhardt, Isabelle, *Notes de Route* (Paris 1921).
Echo d'Alger.
Eisenbeth, Maurice, *Pages Vécues 1940-1943* (Alger 1945).
Eliot, Capt. G. F., "The French Foreign Legion," *Infantry Journal*, vol. xxxii (1928), pp. 407-12.
Eliott, W. J., *see Legion of Hell*.
Enémèsse, "La campagne réactionnaire contre les étrangers habitant Paris," *L'Humanité* (April 10, 1916).
"Etrangers, Les," *Le Temps*, Nov. 29, 1915.
Farteydigungs Komitet fun di Oyslendishe Yidn Gegen Tsurikshikung Keyn Rusland . . . *Biuletin* (London) 1916.
Favrel, Charles, *Ci-devant Légionnaire* (Paris 1962).
Feingold, Boris, *Au Armes! Appel au Peuple Juif*. Préface de G. Dreyfus (Paris 1916).
F.K.B., "The Foreign Legion," *The Spectator*, vol. cxlvi (1931).
Forbes, Reginald R., *Red Horizon* (London 1932).
"Foreign (The) Legion, *"Blackwood's Magazine*, vol. clxxxix (1911), pp. 588-89.
Frappa, Jean-José, "A Few Days With the Foreign Legion," *Journal of the Military Service Institution of the United States*, vol. lvii (1915), pp. 30-53.
Free France.
"Freedom in Africa," *Jewish Frontier*, Dec. 1942, p. 5.
From the Abyss to the Foreign Legion. As told to Edward Clarence Trealawney-Ansel by T. Victor (London 1939).
Fry, Varian, "Giraud and the Jews," *New Republic*, May 10, 1943, pp. 626-29.
Gali, H., "Débusquons-les," *La Liberté*, Aug. 16, 1916.
Genet, *see War Letters*.
G. F. de Ch., "La Voix des Juifs Russes," *L'Echo du 9e* (Paris), July 1, 1915.
Golski, *Un Buchenvald francais sous le règne du Maréchal* (Perigueux 1945).
Gosset, Pierre R., *Algiers 1941-43. A Temporary Expedient* (London 1945).
Guerre (La) Sociale, 1915-1916.
"Haine (La) de l'étranger," *La Bataille Syndicaliste*, April 14, 1915.
Hamonneau, Maurice, *The Foreign Legion* (n.p. n.d.).
Harris, Ted, *Escape from the Legion* (Condor 1945).
Hart, Adrian Liddell, *Strange Company* (n.p. 1953).
Hervé, G., "Au secours de Sarrail," *La Guerre Sociale*, Nov. 25, 1915.
———, "La campagne contre les Juifs russes," *ibid.*, June 28, 1915.
———, "La chasse aux réfugiés russes," *ibid.*, July 1, 1915.
———, "Le droit d'asile menacé," *ibid.*, June 30, 1915.
———, "La France expulsera-t-elle les réfugiés russes?" *ibid.*, June 29, 1915.
———, "Les Juifs russes de Paris," *ibid.*, Nov. 26, 1915.
———, "Le Parlement et les camps d'évacuation," *ibid.*, Jan. 13, 1915.
———, "Pénibles incidents," *ibid.*, Dec. 29, 1914.
———, "Pour l'honneur de la France," *ibid.*, June 26, 1915.
———, "La République et le droit d'asile," *ibid.*, June 5, 1915.
"Hommage aux soldats juifs d'Algérie," *L'Univers Israélite*, Sept. 15, 1916, pp. 669-71.
Hora, Charles, *Mon tour du monde en 80 barrods*. Recuille par Paul Vincent (Paris 1961).
"Humiliated, Starved and Tortured," *New Statesman and Nation*, Feb. 20, 1943, p. 48.
"In der Sahara verschickt," *Aufbau*, April 25, 1941.
["Interview (An) with Dr. David Jochelman,"] *Jewish Chronicle*, Dec. 5, 1919.
Israélites (Les) dans l'armée Française (Angers 1921).
"Israélites (Les) russes et la mobilisation," *Petit Parisien*, June 27, 1915.
"Israélites (Les) russes et la mobilisation," *Le Temps*, June 29, 1915.

"Israélites (Les) Tunisiens et la Guerre," *Archives Israelites,* Sept. 14, 1916.
Jarblum, *see* Anoutin.
Jaeckel, Eberhard, *Morokko in zweiten weltkrieg. Unter besonderer Bernchsichtung der Behandlung und Internlerung von Juden in der Franzosischen Zone,* Gutachten (n.p. July 1960), mimeographed.
Jewish Chronicle (London).
"Jewish Heros of the French Army," *Varhayt,* July 9, 1915.
Jews, do not *be deluded!* (London 1917), in Yiddish, 1 p.; see note 326.
Jochelman, *see* "An Interview . . ."
Jolinon, Joseph, "La Mutinerie de Coeuvres," *Mercure de France,* Aug. 15, 1920.
Journal Officiel.
"Juifs (Les) sac au dos," *Nouveliste de la Bretagne* (Rennes), June 3, 1917.
Kanitz, Walter, *The White Kepi* (Chicago, 1956).
Kaplan, Jacob, "French Jewry under the Occupation," *American Jewish Yearbook 5706* (Philadelphia 1945), pp. 71-118.
Kazniy ruskikh volonterov vo frantsii (Geneva 1915).
Ker, O., *see* "The Martyrdom . . ."
Klose, Fritz, The Legion Marches (London 1932).
Krammerer, Albert, *Du.débarquement Africain au meurtre du Darlan* (Paris 1949).
Krestovskai, Lidia, *Izistorii ruskavo volonterskavo dvizheniio vo frantsiyi* (Paris n.d.).
Lafayette (The) Flying Corps. Edited by James Norman Hall and Charles Bernard Nordhoff (Boston-New York 1920), 2 vols.
Lambert, Cdt., "The Foreign Legion," *The Fighting Forces,* vol. i, 1924.
Landau, Jacques, "Les Etrangers à Paris," *Je Dis Tout,* Aug. 16, 1916.
Lapie, Pierre-Olivier, *La Légion Etrangère à Narvik* (Paris 1945).
Leahy, William D., *I Was There* (New York 1950).
Lebedov, Victor, *Souvenirs d'un Volontaire Russe dans l'Armée Française, 1914-1916.* Préface de Pierre Mille (Paris 1917).
Legion of Hell, by James Mackinley Armstrong, as told to William James Eliot (London 1936).
Legion (The) of the Damned. The Adventures of Bennet J. Doty in the French Foreign Legion, as told by himself (New York-London 1928).
Lehman, Hans Walter, *Die franzoesische Fremdenlegion. Eine voelkerrechthiche Untersuchung* (Munich-Leipzig 1915).
Letters and Diary of Alan Seeger (New York 1917).
Loehndorf, Ernst F., *Hell in the Foreign Legion* (London 1939).
Londres, Albert, *Dante n'avait rien vu* (Paris 1924).
MacGregor, Ch.L., *see* Bowe.
Magnus, *see* M.M.
Maire, *see Souvenirs du Colonel* . . .
Manington, George, *A Soldier of the Legion* (London 1907).
Martin, Arthur L., "An International Force of Tomorrow," *The Spectator,* vol. cxlii (1934), pp. 40-41.
"Martyrdom (The) of the Russian Soldiers in France," *Soviet Russia,* Feb. 7, 1920, according to O. Ker in *La Vie Ouvrière,* Jan. 16, 1920.
Martyre (Le) des antifascistes dans les camps de concentration de l'Afriques du Nord. Préface de Virgile Barel (Alger n.d.).
McLean, Angus, *Vive la Légion* (London 1937).
Mercier, Charles E., *Legion of Strangers* (New York 1964).
Military Service (Conventions with Allied States) Act, 1917 (London July 19, 1917), mimeographed, 1 p.

Millán-Astray, José, *Franco El Candillo* (Salamanca 1939).
———, *La Legión* (Madrid 1939).
Mille, Pierre, *see* V. Lebedov.
Minsky, *see The National Question* . . .
M. M. [Maurice Magnus], *Memoirs of the Foreign Legion* (London 1924).
Moch, Gaston, *La Question de la Légion Etrangère* (Paris 1914).
Monnatte, P., *see "The Russian Soldiers in France."*
Morlae, Edward, "A Soldier of 'the Legion'," *Atlantic Monthly,* vol. cxvii (1966), pp. 383-96, 813-25.
———, *A Soldier of the Legion* (Boston 1916).
Moutet, Marius, "Campagne antisémite," *L'Humanité* (Paris, Nov. 26, 1915).
———, "La question des passeports et les réfugiés étrangers," *ibid.,* June 26, 1916.
———, "Les Russes de Paris et le Droit d'Asile," *ibid.,* July 1, 1915.
Munden, Kenneth W., *Analytical Guide to the Combined British-American Records of the Mediterranean Theater of Operations in World War II* (Rome 1948).
Murphy, Robert D., *Diplomat Among Warriors* (Garden City 1964).
Narcay, Poirier de, "Qu'ils s'engagent ou qu'ils partent!" *La Libre Parole,* Nov. 3, 1916.
Nashe Slovo (Paris).
Nation (New York).
National (The) Question in the Russian Duma (London 1916), translated by E. L. Minsky.
New Republic (New York).
"New (The) Zionism" *New Republic,* March 8, 1943, p. 304.
Notre Volonté. Bulletin de l'Union des Engagés Volontaires, Anciens Combattants Juifs 1939-1945.
O'Ballance, Edgar, *The Story of the French Foreign Legion* (London 1961).
Obey, André, "Camarades Rouski," *Revue de Paris,* Dec. 1920 (a fictionalized account of La Courtine mutiny).
Ouida [Louise De La Ramée], *Under Two Flags,* A novel (Philadelphia 1862); also dramatized as *Cigarette.*
Pages de Gloire de la Division Marocaine (Paris 1919).
Parliamentary Debates (London).
Pellew, *see Dead March.*
Penderel, William, *Parade of Violence* (London 1937).
Pennette, Marcel, and Jean Castaingt, "La Legión extranjera en la intervención francesa," *Historia Mexicana,* vol. xii (1962), pp. 229-73.
Pertwee, Roland, *Gentelmen March* (Boston-New York 1927).
Peuple (le) Juif, 1917.
Poinsot, Maffeo Charles, *Au Service de la France. Les Volontaires Etrangers de 1914* (Paris n.d.).
Les Volontaires Etrangers Enrolés Au Service de la France en 1914-15 (Paris 1915).
Pol, Heintz, *Suicide of a Democracy* (New York 1940).
———, "Vichy's Slave Battalions," *Nation,* vol. clii (1941), p. 529.
"Pour les Juifs russes de Paris," *Les Tablettes des Deux Charentes* (Rochefort), March 22, 1917.
Poitevin, Pierre, *Une bataille au Centre de la France en 1917. La révolte des Armées Russes au camp de La Courtine* (Limoges 1937).
———, *La Mutinerie de La Courtine* (Paris 1938).
Presse Marocaine.
Price, G. Ward, "The Lords of the Atlas Submit," *Saturday Evening Post,* vol. ccvii, Nov. 10, 1934.
Prieto, Carlos, "Legion of 'the Lost Ones' Fights in Spain," *New York Times,* Oct. 18, 1936, p. 7.
Printer, A. D., "Spanish Soldiers in France," *Nation,* vol. clv (1943), p. 489.
Proposed (The) Deportation and Compulsion for Russian Subjects (London n.d.), 2 pp.; *see* note 319.

"Que signifient ces menaces," *La Bataille Syndicaliste,* June 27, 1915.

Ramée, *see* Ouida.

Raphael, Lois A. C., "Dakar and the Desert Road," *Political Science Quarterly,* vol. lix (1944), pp. 15-29.

Ratz, Joseph, *La France que je cherchais. Les impressions d'un Russe engagé volontaire en France* (Limoges 1945).

Reed, John, *Ten Days That Shook the World* (New York 1919), contains an appendix on the mutiny of Russian soldiers in France.

Renaissance (La) du Peuple Juif (Paris).

"Repatriation (The) of Russians in France," *Soviet Russia,* Sept. 6, 1919, according to *Le Populaire,* July 13, 1919.

Report of the Defense Committee . . . (London 1917), in Yiddish; *see* note 326.

Return of Polish Citizens. [*H. J. Res. 291.*] *Hearing before the Committee on Military Affairs House of Representatives. 66:2 (Washington 1920).*

Reveil Juif.

Revue Juive de Genève.

Right of Asylum (London 1916), *see* note 326.

Right (The) Way (Foreign Jews and Military Service), in Yiddish (London 1917), 8 pp.; *see* note 331

Rockwell, Paul Ayres, *American Fighters in the Foreign Legion 1914-1918* (Boston 1930).

Rosen [Carlé], Erwin, *Cafard. Ein Drama aus der Fremdenlegion in 4 Akten* (Munich 1914).

———, *In the Foreign Legion* (London 1910).

Rothschild, see [Appeal . . .]

Rubakin, A., "Situation of the Russian Soldiers in France," *Soviet Russia,* Feb. 28, 1920.

Russian Jewish (French Refugees) Protection Committee (London August 15, 1916), one page leaflet published by The Foreign Jews Protection Committee against Deportation to Russia and Compulsion.

"Russian (The) Soldiers in France," *Soviet Russia,* Jan. 24, 1920, according to P. Monnatte in *La Vie Ouvrière,* Dec. 26, 1919.

Rusishe Nakhrikhtn—Les Echos Russes [Russian News], Paris nos. 1-10, Sept. 26, 1917—Jan. 11, 1918, and *Buleten [Bulletin],* published by the General Russian Colonial [Colony] Committee; published also in Russian, 17 issues.

Sabille, Jacques, *Les Juifs de Tunisie sous Vichy et l'occupation* (Paris 1945).

Sablotny, Richard, *Legionnaire in Morocco* (Los Angeles 1940).

"Sahara Railway . . ." *Life,* Nov. 17, 1941.

"Sans (Les) Patrie," *L'Oeuvre,* July 18, 1916.

Saphir, A., "Les Engagements Volontaires en Août 1914," *Le Volontaire Juif,* April 1932.

"Save the Spanish Loyalists!" *New Republic,* Nov. 30, 1942, p. 700.

Schapiro, J., "With the Russian Jews in Paris," *Varhayt,* July 17, 1915.

Scheftel, Joseph R., "The Russian Soldiers in France," *Soviet Russia,* no. 21 (Oct. 25, 1919), pp. 12-15.

Schwartzbard, Sholem, *In krig mit zikh aleyn* [In the War with Oneself] (Chicago 1933).

———, *see* Bal Hahalomes.

Scott-Kilvert, "The Mercenary," *The New Statesman and Nation,* n.s., vol. xxiv (Sept. 5, 1942), pp. 155-56.

Seeger, *see Letters and Diary.*

Sefer virushuv (Tel Aviv 1970).

Selke, Rudolf, "Trans-Saharan Inferno," *Free World,* vol. ii (1943), pp. 57-62.

"Service (Le) obligatoire pour tous. Obligation politique et morale," *Le Journal de Tunis,* Aug. 3, 1915.

Seville, Charles, "Barcarès-Beyrouth-Roanne-Turin," *Le Combattant Volontaire Juif* . . . (Paris 1971), pp. 18-19.
Shlevin, Benjamin, *The Jews of Belleville* (Paris 1948), in Yiddish.
Silva, Gen. Carlos de, *General Millán Astray. El Legionario* (Barcelona 1956).
Sothern, J. M., "An Outpost of the Foreign Legion," *Cornhill Magazine*, n.s., vol. lxxiv (1933).
Souless (The) Legion. By Ex-Legionnaire 1384, in collaboration with W. J. Blackledge (London 1934).
Souvenirs du Colonel [Fernand V. M.] *Maire de La Légion Etrangère*, recuillis par Jean-Pierre Dorian (Paris 1939).
[Statement by the Committee of Delegates of the Russian Socialist Groups in London.] Aug. 3, 1916, mimeographed, 2 pp.
[Statement by the London Groups of Socialist Parties of Russia, July 1916], 2 pp., *see* note 321.
Stein, Kalman, "Jewish Soldiers in the Polish Army," *Jewish Frontier*, May 1944.
Steinberg, Lucien, *La Révolte des Justes. Les Juifs contre Hitler* (Paris 1970).
Swaythling, *See* [Appeal . . .]
Szajkowski, Z., *Analytical Franco-Jewish Gazetteer 1939-1945* . . . (New York 1966).
———, *Jews, Wars, and Communism*, vol. i (New York 1972).
———, "Jews in the French Army," *Hayalim yehudim bezivot europa* [*Jewish Soldiers in the European armies*] (Tel Aviv 1967), pp. 30-41.
———, "Jews in the Foreign Legion," *Conservative Judaism*, vol. xxi, no. 4 (1966-67), pp. 22-34.
———, "The Soldiers France Forgot," *Contemporary Jewish Record*, vol. v (1942), pp. 589-96.
———, "'1914-1918," *Unzer Shtyme* (Paris), Oct. 22-Dec. 3, 1938.
Sztern, N., "Le Tribut du Sang (Les Etrangers et la Guerre)," *Bulletin de l' Union des Engagés Volontaires, Anciens Combattants Juifs 1939*, [1946], pp. 2-3.
Thiéry, Gustave, "La France aux Français," *Revue Catholique des Institutions et du Droit*, Sept. 1915.
Tchernoff, Juda, *Dans le Creuset des Civilisations*, vol. iv (Paris 1938).
Tiira, Ensio, *Raft of Despair* (London 1954).
Times, New York.
To the Emigrants from Russia (London July 1916), 1 p., published by the Committee of Delegates of the Russian Socialist Groups in London.
To the Jewish Workers—Our Situation (London Oct. 1916), 1 p., in Yiddish; *see* note 326.
To the Jews of London (London n.d.), English and Yiddish, 4 pp.
To the Workers—Refugees from Russia (London, October 1916), 2 pp.; *see* note 325.
Torato, *see* "What Price . . ."
"Trois articles d'Hervé. Pour l'honneur de la France," *L' Univers Israélite*, vol. lxx-2, 1915.
Turnbull, Patrick, *The Foreign Legion* (London 1964).
Ulmer, George Elmer, "Franco Perfected Foreign Legion As Weapon to Seize Rule in Spain," New York *Times*, July 26, 1936, p. 23.
Univers Israelite, L'.
Vagts, Alfred, "The Foreigner As Soldier in the Second World War. II. The Military Use of the Foreigner by France," *The Journal of Politics*, vol. ix, Aug. 1947.
Vanikoff, Maurice, *La Commemoration des Engagements Volontaires des Juifs d'Origine Etrangère 1914-1918* (Paris 1932).
———, *see* Vanino.
Vanino-Vanikoff, M., *Le Temps de la honte* . . . (Paris 1952).
———, "Le Régime des Camps en Afrique du Nord," *Le Combattant Volontaire Juif 1939-1945*, pp. 80-82.
———, *see* Vanikoff.

Verfel, Franz, *Jacobowsky und der Oberst* (Stockholm and New York 1944).
Verité, La (Paris).
Victor Emmanuel Chapman's Letters From France (New York 1917).
Victoire, La (Paris).
Volontaire Juif, 1919 and 1931.
"Volontaires (Les) juifs de 1914," *L'Univers Israélite,* Feb. 18, 1916, pp. 600-602.
Viliers, René, "Heat that Kills," *Living Age,* vol. cccxxxiii (1927), pp. 622-24.
Vincent, Paul, *see* Hora.
Wanikoff, *see* Vanikoff.
War Letters of Edmond Genet (New York 1918).
Waterhouse, F. A., *Five Sous a Day* (London 1933).
———, *Journey Without End. An Autobiography* (London 1940).
Wassilevsky, I., *Jewish Refugees and Military Service* . . . (Manchester n.d.), 8 pp.
What Awaits Those Who Will Be Deported to Russia? (London n.d.). Published by The Committee of Delegates of the Russian Socialist Groups in London and printed by the National Labour Press.
Weil, Bruno, *Baracke 37-Stillge Standen! Ich sah Frankreichs Fall hinter Stacheldraht* (Buenos Aires 1941).
Werstein, Irving, *Sound No Trumpet. The Life and Death of Alan Seeger* (New York 1967).
"What Price Humanity," by Legionnaire "Torato," *Living Age,* vol. cccxxxii (1927).
Wolf, Lucien, "Conscripting the Alien. The New Military Act," *Daily Chronicle* (London), July 13, 1917.
Wolf, Mathieu, "Les Corps des Volontaires Israélites," *L'Univers Israélite,* vol. 70-2, 1915.
World Jewish Congress, Advisory Council on European Jewish Affairs, *Facts and Documents. Collection of Reports and Documents Pertaining to the Jewish Situation in French North Africa* (New York June 1, 1943).
Wren, Percival Christopher, *Beau Geste* (New York 1925).
———, "With the Legion," *Living Age,* vol. cccxliii (1932).
Yellow (The) Press, the Danger of Pogroms and the Home Secretary (London September 1916), 4 pp.; *see* note 323.
Yidishe (Di) Shtime (London), 12 issues, 1916.
Zannutelli, Giutonne, "The Disenchanted," *New Republic,* March 1, 1943, pp. 284-85.
Za pravo ubiezestsha! (London 1916), 7 pp.

INDEX

Aage, Prince 1-2
Abadie, J. 202
Abedovitch, W. 22
Aboulker, H. 210, 215
Ackerman, L. E. 207
Action (L') Française 38, 58, 215
Adams, B. 238
Adrar 88, 92
Africa 2, 6, 10, 15, 87, see also North Africa, Sahara, etc.
AFSC see American Friends Aid Committee 69
Ain 72
Ain-el-Ourak camp 107-8, 112, 166, 175
Ain-Sebaa 182
Ain-Sefra camp 103, 161, 194
Aisne 74
AJDC see American Joint
Akbou camp 201
Alcoholism in the Legion 1-2, 14-15, 74
Alexandre 151, 194-5
— M. 8
Algeria 1, 22, 25-6, 32-4, 43, 52, 83-5, 87-9, 92, 94, 96, 98, 103-4, 106, 113-6, 129, 158, 161, 163, 181, 184, 189, 191-3, 198, 201, 204, 213, Algerian Jewish soldiers, 208-16, and the Allies 85, 88, 115, 215-6, see also Crémieux Decree
Alger Républican 109
Allen, R. F. 183
Aliens in the French Armed Forces *passim*
Almeria 160
Alsatians 34, 37
Alsina 86
American, New York 39
American Friends Service Com. 101, 104, 113, 116, 155, 157, 161, 172, 174-5, 180-1, 183, 202, 206

American Joint Distribution Com. 114, 182
Americans in the Legion 16, 18, 20, 41, 44-5
Americas 88
Amicale des Volontaires 35
Amarcho-Syndicalists 39
Anders, W. 68
Anderson 9
Anfa Conference 221
Anglo-Jewish Assoc. 35, 230
Anglo-Saxons 68
Ansky, M. 84
Anti-militarists 24
Antisemitism 31, 38-44, 58, 61, 64, 83, 128-9, 158, 170, 214-7
Arabs 2, 4, 7, 16-7, 23, 62, 94, 103, 221
Arcadia 51
Archives Israélites, Les 38
Aréga, L. 66
Arendt, H. 218
Argelès camp 69, 83-4, 228
Armistice 44, 59, 84-5, 89, 91
Army, 6th 72, 213; 7th Corps 72
Arras 50
Ashkenazim 63
Assimilation 62
Assoc. of Polish Jews 64
— Tunisienne 27
Astray, D. J. M. 20
Asylum in England 41, 230-49
Atlantic 92
— *Monthly* 48
Atrocities in the Legion and in concentration camps, 2, 7-10, 13, 17-8, 89, 94, 99-100, 102, 107-13, 116, 144-47, 151-71
Aubagne camp 228
Austria 1, 24, 37, see also Refugees
Avelar 112

269

INDEX

Aviation *see* Lafayette Squadron
Avignon 26, 79-80
Azemour camp 84, 107
Azrou camp 198

Back, Rabbi A. 129
Bailby, L. 34
Baker, R. 10
Baku 86
Balkans 47
Bamako 89, 92
Barcarès camp and military training center 69-70, 134, 136, 159
Barcelona 53
Barcy 213
Basch, V. 38, 40
BPI *see* Bataillons
Bataille (La) Syndicaliste 32
Batallions des Pioniers Israélites 208
Bayonne 123
Beaucaire camp 81
Beau Geste, 2, 49
Beaune-la-Rolande camp 77
Béchar River 95
Bedeau prison 208-11
Beirut 85
Belahsen 213
Belgians in the Legion 10-11, 26, 41, 91, 93, Belgium 72, 66, 71
Bellah, J. W. 3
Benaatar, H.N.C. de 114, 182
Ben Guira 217
Beni-Abbès 88, 92-3
Beni Mellal 217
Beni-Ounif camp 162-3
Bercy, L. de 24
Bergeret, Gen. 192
Berguent camp 105, 110-11, 153-55
Berkovitch, P. 37
Berliner Volkszeitung 169
Bermuda Conference 205-7
Bernard, G. 41
Berrouaghia camp and prison 84, 113, 184, 189, 201
Besson, Col. 71
Blum, Léon 66, 68, 73
Bidon II camp 97-8
—V camp 98
Bienstock 111
Billat, B. 35
Birkenwald, M. 113

Blida 174
Bloch, Rabbi A. 129
Board of Deputies 35, 230
Bocca, G. 22-3, 45
Boëgard, Baron de 1
Boghar camp 187, 193, 201
Boghari camp 113
Bohar *see* Boghar
Boisseau, Gen. 172, 211
Boitel 209, 211
Bonestell, C. H. 183
Bordeaux 79
Boston, 52
Bou-Arfa camp 84, 88, 94-99, 105, 107-8, 110-13, 145, 151, 153, 156, 160, 162, 193, 197, 201
Bourg-en-B. 25
Bourtzev, V. 33, 126
Bouton, P. 215-6
BPI *see* Bataillions
Brazil 88
Brelet, 34
Brennmann 111
Brenon, H. 2
Brens camp 28
British 30, 45, interned in North Africa 104-6, 156, in the Legion 2-4, 7-8, 42, 85, 91, 93, British Pioneer Corps in North Africa 116, 173-6, 185, 188, 200
Brister 116
Brooklyn 46
Brussels 25
Brutality *see* Atrocities
Buisson, F. 35, 40
Bulgaria 35
Bulletin . . . d'Algérie 213
Bullit, W. Ch. 180
Butterworth, F. S. 53-4
Bukovina 37
Bund, Socialist 137

Caboche, 107, 116
Cafard 9, 12, 14
Café Globe 24, Weissman 44
Caffareli fortress camp 107
Cameron 1
Camps, concentration camps, forced labor camps, prisons in France and North Africa 31, 34, 37, 58-9, 69, 76-8, 81-6, 98-9, 101, 105-7, 113,

INDEX

115-6, 144-9, 152-3, 155-7, 161-2, 166, 178, 185, 227, death camps 76, 83, escapes 83, refugee camps 58-59, 206, in Spain 176, *see also* Atrocities, Trans-Saharian, and the individual camps Ain-el-Ourak, Ain-Sefra, Akbou, Argelès, Aubagne, Azemour, Azrou, Barcarès, Beaucaire, Beaune-la-Rolande, Bedeau, Beni-Ounif, Berguent, Berrouaghia, Bidon II, Bidon V, Boghar, Boghari, Brens, Caffareli, Casablanca, Catus, Cherchell, Colomb-Béchar, Coupiac, Djelfa, Djenien-bou-Rezg, Djérada, Drancy, El Aricha, Foum de Flah, Gurs, Hadjerat M'Guil, Im Fout, Kasba Tadla, Kef, Kenadsa, Kerras (Khesas), Lambesc, Lambèse, Magenta, Maison Carrée, Mascara, Mauriac, Mechata, Meknès, Menabba, Mengoub, Merchària, Midelt, Les Milles, Missour, Moulay- Bou-Azza, Montguyon, Oswego, Oued-Akreuch, Oued Zem, Oujda, Pithiviers, Port Lyautey, Port Vendres, Rieueros, Saida, Saintes, Septfonds, Settat, Sidi-el-Ayachi, St. Cyprien, Le Vernet
Canadian forces 45, 54
Condace, G. 34
Carency battle and revolt 30-7, 57-8, 125-6, 133, 227
Caro, K. 169
Carpentras 79-80, 143
Carpinteria *Herald* 53
Carreau du Temple 33
Carret, M. 175
Carboux, G. 226
Carusso, G. 53
Carvell, J.E.M. 183
Casablanca 3, 90-1, 115, 148, 152, 154-5, 167, 173, 181-2, 197, 220, prison 201
Casualties among legionnaires 26-7, 30, 74
Catholics 38
Catus camp 228
Cau, Col. 172
Cavalry units in the Legion 57
Celler, E. 224
Censorship 39, 204
Centa 20

Chadenson 92
Chambry 213
Chapin, S. 206
Chaplains 38, 64, 130, 209, 211
Chapman, J. H. 183
— V. E. 22
Charlie 50
Chatekoff, H. 46, 48
Chatel 164
Chatt, N. 142
Cheatham, A. R. 183
Chemin des Damnes 72
Chenelière 183, 199
Charagam *see* Chéragas
Chéragas, 192, 209, 211
Cherchell camp 160
Childs, J. R. 226
Chinese in the Legion 38, 45
Christian Science Monitor 212
Churchill, W. 115, 206, 221
Citizenship of legionnaires, 5, 11, 19, 24, 27, 29, 38, 56
Civilian prisoners and internees, 69, 121, *see also* Alsatians
Civil War 54
Clark, A. M. 53
Coehen, H. 169
Cohen, I. 39-40
— J. 216
Cole, F. 97
Colomb-Béchar camp 10, 77, 84-5, 87-8, 92-98, 102-3, 113, 116, 144, 161-5, 169, 186-7, 193-6, 201
Colonies, colonial wars 4, 13, 87
Columbia University 49
Combat group 192
Comité d'Aide . . . 166-67
— de Propagande . . . 40
— Français . . . 40
— Juif Algérian . . . 209-10, 216
— Juif d'Aide . . . 114
Committee of Jewish Widows . . . 140
— of National Liberation 189
— of Political . . . 34
Communists 60, 62, 64, 67, 74, 99, 102, 106, 152, 176, 200, 204, 219
Comtat Venaissin 79-80
Confederación . . . 155
Conjoint Foreign Com. 35, 37, 230
Conod, E. 183

Conscription of aliens in England 40-1, 130, 230-49
Consistory, Paris 213
Constantine 210
Cope, T. P. 174
Cordoba 8
Corps Franc in North Africa 153, 172-4, 185-6, 181, 185-6, 213
Corsicans in the Legion 102
Costaud 217
Coster, D. 183
Council of State 35
Coupiac camp 78
Courtin, Mme. 166
Court-martial at Carency 30, 42
Crawford, K. G. 151, 160-1, 165-6, 220
Creek, H. P. 52
Crémieux Decree 213, 218-26
Crippen, R. 50
Criticism and praise of the Legion 19-20, 29, 49
Cruelties *see* Atrocities
Cruker, E. 36
Cuiry-lès-Ch. 46
Culebras, A. 113
Cuttoli 219
Czapski 113, 176
Czechs in the Legion 85, 91, 97, 113, 138, 156-7

Dachau camp 99
Dahomey 92
Dakar 87-8, 156
Damascus 18
Danes in the Legion 9
Darlan, F. 115, 162, 164, 180, 191-2, 198, 219
Daudet, L. 38
Dauphin 204
Day, The 40
Death in the Legion 11-3, 15; 46, 52, 139, in the Spanish Legion, 21, *see also* Suicides
Delmayne, A. 85
Demobilization 76-8, 84-5, 92, *see also* Discharge
Denikin's army 43
Denmark 1
Dentz, 75
Dépêche Algérienne 118
Deportations 23, 31, 35-81-2, 230-49

Desert, African 4, *see also* Sahara, Trans-Saharian
Desertion, escape from the Legion 9, 14, 18, 53
Devalon 92
Dijon 64
Discharges from the Legion 4, 15, 22, 49, 64-5, 92, 180, *see also* Demobilization
Disciplinary units, discipline 7, 10, *see also* Atrocities
Discrimination against old-time legionnaires 114
Division, 8th 72; 45th 213; 86th 85; Moroccan 30
Djelfa camp 83-4, 106-7, 113, 116, 150, 157-60, 176, 178, 186, 201
Djenien-bou-Rezg camp 20, 204
Djérada camp 113
Dotti 165
Doty, B. J. 18, 53
Doubs 25
Dourmanoff 105
Drancy camp 139, 142
Dubnow, S. 63, 80
Dubois, M. 3
Dugan, W. E. 50
Dugardier, M. 206
Duke of York 3
Dupuy, E. E. 49
Durkheim, E. 35
Dutch Legion in the East Indies 20, 38

Eastern Europe 83
Eberhardt, I. 3
Echo (L') d'Alger 114
— *du 9e* 34
Ecole Libre. . . . 22
Ehrlich, F. 111
Eisenbeth, M. 225
Eisenhower, D. D. 178-80, 191, 202, 205, 219
Ekmul 210
El Aricha camp 201
El-Guerrah 210
Elishkovsky, S. 36
Ellis, B. 4-5
—, S. 4
El Méridj 211
Emergency Rescue Com. 179
England, 4, 35, 71, 179 *see also* British

INDEX

Enemesse, Dr. 33
Entrepilly 213
Equatorial Africa 87-9, 176
Erg Ergatolis 92-93
Erlich, M. 22
Executions 30, 40, 42, 126 *see also* Carency
Extradition 77

Fascist 58, 79, 111, 161
Fédération des Engagés Volontaires 79
— of Jewish Societies 60
Fédalah refugee camp 206
Ferrier, A. 111
Fez 204
Films, The Legion in 2-3
Finidori 111, 165, 204
Firemen as cadre of the Legion 26
Fismes 46
Fitzerald, J. J. 4
Flax, J. 24
Fleg, E. 122
Food in the Legion 28-9, 32
Forbach 56
Forbes, R. R. 7, 19-20
Forced Volunteers 64-65
Foreign Jews Protection Com. 41, 130
Foreign Legion *passim*
Foum de Flah camp 110, 113
Four Communities 79
France *passim*
Franco, F. 21, 80, 178
François, Gen. 73
Franco-Russian agreement on military service 43, 131
Frankfurter, F. 221
Frederic Douglas Council 52
Free French Forces 71, 191, *see also* Gaullist
Freemasons 21
Freiburg 20
France passim; French army, mutinies 43, native Jews in the 60
French Republican Com. 212
Friedman 29
Friedmann, Is. 37
Frydman, Mrs. 84
Fuller, A. T. 52
Fullerton, H. S. 154
Funerals 150

Galicia 37
Galli, H. 34
Gallieni, J. S. 213
Ganz, C. 173-4
Gao 92, 95, 97-98
Garibaldi Brigade 26, 173
Gaulle, Ch., de Gaullist 67, 117, 156, 163-4, 191, 197, 213, attitude to volunteer legionnaires 176 *see also* Free French Forces
Gazette, Westminster 39
Genet, E. 11, 42, 45
Gentlemen March 2
German Jews *see* Refugees
Germans in the Legion 16, 19, 22-3, 56, 79, 83-4, 89-91, 94, 102, 108, 111, 114, 195
Germany *passim*
Gibraltar 176
Giraud, H. H. 156, 172, 178, 187, 192, 205, 208, 212, 218-19, 221-22, 225
Glasgow *Herald and Globe* 39
Glatstein, J. 62
Goldbeck, W. 3
Goldfarb, P. 29
Gordon, P. W. 174
Gorky's (Maxim) son in the Legion 1
Gosset, R. P. 117, 209
Gozlan, E. 114
Graetz, H. 63
Grandjean 32
Greeks in the Legion 31
Grenoble 78
Groupement des Travailleurs Algeriens
— — Israélites 208
Gruen 111
GTA, GTI *see* Groupement
Groupements des Travailleurs Etrangers (GTE) *see* Camps
Guerre (La) Sociale 24, 32, 39
Guardian, Manchester 39
Gurs camp 83, 101, 228

Habicht 112
Hadjeràt M'Guil camp 62, 107-8, 162-5, 175, 195, 204
Half-brigade (13th) 71, 74
Hall, M. 2
Haller, J. 54
Hallsley, R. G. 180
Hannes, E. 179

INDEX

Harris, T. 83
Hart, A. L. 22, 48
Hartley, D. S. 167, 169-70, 180, 183
Harvard 45
Havre, Le 50
Heath, L. O. 101, 104, 196, 116, 152-3, 170, 172, 181, 183
Hebrew 22
Heisler, Ch. H. 10
Heller 177
Henry, Sgt. 74, 137
Heroism 7, 9
Hertz, Rabbi J. H. 240
Hervé, G. 32, 39, 42, 211
Heyer, D. 2
HICEM 59, 84, 114, 172, 228
Hill-Dillon, S. S. 183
Hindus 45
Hirsch, M. 37
Hirschler, R. 64, 137
History of the Legion 1
Hitler 58-59, 61, 66, 210
Hohler, F. K. 183
Hoffenheimer, Col. 107
Hoffman 220
Holschuler, F. 176-7
House of Commons 158
Hufnagel, L. 64
Hull, Cordell 179, 203, 215
Humanité, L' 24, 33, 39
Hungarian Jews declare hunger strike in camps 175
Hyslop, E. 179

Im Fout camp 113, 154, 166, 186
Immigrants' Committee 34
Immigrants, Illegal 22
Im-Tassit 92
Indians 45
Indochina 22-3
Innes-Irons, Brig. 200
International Brigade 69, 83, 102, 158, 160, 176-8, 180, 185, 200
— Migration service 113
Internments *see* Camps
Intransigeant, L' 34
Israel, Israelis 22-3
Italian immigrants, Italians in the Legion, Italy 24, 26, 31, 57, 70, 85, 111, 170
Itzkovitz, E. 23

Jacob, P. 212
Janny 122
Jansen, Lt. 111-12
Jansens, Maj. 100
Je dis tout 126
Jew-Bolshevik Bogey repeated by Murphy 219
Jewish Frontier 115, 226
Jewish Legion in the British Army 245-47
Jewish legionnaires, volunteers for the duration of the war *passim;* old-time legionnaires 22-3
Jews of France, The 79
Jochelman, D. 247-49
Johnson, E. C. 212
—, E. W. 175, 183, 193, 202
Joint Anti-Fascist Com. 154
— Commission on Political Prisoners 151, 154, 180, 183-207, 214
Joseph, Emperor 1
Journal Officiel 57, 82
Judenrat 81
Juin, A. P. 192

Kabyle, natives 98
Kahan, L. 36
Kahn, G. 81
Kanitz, W. 2, 19, 77
Kasba Tadla camp 84
Kef(Le) camp 86
Keitel, W. 77
Kellog, F. B. 51
Kenadsa camp 88, 92-3, 95, 97-8, 102-3, 108, 113, 115, 145, 149, 161-66, 173, 177, 186-7, 193-5
Kenadza *see* Kenadsa
Khersas camp 102, 111
Kerras *see* Khersas
Kiesele 107, 112
Kiesler, 197
Killgore, W. F. 50, 52
Kimberland, K. G. 167, 170, 175, 183
King, Dave 45-6
—, J. 238
Kingdon, F. 179
Kleinkopf 112
Klose, F. 20
Klotz, Lt. 210
Knight, E. F. 48
Kohn, M. 24

INDEX

Kolonial Komitet 42
Koestler, A. 196
Koulikoro 87-8
Kruker *see* Cruker
Kulman, M. 36
Kunitz, W. 74
Kuttner, A. R. 49
Kyzonois 111

Lafayette Squadron 42
Lake Tschad 75
Lambert, R. R. 58
Lambesc camp 228
Lambèse camp 189, 201
Lancaster, B. 3
Laseroux 212
Laserre 194-5
Latin Americans 54
Lax, Î. 36
Leahy, I. W. D. 219
Lebanon 85
Leclerc, Gen. 75
Leder, Z. 24
Legion, legionnaires, *passim*
Legion of Strangers 72
Leibovitch, M. 36
Leibovitchi 25
Lemoine 211
Lensch, A. 20
Lerner, Sch. 113
Letor, Lt. 166, 195
Letste Nayes 24
Leugues, G. 40
Leven, N. 213
Levi, I. 40
— S. 40
Levin, 113
Lewinstein, G. 164-5
Libertarion Party of Tunisian Italians 204
Liebray, Col. 194-5
Life 100
Ligny 71
Ligue Pour la Défense . . . 35
Limoges 81
Litwak, L. A. 39, 123
London 155, 176, 178, 191
Londres, A. 10
Longuet, J. 35
Looting 17-19
Lorraine 37

Los Angeles 48
Louisiana 50
Luart, L. de 90, 106
Lucha 160
Luchet, Gen. 212
Lupy, Col. 194
Lyautey, L.H.G. 198
Lyon, W. 49
Lyons, 61, 64, 71, 81, 84

Macabees 25
MacMillan, H. 184, 214
Madagascar 209
Magenta camp 211
Maire, F.V.M. 1
Maison Carée prison 189, 201
Makins, M. 184
Malinets, S. 24
Malvy, L. J. 42
Manchester, Duke of 2
Mandel, G. 59, 228
Mandemont 213
Marching in the Legion 12-3
Marin-Chencerelle 113
Marinha Grande 169
Maritain, J. 222-3
Marne front 72, 213
Marrakesh 48
Marseilles 3, 78-9, 81, 85
Marshall, G. L. 219
Martinique 80
Marty 112
Mascara camp 25
Maunoury, Gen. 213
Mauras, Ch. 58
Mauriac camp 139
Maximilian 1
Mechata camp 169
Mediterranean 90, 107
— Nigerian railway *see* Trans-Saharian
— Niger
Meknès prison 21
Menabba camp 113
Mengoub camp 113
Menthon, M. de 226
Mercenaries 1, 4, 32
Mercheria camp 201
Mercier, Ch. E. 23, 72-73
Meuse 72
Mexicans, Mexico 1, 54, *see also* Spanish Loyalist

Meyer, G. 46
Middle East 6
Midelt camp 198
Mikhovsky, A. 36
Miller, J. P. 52
Milles (Les) camp 228
Missour camp 104-5, 113, 184, 198
Moulay-Bou-Azza camp 113
Mon Légionnaire 3
Monnet, J. 221
Montagu, Lord Ed. 2
— Lady L. 2
— Swaythling, Baron L. S. 241-2
Montauban 79
Montguyon camp 228
Montluel 135
Montmartre 25
Montpellier 81
Montviso 86
Moreno 165-6
Morganthau, H. 220
Morlae, E. 48
Morteaux 25
Moore, K. 3
Moreno 111
Morocco 15, 19-21, 26, 30, 32-3, 53, 71, 75, 79, 84, 86-91, 96-100, 103-4, 108, 113-4, 152, 155, 173-4, 181, 184-5, 187, 189, 201-2, 204, 213, 220
Mosabert, Gen. 191
Mosca 111, 165
Mossi 92
Moutet, M. 33-4, 40, 42
Munich Agreement 56, 58
Murphy, R. D. 89-90, 98, 15, 161, 169, 174, 176, 180-1, 183, 191, 193, 198, 202, 205, 215, 218-20
Muslims 214, 217, 219, 225-6
Muster 112

Naidman, M. 36
Narcay, P. de 34
Narvik 71, 74
Nassariaz 111
National Maritime Union 180
Nationality, naturalization of legionnaires see Citizenship
Nazarian 105
Nazis 22-23, 71, 77, 83, 85, 115
N.C.O. see Non-Commissioned Officers
Négrier, Gen. 11

Negroes in the French army 52, Legion 45
Negroni, A. 173
Neumeyer, G. 6
Neutral countries 32, 39-40
Newman, H. 49
New Republic 117-18, 179
New Statesman and Nation 178
New York 8, 45, 88, 89
Niamey 88, 92
Nice 78
Niger 88, 92, 95, 97, 105, 151
Nîmes 81
Nogues, Ch. A. 155
Non-Commissioned Officers in the Legion 15, 26, 28, 31-2, 47, 52, 57, 61, 108, 163, 165
North Africa 3, 10, 12, 14, 22, 28, 56, 58, 61, 82-85, 88, 90-1, 93-4, 96, 101-229, see also Algeria, camps, Morocco, Tunisia
Northern Russia 43
Norvay 113
Nourrices 65
Novels, The Legion in 2

Obrona Com. 43
Odessa 36
Oettinger, J. 114, 172, 174, 207, 258
Oeuvre, L' 59
Office of Strategic Services see O.S.S.
Officers in the Legion see N.C.O.
Oran 83, 97, 117, 119, 160, 165, 192, 196, 208, 210-11, 213
Orenstein, H. 175
Orinstein, A. 142
—, F. 142
Ortiz, Philip 49
—, Pierre 49
O.S.S. reports 83, 108
Oswego camp for refugees 206
Ottoman Empire 25
Oued-Akreuch camp 113, 169, 197
Oued Zem camp 84, 113
Ouida see Ramée
Oujda camp 112
Oyfn Schweiweg 62-3

Palestine, Palestinian forced labor groups, 81-2, 139-175
Papal Province 80

Parades of the Legion 3
Paratroopers 22
Paris 1, 3, 15, 22-3, 31, 33, 40, 48-50, 56, 59, 69, 73, 79-80, 213
Pariser Tageszeitung 169
— *Yidishe Vokh* 41
Paris Soir 73
Parliament 34
Passower seder 73, 136
Pay in the Legion 14-16
Pehle, J. W. 207
Peixotto, G. 46
Pellew, M. 7
Penal battalions of the Legion 10, 77, *see also* Atrocities
Pennington, L. T. 214
Pensions 16
Peral, J. C. 160
Perpignan 69, 71
Pertwee R. 2
Peru 1
Pessin, M. 29
Pétain, P. 67, 77-8, 87, 91, 156, 160, 162, 192
Petit Parisien 33
Petlura 28
Peyrouton, M. 218, 220, 225
Phelizot, R. 46
Philadelphia 181, 202
— *Record* 14
Pioneer Corps *see* British
Piraud 76, 79
Pithiviers camp 77, 139-40
Pogroms 17, 28, 32, 54, 80, in Palestine 62
Pol, H. 20, 88-9
Poland, Poles 17, 37, 62, 113, Polish Legion 54, army in exile 65-68, 176, antisemitism there 150, 152, 166-68, 176-77, Socialists 24, Poles in the Foreign Legion 85, 91, 93-94, 97
Poliakov 37
—, S. 36
Political refugees in England 230-49
Poniatovski, M. 183
Pont-sur-Yonne 74
Port Lyautey prison 189, 201
— Vendres camp 83
Portugal 169
Posner, H. 166
Post, New York 208

Poverty in the Legion 14, *see also* Pay
Prades 84
Presse Marocaine 114
Prince, N. 47
Printer, A. D. 84, 101, 178
Prioux, R. J. 212
Prisons *see* Camps
Prisoners of War 78, 142
Propaganda 1
Psenin 122
Pugh, Col. 152
Punishment *see* Atrocities
Punitive expeditions 18, 85, *see also* Atrocities
Pyrénées Orientales 84-85

Quakers *see* AFSC

Rabat 90, 98, 105-7, 112, 152, 169, 172, 206
Rabbinate 82, *see also* Chaplains
Radical Party 87
Rakover, J. 33-4
Rambervilles 129
Ramée, L. de la 2
Ransdell, J. M. 50
Rapes, 17-9
Rapoport, Ch. 63
Rathenau's (W.) murderer in the Legion 5
Ratz, J. 60
Recruitment in the Legion 2-6, 15, 19-20, 22, 48-9, 56, 85, 172-7, 186, 206
Red Cross 18, American 175, French 155, International 104-5, 107, 153, 183, 203
Refuge for criminals in the Legion 4
Refugees, Austrian and German in the Legion and camps 4, 58-9, 62, 80, 82-86, 91, 93, 101, 112-115-16, 159, 164, 173-5; refugees from and in Spain 31, 205-6, *see also* Fédalah and Oswego
Reggan 92
Regiment, 1st 26, 30; 2nd 26, 31; 3rd 1, 26; 6th 71; 11th 71; 12th 71, 73; 21st 71; 22nd 71; 23rd 71, 79; Zouave 85
Reibel, Ch. 57
Reid, W. S. 90
Rent, Col. 192

Repatriation of Soviet citizens 190
Representative Com. of French Jews 213
Republican Party of Italians in Tunisia 204
République 26
Revolt of Carency *see* Carency
Revue Juive de Genève 58
Rheims 46
Richardson, W. U. 51
Richmond, H. 203, 183, 203
Riepp 111, 204
Rieucros camp 59, 228
Riffs, War with the 21, 49
Riga 37
Riots in the Legion 10
Riom trial 73
Rocha, J. 113
Rockwell, P. A. 42
Roland, G. 3
Ronin 183, 203
Roosevelt, F. D. 115, 149, 151, 155, 163, 179, 191, 206, 209, 219, 221, 226
Rosen, E. 8, 16, 22
Rosenberg, S. 46
Rosenthal 112
Rothberg 122
Rothenstein, G. 162
Rothschild, Ed. 221-2
—, L. 241
Rotstein, M. 36
Rothsztein, A. 65
Rouen 26
Rumania, Rumanians 22-5, in the Legion 37-8, in camps 175, antisemitism 23
Russel, H. E. 90-1, 95, 174, 206
Russia 17, 32, 41, embassy in Paris 24, Revolutions 43, 62-63, Russian-Jewish emigrés 24, 62, Russian-Jewish (French Refugees) Protection Com. 40-41, 130, Russian Jews 22, 24-32, in England, 40-41, 130, 230-49, Jews and non-Jews in the Legion, 25-6, 31, 39, 42, 70, 97, *see also* White Russians
Saarlanders in the Legion 56
Sadek, W. 4-5
Sahara 88-9, 95-98, 102, 111, 151, 160, 178, *see also* Trans-Saharian

Saida camp 34, 103, 116, 162
Saintes camp 228
Salvation Army 46
Samuel, H. 40, 235, 240
Sandhurst, Lord 249
Sandlersz, L. 76
Santucci, Lt. 111, 204
Sarreguemines 56
Saville, L. 49
—, M. H. 49
Scharf, E. 113
Schmidt, G. 174-5
—, H. 174-5
Schnek, F. 115-6, 164-5
Schwabe 195
Schwartzbard, S. 10-11, 25, 30, 41, 58, 80, 124
Secours Populaire Algérien 148
Secularism 62
Sedgwick, E. 48
Seeger, A. 41, 45-6
Segou 88
Seine River 72
Self-mutilation in the Legion 10
Selke, R. 107
Selo 112
Sengalese troops 31, 88, 94, 100-1
Septfonds camp 76, 228
Ser, Ch. 85
Serbia 1
Settat camp 113, 167, 197-8
Sexual life in the Legion 3, 14-5, 65-6, 195
Sfaïa 92, 95
Shat, J. 37
Sheffield, Lord 236
Shlevin, B. 61, 65
Shonberg, M. 36
Siberia 33, 126
Sidi-bel-Abbès, 1, 34, 161, 208
—el-Ayachi camp 104, 106, 113, 152-3, 150, 170, 184, 201
Signard, M. 194-5
Sikorski, W. 67-8
Simons, H. 161
—, W. H. B. 161
Slavic legion 54, Slavs 24, 40
Sloutchewsky, M. 30, 125
Smith, W. B. 202, 214
Snowden 238

INDEX

Socialists 24, 34, 39, 62, 137, 204, 230-49
Society for Momentary Aid 121
Soissons 73-4, 213
Solidarité des Volontaires Juifs 44
Solothurn 20
Songs in the Legion, 3, 13, *see also* Spanish songs 12
Sothern, J. M. 7
Soviets 158, 178, 200
Spain 44, 57, 174-6, 213, refugees in 31, 44, 205-7, Spanish Legion 20-1, 53, Spaniards and Loyalists, Spanish refugees in the Foreign Legion and camps in France and North Africa 20-21, 31, 56, 69-75, 80, 85, 89, 93-4, 97-8 101-2, 113, 155-59, 178, 180-2, 185-7, 194, 196, their emigration to Mexico 89, 116, 156, 158, 187, 202, Spanish Songs 12
Spartansburg 54
Stanescu 23
St. Cyprien camp 69, 83, 228
Stein, K. 67
Stern, T. 169
Stimson, H. C. 212
St-Maurice-de-G. 65, 70, 135
Stuart, B. 5
Suchet 211
Sudan 87-9, 97
Suez 23
Suicides in the Legion 14
Sultan of Morocco 226
Sulzberger, C. L. 212
Svirsky, A. 36
Sweeny, Ch. 49
Swiss in the Legion, Switzerland 19, 20, 25, 29
Synagogues 129
Syria 18, 71, 75, 176, 209, Syrian Jews 25, prisons 85, Syrian legionnaires 38

Taba 111
Taghit 92
Tangier 226, Jews 213
Tarhit *see* Taghit
Tassit 88
Tauber, A. 84
Taxes 18
Tcherikower, E. & R. 62-63, 74, 79-80
Teller, G. W. 206

Temps, Le 34
Ten Tall Men 3
Teran, L. de 161
Tercio *see* Spanish Foreign Legion
Thiéry, G. 38
Third Republic 91, 107
Thompson, H. 2
Ticko 204
Tiflis 86
Times, London 37
Tog, Der 40
Tomb of the Unknown Soldier 133
Torch Operation 115
Tosaye 92
Torrès, H. 213
Toulouse 26, 78, 81, 87, 173
Tours 121-22
Transafrica railroad *see* Trans-Saharian
Transfers from the Legion to regular units 25, 29, 30-1, 34-5, 37-8, 41-3, 46-7
Trans-Saharian railroad 85, 87-100, 103, 107, 144-6, 151-2, 161, 194, 196-7
Trepier 72
Trets-Fuveau 79
Tripoli 85
Trojman, Rabbi 211, 213
Trois, M. F. 154
Trumbo, D. 179
Tunisian Jews 10, 25, 27, 86, 204, 224
Turkish Jews 25, Turkey 170

UGIF 181
Union . . . *see* UGIF
Ukraine 28, 80
Underground organizations 141
Under Two Flags 2
Union Nationale des Officiers 57
Unione Democratica Italiana 204-5
Union Sacré 38-44, 129
United Nations 8
United States 5, 10, 18, 20, 31-2, 42, 47, 50-2, 54-5, 75, 79, 84-6, 90-91, 97, 161, 174, 179
Unterman, J. 123
Univers Israélite, L' 25, 29, 38-9

Vaeddes 213
Valbonne, La 61, 70-71, 135, 137
Vancia 61, 64
Vanikoff, Vanino *see* Wanikoff

Varene 192
Varhayt 40
Ventura, I. 36
Verdun 37, 46
Verfel, F. V. 67
Vernet (Le) camp 83-4, 101, 159, 228-9
Veterans 76-9, *see also* Camps, etc.
Vichy regime 73, 75-6, 78, 81-2, 84, 85, 87-90, 90, 92, 102, 107, 155, 162, 170, 191, 200, 209-10, 212-3
Vic-le-Comte 81
Victoire, La 37
Vienna 85, 115-6, 164
Vietnam *see* Indochina
Vilna 62
Vivier 112
Voelkischer Beobachter 21
Vogue 49
Voix d'Amerique, La 100
Volunteers *passim*, for the duration of the war 25-26, 28
Vosges 11
Vust, R. 183

Wadsworth 54
Wanikoff, M. 112, 113
Warburg, Paul F. 183, 203, 214, 220-21, 223-25
War Refugee Board 200, 206-7
Warsaw 29
Waterhouse, F. A. 4, 9, 18
Weil, B. 229
Weill, H. H. 162
— J. 58

Weinberger, S. 180
Welles, Sumner 221
West Africa 87-9
West Indians 54
Weygand, M. 89-90
White Russian emigrés in the Legion 43, 56-7, 83, 85-6, 163
Willey, S. H. 183-4, 195, 201, 203, 221-2
Wise, Rabbi S. S. 212
Wolf, J. 85
— Lucien, 230, 243
—, M. 38
World 49
— Jewish Congress 99, 101, 111, 216
World War I 10-11, 16, 23-7, 43-45, 54, 57, 61-3, 211-3, 227, 230-49
— II, 17, 22-3, 60-229
Wren, P. C. 2, 4
Wyoming 86
Wyss-Dunant, E. 104-5, 153, 183, 203

Yellow Star 142
Yiddish 22, 24, 42, 60, 62, songs 12
YIVO Institute 62-3, 79-80
Yom Kippur 28, 123
Young, R. 53
Younger, K. G. 183, 193-4, 197-8, 201

Zannutelli, G. 118
Zaoui 209
Zinn, F. W. 49-50
Zionists 62
Zone, Free 79. 81, Occupied 77